OUT OF THE BOX AND ONTO WALL STREET

OUT OF THE BOX AND ONTO WALL STREET

Unorthodox Insights on Investments and the Economy

MARK J. GRANT

WILEY

John Wiley & Sons, Inc.

Published by John Wiley & Sons, Inc., Hoboken, New Jersey.
Published simultaneously in Canada.

For general information on our other products and services or for technical support, please contact our Customer Care Department within the United States at (800) 762-2974, outside the United States at (317) 572-3993 or fax (317) 572-4002.

Wiley also publishes its books in a variety of electronic formats. Some content that appears in print may not be available in electronic books. For more information about Wiley products, visit our web site at www.wiley.com.

Library of Congress Cataloging-in-Publication Data:
Grant, Mark J., 1950-
    Out of the box and onto Wall Street: unorthodox insights on investments and the economy / Mark J. Grant.
        p. cm.
    Includes index.
    ISBN 978-1-118-01810-1 (hardback); 978-1-118-05665-3 (ebk);
    978-1-118-05664-6 (ebk); 978-1-118-05663-9 (ebk)
        1. Global Financial Crisis, 2008-2009.   2. Finance—History—21st century.
    3. Investment analysis.   I. Title.
    HB37172008 .G733   2011
    332'.042—dc22

                                                                    2010051232

Printed in the United States of America
10 9 8 7 6 5 4 3 2 1

This book is dedicated to the fine people on Wall Street whom I work with each day. Regardless of comments made in the press or barbs thrown about by politicians, most of the people on Wall Street are honorable people who make every effort to do "the right thing." The financial community is made up of people from all over the world, and your family name, your point of origin or the school that you attended make little difference. In the end, you are either bright enough to carry the torch or you are not. On Wall Street your reputation is not just a thing—it is everything; while we have a few bad apples, as in every profession, for the most part there is not a finer group of diverse people to be found on this planet. Our community is different in one very real sense—it is a profession of results. There is no trying; trying is for other areas of endeavor. Either the task is accomplished or it is not, and that is deeply inscribed in the bedrock in very stark black and white.

I am a guy that started at the bottom and made it somewhere toward the top. There are richer people, to be sure, and someone always has a bigger boat; but I had the opportunity, was given the chance, and was able to move myself to higher ground. The bright-eyed kid over time became a senior statesman and I dedicate this book to all of the people, over the years, who saw some promise and encouraged me on in my adventures. To all of my friends and clients: Please allow me to express my gratitude and dedicate this book to all of you!

■ *Contents* ■

PART II   LEARNING TO DANCE UNTIL IT MOVES

CHAPTER 6   CPI LINKED SECURITIES   153

CHAPTER 7   THE WISDOM OF BUYING SENIOR DEBT TO PREFERRED STOCK   173

CHAPTER 8   AIG DEBT   203

CHAPTER 9   FIXED-TO-FLOAT BONDS   231

CHAPTER 10   GRANT'S GAMBIT   255

PART III   MARKET ISSUES

CHAPTER 11   BEAR STEARNS AND LEHMAN BROTHERS   269

CHAPTER 12   THE AMERICAN CREDIT CRISIS   291

CHAPTER 13   THE BAILOUT   319

PART IV   THE GREAT GAME

CHAPTER 14   POLITICS   341

■ *Acknowledgments* ■

I have lived my life by two guiding principles:

1. Have a great adventure, and if it is not good, then you are doing something wrong and it should be changed.
2. Surround yourself with people who you love and who love you.

Of all of the people on this Earth who have encouraged me in my endeavors, added joy to my adventure, and loved me through the bright and dark days of life, it would be my mother, Carlyn Pollock, to whom the greatest debt is owed. As she would tell you, if not for her I would never have had an opportunity to have this adventure, and, as any mother would tell you, she is right, of course. Consequently, I acknowledge my shining star, my mom, for her contribution to me and this book, and I also give thanks to my father, Stanley Grant, who has left us here and is off on his new adventure somewhere else in the universe. Better parents a son could not have had!

I have two fabulous assistants that work with me: my junior partners, the Sorcerer's apprentices. I wish to thank them both for their hard work—Angela O'ffill for handling more than her share of the workload as I got the book ready to be published, and Tara Schuerman for helping to organize the book. There would have been no book without their invaluable assistance, constant loyalty, and late hours worked. I doff my Wizard's cap to both ladies and say "thank you" with great affection and humility as they both fit into the category of surrounding myself with people that I love.

Finally, there are Bill Gross and Paul McCulley at Pimco, Pimm Fox at Bloomberg News, Andy Heiskell at Mutual of America, Cliff Noreen at Babson/Mass. Mutual, and Howard Potter at the Capstone Funds to thank. Without their encouragement and prodding, this book would never have been written. They pushed, pulled, and gave their support to this book as I often wondered if anyone outside of the professionals with whom I do business would have any interest in my meanderings. Finer people there are not on Wall Street, and each is a "stand-up guy" who carries his values and high standards to our profession. Thank you, my friends.

■ *Introduction* ■

or almost four decades I have been working on Wall Street. There have been great joy and moments of incredible aggravation. I climbed up the ladder step by step, starting from the first rung, and made every effort to continuously pull my way higher. All of the content that you will find here was written for investment professionals. You may not understand each and every subject or nuance, but I believe the general concepts can be easily understood. My commentary is reflective of 10 years where the only distribution was made to professional money managers of one type or another. This is the first instance where *Out of the Box* has been made available to the public.

My book is not about the stock market, though certain principles apply, or the bond markets, where I have spent most of my time; but it offers some methods for investing that are often not taken up in the news of the moment. Many of my views, I am not apologetic to tell you, have been formulated through long experience. I have often felt that, regardless of any person's intelligence, there is just no replacement for having lived through the battles of the markets, and I wear each scar proudly; each has shaped my vision of how to win at the Great Game. There is a subtle but very real difference between "being right" and "winning," and I have always played to win.

I am up each day at 4:00 A.M. to write my commentary; this is what it takes to get it right. Every single morning, I bounce out of bed and head to the computer to see what has happened overnight. From day one until this moment, I have found it exciting. Wall Street is the biggest sandbox in the world, where you get to come and play with the boys and see if you can scramble to the top. As I am a giver of advice, I get to interact with some of the best and brightest minds on the planet, and here—besides making money, which is always fun—is one of the aspects of my life that I have always cherished. It is amazing, really: some guy from Kansas City, another from Pakistan, a trader from Iowa, a saleswoman from some small town in France. Some coming from the local college and some out of the London School of Economics, and the playing field is leveled with your ability to either earn your own way in or not. There is no place for losers and no place for crying, and the Great Game takes no prisoners.

You may note certain conjuror's tricks in this book. It all seems like magic until it is explained, and then everyone goes, "Oh," and the magic is replaced with knowledge and it appears oh so easy. There are Grant's Rules and the experiences of living through financial crises and how one deals with inflation and many other life experiences that I share with you as you walk through the chapters. My musings are not a point-and-click methodology for making money, but carefully read, I believe it will help you in how to manage your own personal finances—especially those directed at investments. There is no quick way to accumulate knowledge and no reliable way to increase your capital in a short period of time except by the learning of life's lessons. What is written in this book cannot be learned in school, any school, and there is no teacher of this course except the longevity of experience.

One of the important lessons to be found in this book is the importance of the capital structure. Equities are at the very bottom of what is possible to purchase by any institution or individual and that has been a maxim lost upon the general public for generations. It has often seemed to me that most people were not savvy investors because they were peering into the wrong pigeon hole. You should own bonds for "capital preservation" and stocks for "appreciation," and your holdings in debt instruments should always significantly outweigh what you own in equities. This has been proven time and time again by financial difficulties, and if there is one guarantee that I can provide you, it is that the markets have always and will always go through cycles, with booms and busts and economic crises as part of the process. You do not own stocks for their dividends; you buy bonds for yield and to keep what you have labored so hard to make, and equities are never the cake but the icing that is layered upon it.

I have always believed that the best and most important concept in investments was a warning. This is a well-reasoned approach to what not to buy, and this is not often found in anything that is available to the public because everyone has some axe to grind. In the bond markets or the stock markets, you make money in decimals, but you lose money in points. To make money is a long grind upward, but on the downside the G-forces are massive and increase exponentially. Consequently, you will find a good portion of this book concerned with what not to own or what not to buy, as my approach has always been to work with my clients on a long-term basis to help them to achieve the best results. What I have suggested they purchase never had anything to do with my firm's inventory or some new deal but was grounded totally in what I thought had some advantage. I have done very well in my world—better than I ever thought was possible—but I did it in my own way with no sacrifice of my standards or ethics.

For 10 years now, through my commentary, I have tried to add value to the proposition. That is what I do, and many of the largest financial institutions on the planet have listened and continue to listen. They do not always agree with my viewpoint, as you might expect, but they give my opinion some thought and then they pay for it by doing business with me. I warn and I cajole, and I look at massive portfolios with an eye toward the future and occasionally some sector or play seems undervalued, and I try to point them in that direction. Every day, I give my friends and clients my very best and my thoughts are not contaminated by anything except my own ability to think. In some sense, it is rather like being the Sherlock Holmes of the investment world as sensible deductions are often the magic key upon which the world turns and upon which a solid investment foundation is built. It is never the news but what the news means, and if I have any abilities, it is there that my abilities rest.

If you are looking for a book on how to gamble or some new methodology for speculating, then this book will not fulfill your desires. If, however, you are looking for some grounded principles of how to prudently invest your money, then you may find that some of the Wizard's secrets, presented here for the first time to the larger audience, will help to light your way down the treacherous road. What you know will always help you but what you don't know can sink your ship before it has left port. It is my hope that *Out of the Box and onto Wall Street* will increase your knowledge base so that your capital can increase along with your understanding. There is nothing on Earth like the Great Game, and I invite you to join me on my journey as I seek to master the playing field.

The Formative Years

After I left law school I wandered into one of the largest banks in Kansas City. I began my professional life here as a trainee, working in the credit and bond departments. It was 1974 and the market was horrible. Interest rates were rising very slowly but continuously like some Chinese water torture. No one was making any money. There were no computers in the whole place, and people were using yield books to figure out prices. There was yelling and screaming and phones in everyone's ears. What seemed, at the time, like large amounts of money were moving around, and someone continuously updated the chalkboard. I had no idea what was going on—but I was fascinated and I was hooked!

I had to find out. I needed to find out. All these guys in suits and ties sitting, standing, moving, pushing, yelling, screaming, and bells were ringing at various intervals. There was the clack, clack, clack of some machine and paper was pouring out on some undecipherable tape. Young men and women were scurrying from one desk to the other and collecting some multiple copied papers. I had a chance to look at one. Who knew what it said. It might have been written in Mandarin for all I knew. No one seemed to agree on anything, and everyone was spread out on long trading desks. I was told that there were traders and sales-people, and that guy over there was the manager. They were all frantic. They were all disheveled. They were all hard at work, but at some work that I had never experienced in my entire life. God, it was exciting! When I think back about it all these years later, I still find it exciting. I have always found it exciting. It is the Great Game, and my ability to experience it would change my life forever.

I knew nothing about what these people were doing. I had no guess as to how it all worked. My father, after all, had been in advertising.

I arrived at 7:30 in the morning on my first day. I expected to wander in and be among the first people in the trading room. I was hoping to ask a few questions and get some idea of what I was supposed to do. But that wasn't going to happen as everyone had been there for hours. You must understand, the bond markets don't close except on the weekends. They begin Sunday night in Tokyo and keep going until Friday night in New York. Different trading desks in Tokyo, London, and New York City pick them up as the sun shifts around but during the week, the sun never sets on them. Bonds are used to hedge positions and acts of terror-ism, moves by various central banks, revolutions, and various dislocating political events need to have somewhere to go to lay off the bet. Every significant happening in the world causes a reevaluation of interest rates and risk. Every trader in the world has a position and is at risk. That risk must have someplace to be balanced, and that is why the markets are open. On top of that is the fact that our currency is the money of the world and our bonds are the watershed benchmark. Financial institutions in every place on the globe, from Ghana to Greece and from Finland to France own American bonds. They have to be able to trade them somewhere and do so when they are awake. It is very difficult to trade bonds when you are asleep. I have tried it. Not an easy thing to do!

I showed up every day as early as I could. I sat with traders and salespeople alike and tried to understand what they were doing. I learned to read the bond tables, calculate yields, and calculate prices. Most of the guys on the floor were nice to me. They had been though it themselves. They knew the drill. I was prodded and pulled and given every crummy task that could be given me and I grinned and bore it. I finally understood that those pieces of paper represented tickets or transactions between the bank and the clients. The back office stuff—or where the tickets get cleared and where the money changes hands—still eluded me, but I was getting the hang of it. I was on my way.

But I nearly derailed my career before it started. My department dealt in certificate of deposits (CDs). We bought them and sold them as well as various other short-term instruments. This means that the maturities on these things were days or weeks and not years. I began to formulate an idea and went to see the executive vice president of the bank to present my idea. He listened politely but immediately rejected my idea, noting that "Commerce Bank is not going to change the financial markets, Mark," I was told politely. "We are an old-line and conservative institution. We do not create new financial instruments and we follow along and make our money in the time-tested ways."

Soon after, the manager of the bond department called me into his office to berate me for going over his head. I thought I was going to lose my job, but somehow I wasn't fired. I learned to never jump over someone's head again. It is not well taken, probably not in any business, and certainly not in the financial community. I survived the moment, however. It may have been the first time that it happened to me, but certainly not the last time that someone asked me what the hell I was doing.

Sometime later, as I recall, I was put into sales. I was given the smallest of country banks to call on. I would have strict supervision. My conversations would be monitored. I was to be mentored by one of the more senior guys. He would review each ticket, if there were any. I was on my way! It was that year, my first year in the business, and I was the richest that I have ever been before or since. As I recall, and I might be off on this, I made about $48,000 in my first year of production. I went off my salary as soon as I could and starting getting paid based on my production. It was a wonderful experience and one that frightens most people. If you produce, then you get paid; if you do not produce, then you do not get paid. I learned that I could produce. I learned how to sell, and my sales shot up as I gathered more experience.

Somewhere along the line, I was invited to interview at Stern Brothers & Co. It was a fine old investment bank of good reputation that was headquartered in Kansas City. I was to spend the next 14 or so years of my life here, and I never, ever, thought I would leave. As I look back on it now, as I muse about those glorious days at Stern Brothers, I am filled with delight and boyish enthusiasm about where I really started my career.

The advice I got from two Stern executives—Julian Gumbiner and Bill Wall—has stayed with me over the years: Study the numbers and have good relationships.

Treat your account as you would wish to be treated. No one sale is that important. A sale is the conclusion of making good choices that benefit your clients. If there is no benefit to the client, then do not make the sale. Endeavor to be a partner with your client to help him win the game. A good relationship is a dialogue that helps the client make more money than by doing something else. Add value to the process and just don't sell a bond.

When I was still a young pup, I first developed a work ethic that has survived all of my years in the business. I got to the office somewhere between 5:00 and 5:30 in the morning. I always figured that there were people a lot smarter than I on Wall Street, and I would need some extra time to keep up with them. I used to go through everyone's inventory and try to figure out who owned cheap bonds. The Street was less efficient in those days, and it was possible to find a few offerings that were better than the others. Then I would call my clients and point out the value of what I had found and, sometimes, make a sale based on my knowledge. This was to be the start of my analytical background as I tried to identify value not only on price but on the fundamentals of the company. I read book after book that espoused Modern Portfolio Theory and tried to make sense of it and apply it to various credits. I quickly concluded that cash flows were the mainstay of how a company was doing. I still base most of my thinking on this part of a credit's analysis, and I learned to run cash ratios in all manner of ways—cash flow versus assets, versus revenues, versus gross profit, versus net profits, versus historical models and several other scenarios that helped identify how a company was actually doing in terms of making money. Stern Brothers was too small to have in-house analysts, and I taught myself how to run the numbers. The more senior people at the firm couldn't understand what I was doing and often chided me about it and told me that I should spend my time selling bonds, as that is what I was paid for, but I kept at it diligently. Soon, I was opening new accounts and doing business with several major institutions because they liked the viewpoint that I brought to the table.

I also learned, somewhere around this time, that getting an institutional client was one of the more difficult things to accomplish and that if you got one, and the buyer liked you, then there were all kinds of ways to expand your relationship. The person probably bought all kinds of bonds and you were involved with only one aspect of what he and his colleagues were doing.

My career at Stern was flourishing—I did business with some of the bigger players on the Street when I went to New York. I learned valuable lessons from people, including Larry Tisch, then CEO of CNA, and a wonderful guy known on The Street as Ricky Perretti. He was the number two guy on Merrill Lynch's trading desk and eventually became a very powerful man at the firm.

As my career flourished, I had a number of good friends and colleagues who helped along the way; their names may not mean anything to you, but they were important to me—Mike Telerico, Al Milano, Jimmy Quigley, and Patrick Price, who became my boss at my current firm.

Enough of my reminiscing. Suffice it to say that I've had a great run and I've been helped enormously by many people. I've learned that a solid work ethic is mandatory for success, but a solid play ethic is also a necessary part of winning. Everyone needs to clear his or her head. Time off is good for the soul, good for your head, and, ultimately, good for your work. Sometimes perspective can be a valuable part of great achievements, and play time often adds new or different perspective.

—MARK J. GRANT

Part I

The Wizard Calls the Ball

Chapter 1

The Implosion of the Housing Agencies

It was in 1938, during the Great Depression, that the U.S. Congress, in its wisdom, established the Federal National Mortgage Association (FNMA). Its sister agency, also a federally chartered corporation, Freddie Mac, is also a government-sponsored enterprise (GSE), as is FNMA, and to truly understand these housing agencies you must bear in mind that they were created by the government no matter what hallucinations our politicians bring to us so many years later. I would say that, since inception, these two corporations have been mismanaged, used as whipping posts by one party and the other and carefully kept off the books of the country so they will not directly impact America's balance sheet.

These two congressional creations have been a convoluted scheme since inception, and while they do not carry an "implicit" guarantee of the government, they do carry an "explicit" guarantee so that they always trade right on top of United States Treasuries.

This gives them lower costs of funding, but what this guarantee is actually worth has been anyone's guess since the companies were first created.

For 72 years, Congress has been involved with all kinds of shenanigans with these corporations, which has even included allowing the banks to buy them—prodded them to buy their debt, in fact—and gave their bonds a zero risk weighting so that the banking system in America is loaded up to the gills with their debt. Now what happened over time was that these two agencies became quite powerful and had big lobbying organizations, and they have been prime examples of public/private entities, as they had publicly traded stock and their own preferred stock plus both senior and subordinated debt. Finally, in a fit of angst, Congress turned against its own creations, much as the creator in Frankenstein turned against the monster it had created, and in 2008 began severing limbs. What took place, in my opinion, was a travesty that caused not only the unnecessary loss of wealth for individuals and institutions alike, but actually caused the bankruptcy of a number of banks as the result of quite capricious actions by Hank Paulson, then secretary of the Treasury, and others who made decisions that effectively bankrupted these entities as they threw out most of the management of these companies based on the fact that they were losing money, even though Congress and the administration were issuing policies and writing laws that were the cause of the losses.

In some kind of fit of rage and one of the worst financial decisions made in this century, the secretary of the Treasury decided to quit paying the preferred dividends of both agencies, which caused irreparable harm to both of the companies and brought into question, quite unnecessarily, the guarantee of the country which sent a tidal wave of doubt and suspicion throughout the world.

These two housing agencies may not have carried the "full faith and credit" guarantee of the United States, but it had always been thought that the "explicit" guarantee was close enough so that when the choice was made to quit paying the dividends of the preferred stock issues, some of which were brought to market just months before, all hell broke loose and the denizens of doubt were unleashed on the plains. The situation can only be described accurately by imagining Sauron, in *The Lord of the Rings,* emerging from his black castle and wreaking havoc with absolute abandon on all of the people of Middle Earth.

It is a strange fate that we should suffer so much fear and doubt over so small a thing. Such a little thing.

—Boromir,
The Fellowship of the Rings,
J.R.R. Tolkien

The travesty for the United States, which represents the safest bonds in the world and is the reserve currency of the world, was that our international reputation, centuries in making and protecting, was thrown under the bus by the actions of one man and his minions, who in one fell swoop tossed the reputation of America close enough to the edge to make everyone shudder and to question the financial viability of the nation. If you think I am being too strong in my presentation, I am not; Henry Paulson utilized some of the worst judgment that has been seen in the history of our country. What he did was absolute idiocy, in my opinion, and from that day to this one I hold him accountable for the reverberations that are still being felt from this decision. He may go down as one of the worst secretaries of the Treasury since its inception—and he should!

Get Back to Where You Once Belonged

August 11, 2008

I would like to take up the issue of the FNMA and Freddie Mac preferred issues once again, along with their subordinated debt. It is my belief that many people have this wrong and that these two federally chartered agencies will make good on their obligations—all of them. The United States can ill afford for any of its agencies to not pay their debts. As I have said all along, the dividend of the common stock is one issue that is not a stated commitment to pay, but all of the other classes of securities that are senior to the equity carry an obligation of the agency and now, perhaps, the government. For the paltry amount of the preferred dividend, do you think America is going to damage its credibility with its citizens and the rest of the world? Secretary Paulson is not that that moronic!

Let me state that I personally own some of these securities, my mother owns some, and there are some in the money I personally manage. Now, if you take the time to look at the indenture of, say, the FNMA 8.25 preferred (FNM.S), you will find that it is stated quite clearly that this preferred is Tier I Capital. You may also wish to note that in the recently passed legislation and in all of the comments from the Treasury, all of the statements refer to backing the agency and there is no discrimination as to the kinds of debt. The ratings agencies may well make proclamations about the financial condition of these two agencies and then look at the various classes of debt and regard the preferred as compared to the subordinated debt or senior debt, but, in my view, that path does not lead to Rome. These are agencies of the government, not private corporations, that were asked recently to expand their lending to help American homeowners, and now we are not going to pay their obligations? Even in the drop-dead scenario that the United States would take over FNMA and Freddie Mac, it is my opinion that the government would continue to pay all debts—preferred, subordinated, and senior. If you make the assumption that the preferreds would then be trading to the 2010 call at the 5-year +200, then you get a yield of 5.20 percent and a dollar price of $26.94. While it is certainly true that the preferred dividends are subject to certain capital requirements and a declaration by the board of directors, it would be a travesty for all of the U.S. agencies not to pay the debts of these GSEs, and I believe this card will trump the short-term economic weakness that is taking place in the housing markets. It hardly makes any kind of rational sense to ask these agencies to expand their role and then have them not pay their obligations. It is quite obvious, given the price of the preferred, that there is another viewpoint here, but this is mine, and I see the present pricing as an opportunity to enhance Grant's Rule 2: "Make Money." Over the weekend, Secretary Paulson announced that the government has no need to invest money into either of the housing agencies at this time, and given that there is still a common stock dividend, this is one more sign that the preferred dividend is intact. I would even make the argument, given the scope of problems in the housing sector, that the recent losses reported by FNMA and Freddie Mac are fairly paltry given the size of their portfolios.

Finally, let me make this observation: If I am wrong and FNMA and Freddie Mac do not pay their obligations, then all of the agencies' subordinated debt and preferred debt will be no more than commercial obligations. The federally chartered sponsorship will have lost its meaning, and you can expect to see all of these classes of debt for all of the agencies descend into a sinkhole.

Watch the Euro Zone

The dollar has now appreciated almost 8 percent from its low point against the Euro. Oil is down to $115.20, and the entire Commodity Research Bureau (CRB) Index is down 18 percent from its highs. The long commodities, long oil, and long euro trades have now turned into major losers. The game is changing as Europe is at the starting blocks for higher inflation, devaluing housing markets, and weaker economies. If you take the conventional wisdom that the equity markets are leading indicators, it is interesting to make some observations.

For the United States the Dow Jones is now down 11.54 percent for the year, with the Standard & Poor's (S&P) Index down 11.72 percent and the Nasdaq is down 8.98 percent. Not good numbers, but let us put this in perspective: The DJ Euro Stoxx is down 22.53 percent, with the Financial Times and London Stock Exchange (FTSE) down 14.99 percent and the CAC 40 down 19.99 percent and the German DAX down 18.66 percent, so America is not doing quite so badly by comparison. Even in the Far East, the Nikkei 225 is down 13.98 percent while the Hang Seng Index is down 21.31 percent.

GMAC

Let me quote from their recent statement released on Friday, August 8, 2008: "There continues to be a risk that the company will not be able to meet its debt service obligations and be in a negative liquidity position in 2008." The rest of their press release was full of hype and hope, and this proclamation, I would certainly guess, came from their legal advisers as a prelude to several possible outcomes of their financial situation and none of them good. On July 31, GMAC posted a $2.48 billion second-quarter loss, including a loss of $1.86 billion at ResCap. The mortgage lender has lost money for seven straight quarters, losing $7.2 billion over that period. Caveat emptor!

Write-Offs

In the first quarter of 2008, I said that the majority of the write-offs would be done by quarter three. I have vacillated in my own mind about this since then, but think I will be close—it could be quarter four, but the end is coming soon. The worst of the hits have already been taken, and those are the most severe of the catastrophes, the ones where the bet was leveraged and the equity has already been wiped out. What will happen next is the appearance of markups where the market has stabilized and the value has bounced off the bottom. It will appear first in some bank or investment bank, and you will get the initial look at credits that have begun to appreciate and then all kinds of good numbers will show up. If you wish to profit from the turn, then I think we are very close to a jump-off point to get back into the game!

The Cost of Not Honoring Obligations

August 19, 2008

The financial world is currently under siege. I am not sure if there is a better way to put it, but it might as well be an economic jihad fostered by some terrorist group. There is certainly no letup in the press, and I wonder who is making what bets after reading some of the commentary provided by the tribal leaders and warlords of the global marketplace. Some of the more recent articles such as the ones recently in *Investor's Business Daily* and *Barron's* struck me as so short-sighted as to lack common sense.

On the agency front, the mistake is this: These are not totally private companies, and yet the mentality of these and other articles are treating them as if they were no different than GE or IBM. The

> *Common sense is not so common.*
> —Voltaire

viewpoint is also so skewed, in my opinion, that they do not understand the ramifications of what they are suggesting. If a GSE were to default on one of its obligations, anywhere in the debt structure, the trust would be broken. This could be at the preferred level or the subordinated debt level because if an agency were to default there, then why would any person think their promise to pay was valid at any other place or point in time? The point is clear to me: If an agency of the U.S. government does not honor its obligations, then there is no value in the federal charter. Further down the path of rational thinking, if one American agency does not honor its commitments, then why would any investor expect any other American agency to honor its commitments? It seems to me that the fallout from FNMA, as an example, of not paying its preferred dividend would be disastrous for not only the credit of FNMA but also

Freddie Mac, Federal Farm Credit Bank (FFCB), and the home loan banks. The violation of a payment of debt by any agency will forever invalidate the meaning of a GSE and, in a larger sense, the reputation and honor of the U.S. government, and yet that is what recent articles have suggested to minimize the short-term difficulties of agencies that support and fund housing in the United States.

In my opinion the viewpoints recently expressed in these and other articles take no consideration of the extreme fallout that would accompany an agency not paying its debts—any of its debts. The price of the equities of FNMA and Freddie Mac were down 22 percent and 25 percent just yesterday, and the falling knife has become the meat cleaver in a nosedive. I have noticed in life that it may seem like the easiest course not to meet one's obligations. There seems to be a rather large group of people who feel that temporary setbacks can allow you to not stand up to your responsibilities. I have always felt that our government and the agencies represented by federal charter followed a higher standard, and I pray that I am correct in this assumption because the notion that they should not pay their debts would be a travesty for America—an absolute and final statement that the value of a GSE was null and void.

All the perplexities, confusion and distress in America arise not from defects in their Constitution or Confederation, nor from want of honor or virtue, so much as downright ignorance of the nature of coin, credit, and circulation.

—U.S. President John Adams

If some U.S. agency does not pay its debts, then the greater sadness will not be in the loss to portfolios but in the loss of common sense of our political leaders and the resultant loss of trust by investors in America and in the rest of the world who will learn quite conclusively that the United States does not honor its obligations. If you think that is too harsh, then so be it, but I choose to believe that a GSE has a meaning and that a federal charter invokes an obligation of the federal government. To be more pointed, I am ashamed and disgusted that Bernanke or Paulson or the president has not stood up and said, unequivocally, that the American government will support, if necessary, all of the debts of a U.S. agency. The rhetoric to date has been jumbled and unclear and misleading, either by attempt or construction, and I find it disheartening as an American citizen. I am happy to share the burden of increased taxes if necessary to support an obligation of my government, any obligation, as I expect the politicians that represent our country to be honorable in their statements and actions and to pay the bills of the federally chartered agencies as they would pay the direct obligations of the debt that is guaranteed in our Constitution.

Congress has asked FNMA and Freddie Mac to assume a greater role in housing given the current difficulties, and then the government is supposed to abandon them when they have financial issues as a result? There is no claim of fraud or mismanagement beyond the normal political barbs of those of different stripes, and yet supposedly responsible people in national publications are calling for the abandonment of obligation under fire. To be honest, I am greatly saddened by the rhetoric of many of these people and amazed at their lack of judgment and inability to grasp the stark reality of what they are suggesting.

Government loses its claim to legitimacy when it fails to fulfill its obligations.
—Martin L. Gross

The Agencies and Uncertainty

August 25, 2008

FNMA and Freddie Mac: The Uncertainty Principle

In quantum physics, the Heisenberg uncertainty principle states that locating a particle in a small region of space makes the momentum of the particle uncertain and, conversely, that measuring the momentum of a particle precisely makes the position uncertain. This postulate in the scientific world seems to have some relevance to the present state of affairs with these two agencies. The paradigm is convoluted by the structure, privately owned corporations with federal charters, government sponsorship, and a congressional mandate to provide affordable housing to the citizens of the United States. Allow me to point out that it was Congress that created this structure, which, in my view, makes the government responsible for the obligations of what they have created. The exact location or specificity, then, of these entities' obligations has become increasingly uncertain, as there are large and pertinent questions about what their obligations exactly mean to any and all parties who accepted the notion of a federally backed agency. One could argue, with some validity, that the notion currently being adjudicated and settled involving auction-rate bonds and variable-rate bonds has some bearing on the issues with these two agencies, as securities of all classes were sold with the understanding that they would get paid by these agencies of the government as the auction securities were sold with the understanding that there would be auctions. This is clearly a case where the government has taken the position that false or unwarranted claims or promises cannot be made without consequences, and, at a minimum, that standard should be held when there are governmental representations about the debts of these two agencies.

It seems clear that the right thing to do—the only thing to do as a matter of economic practicality—is then for the government to honor all of the obligations of FNMA and Freddie Mac while making sure it gets paid back for helping them out of their current crisis, which Congress from inception onward helped create. Congress has allowed, if not encouraged, commercial banks to own the preferred stock of these agencies and allowed it to be part of their capital structure, and there are no other preferreds in this class, so one must conclude that Congress was indicating that this class of securities was money good along with the subordinated debt and the senior debt. If, at any point in the financial structure, the government would cause these agencies to not live up to their obligations, then the reputations of any and all of the agencies has just been negated and the trust broken with the commercial banks, the investment banks, foreign governments, and the individuals who bought these securities relying on their federal charter. The government cannot have the Securities and Exchange Commission (SEC) and others mandated to protect the individual investor from unwarranted claims and then take a different tack when it is the government's unwarranted claims that are called into account.

It also seems that there is an argument here centering on the question of supervision. These agencies have had federal oversight since inception, with the presumed blessing of the government each time they issued a securitization, derivative, preferred stock offering, or any other obligation that these agencies have undertaken. The SEC routinely and with vigor pursues those people in supervisory positions who have had people in their capacities who have not lived up to their responsibilities, and have mandated fines for individuals and firms that have not provided adequate oversight for their employees who did not fulfill their obligations—should we now have a different standard, a lower standard, when it comes to governmental oversight? The central government has acted, in fact, as the office of supervisory jurisdiction, and that fact cannot be ignored. If you take the position that certain obligations should get paid and others not paid, then the value of a GSE becomes worthless and void. These two agencies have a supposed exposure of over two trillion dollars' worth of derivative counterparty obligations, and where do these rank in what should be paid? If you start slicing and dicing the obligations, then you negate the supposed responsibilities that come along with a federal charter, and you pronounce the governmental oversight valueless. Each and every day of FNMA's and Freddie Mac's existence, the U.S. government has overseen their actions; if nothing else, the government must live up to the economic reality of deciding to be in that position.

The uncertainty that now surrounds FNMA and Freddie Mac has become devastating. Everything but their most senior obligations is trading like junk, and the ratings downgrades are only adding fuel to the fire. To date, the inconclusive behavior of the Treasury and the Fed has only increased the worry and speculation that surrounds the Agencies. This cannot continue and should not continue, as the government's inaction is causing additional suffering for many classes of investors. Chart the course, Secretary Paulson, and then execute the plan, and please leave our country's reputation intact!

We're all trying to get our heads above the battle smoke and look for the real meaning of Enron to put it in perspective.
—Henry Paulson

The GSE Agencies as an Opportunity

August 27, 2008

I recently talked to a friend of mine who is quite senior at one of the agencies, and the topic was the equity infusion problems. The fear, and understandably so, is that the central government could show up and preempt any new capital, and this would be disastrous for obvious reasons. The idea that I floated was a convertible preferred that was structured in a novel manner. I suggested a reasonable coupon, language providing parity with all of the other preferred issuances, and then a conversion into senior debt if the Treasury interceded. I have spoken with several large institutions who are clients of mine about this concept, and there are a number of people who have expressed interest.

I want to circle back to the agency oversight discussion that I began several days ago. I think this topic is quite relevant to the current situation and has not been discussed anywhere else that I have seen. Freddie Mac and FNMA report directly to the federal government and have oversight or supervision provided by the central government. The government has in fact and without denial approved either de juris or de facto each and every issuance of preferred stock or subordinated debt that has been issued by either agency. These agencies are regulated by federal charter and overseen by the federal government, and I find it then problematical that the American government would not pay all of the obligations of these agencies without massive legal issues that would extend past the agencies and to the supervisory agency (the Office of Federal Housing Enterprise Oversight [OFHEO]) mandated by Congress. The SEC avidly proclaims that those people or institutions in a supervisory role are responsible, and there is a wealth of case law to support this concept, so I ask the pertinent question: How could the SEC not hold the oversight division of the central government responsible for the exact same criteria if they approved the issuances of these debts and then if the agencies were forced by the Treasury to not pay their obligations?

The instance most often cited when discussing the perils of the junior debt of FNMA and Freddie Mac is the Continental Illinois Bank failure. Let me point out the obvious distinctions:

- The bank was a totally private corporation without federal charter and without government sponsorship.
- The bank was not created by an act of Congress.
- The bank was not requested by Congress to expand its role in providing affordable housing to the citizens of the country.
- The bank did not have congressionally mandated oversight that was specific and limited to the two GSE agencies.

Given the yields presently available for the preferred stock and the subordinated debt, there is a large opportunity to make money with a risk that is de minimis when all aspects of the risk are carefully considered, and I do not think that the rating agencies and others have fully appreciated the legal consequences, much less the economic problems and reputational issues that would present themselves if the agencies, with stipulated federal supervision, did not meet all of their obligations. Let me quote directly from the mission statement of OFHEO so that you can fully appreciate the context of the point I am making here:

OFHEO's mission is to promote housing and a strong national housing finance system by ensuring the safety and soundness of Fannie Mae (Federal National Mortgage Association) and Freddie Mac (Federal Home Loan Mortgage Corporation). OFHEO works to ensure the capital adequacy and financial safety and soundness of two housing government-sponsored enterprises (GSEs)—Fannie Mae and Freddie Mac. . . . Fannie Mae and Freddie Mac are Congressionally-chartered, publicly-owned corporations whose shares are listed on the New York Stock Exchange. Under terms of their GSE charters, they are exempt from state and local taxation and from registration requirements of the Securities and Exchange Commission. Each firm has a back-up credit line with the U.S. Treasury. . . . OFHEO's oversight responsibilities include: conducting broad based examinations of Fannie Mae and Freddie Mac; developing a risk-based capital standard, using a "stress test" that simulates stressful interest rate and credit risk scenarios; making quarterly findings of capital adequacy based on minimum capital standards and a risk-based standard; prohibiting excessive executive compensation; issuing regulations concerning capital and enforcement standards; and taking necessary enforcement actions. . . . In its safety and soundness mission, OFHEO has regulatory authority similar to such other federal financial regulators as the Federal Deposit Insurance Corporation, the Office of the Comptroller of the Currency, the Office of Thrift Supervision and the Board of Governors of the Federal Reserve System.

Given the strictures of the U.S. Constitution, the arbiter of last resort in the case of the two GSE agencies not paying all of their obligations would be the judiciary. Regardless of any preemptive actions by the Treasury that would erase the obligations of the GSE agencies, which I certainly hope does not become a reality, I find it hard to believe that the courts would side with a cancellation of debts that had been approved by the oversight office mandated by Congress. Given the current yields on the preferred stock and the subordinated debt, I realize I am taking the minority view, but I find much more opportunity here than risk, though I am pointedly aware that there are different viewpoints; but also bear in mind that those viewpoints are what has created the opportunity.

> *When written in Chinese the word "crisis" is composed of two characters— one represents danger and the other represents opportunity.*
>
> —John F. Kennedy

What Is Given Can Be Taken

September 8, 2008

The biblical text seems to ring true today, just as it provided the wisdom of millennia past. Here, we have an encapsulated rendition of the crux of the problem at hand and the foundation for the modern-day parable of FNMA and Freddie Mac, who were forced by statute to serve two masters.

> *No one can serve two masters, because either he will hate one and love the other, or be loyal to one and despise the other. You cannot serve God and riches!*
> —Matthew 6:24

One of the amazing parts of this unfolding story—to me, in any event—is that Congress asked these agencies to expand their role in housing and then axed them by Treasury fiat for fulfilling their mission. If that is not problematic on its own merits, consider that they had federal oversight the entire time from exactly the same agency, the Federal Housing Finance Agency (FHFA), that has now taken them over. Did not this same oversight agency tacitly approve the December 2007 issuance of the FNMA preferred stock and the December 2007 issuance of the Freddie preferred stock? Under U.S. securities law and regulation, does the supervisor have no culpability for the actions of what they supervised? The answer, of course, is apparently not, though the capricious exercise of power by the Treasury will still fall to the scrutiny of the judiciary and the Congress, as both will be called to task. I have no issue with the line being drawn at the equity holders, though some very high-powered money managers might disagree, but to draw it to protect the subordinated debt holders and deny the rights of the preferred holders both seems ethically wrong and an injustice to many who relied on the pronouncements of the GSE agencies when purchasing those shares.

One of the more amazing parts of the story here is that banks were encouraged and legally allowed to own the preferred shares of the federally chartered agencies as part of their capital structure, and now they are being rather severely penalized for following the government's lead. Make what argument you like, but the allowance of utilization here was not meant to discourage the use by the banks but rather to prop up and help support the preferred issuances when they came to market, which has now been shown to be nothing more than a governmental fabrication by Mr. Paulson's actions. It is my view that the action of the Treasury to not include the preferred holders as part of the bailout was morally, ethically, and legally wrong, and the last is yet to be determined.

The other problem I have with the entire bailout package is the oversight issue regarding the financials. Clearly, Paulson stated that they had found irregularities and uncovered new concerns; where was this oversight agency, the same agency that just assumed control of FNMA and Freddie Mac, during this whole process? Why should we think that their abilities as operators will be any better than their abilities as overseers? Does not the government as supervisor have legal liability for "failure to supervise" as much as the SEC and others have mandated these responsibilities for commercial and investment banks? So, one must ask if FHFA is above the law.

The large losers in the preferred debacle are some names whose stock and capital may be impaired by the nonsensical line in the sand where the Treasury decided to draw the line. American International Group (AIG) and Hartford Financial Services Group were the largest institutional preferred stockholders of Fannie and Freddie, as of year-end 2007, with AIG holding $313.99 million in Freddie Mac preferred shares and $266.73 million in Fannie Mae preferred stock. Of the large-cap banks, M&T Bank, Fifth Third Bancorp, and National City along with Sovereign—which may actually have the largest exposure, though you have to look in several places to find it—it appears as if their ownership equates to about 13 percent of their tangible assets. It appears that M&T has $120.0 million, or 4 percent of its tangible capital, in the preferred stock of Fannie and Freddie; Fifth Third has $55 million, or 1 percent of its tangible capital, in their preferred stock, while Fifth Third took $13 million in other-than-temporary impairments on their stocks in the second quarter. The regional banks have even greater exposures to these preferred shares of Fannie and Freddie. Gateway Financial Holdings has a $38.5 million exposure to Fannie and Freddie preferred stock, or 34 percent of its tangible capital. Midwest Banc Holdings has $62.0 million in preferred shares, or 32 percent of its tangible capital, and Westamerica Bancorp has $44.5 million, or 16 percent of its tangible capital, in their preferred stock. I am sure that the smaller banks all thought they were maintaining conservative positions given the guarantee of the GSE agencies, but now the Treasury has reneged on its obligations and impaired these smaller banks.

In general, I applaud the plan but decry the execution!

We Have Been Grievously Misled

September 9, 2008

t is my opinion that the judiciary will weigh in on the FNMA and Freddie Mac takeovers before this is all over. America is a country of laws, and even the government is not above the law. This is what we teach in schools and tell our children, and this is how we hold ourselves up to the rest of the world. Politicians may blunder and err in judgment, and mistakes can be made, but, in the end, the law is supposed to hold to protect the public.

Part of America's legal system rests upon case law, which has a postulate called "reliance." If you can prove that you relied on someone's assertions to do something or that their pronouncements caused you to undertake an action that you would not have otherwise engaged in then, there is legal liability.

Now let us examine the statements of the last 48 hours. Everyone, from Paulson to Dodd to the members of the Fed, is dancing around saying that all kinds of irregularities were just found that necessitated the actions of the secretary of the Treasury. One moment, please—both of the GSE agencies in question have had federal oversight and supervision this whole time. No one has accused anyone at the housing agencies of fraud or hiding anything, and the financial statements have been released quarterly under federal supervision,

Reasonable reliance is usually referred to as a theory of recovery in contract law. It was what a prudent person might believe and act upon based on something told by another. Sometimes a person acts in reliance on the promise of a profit or other benefit, only to learn that the statements or promises were either incorrect or were exaggerated. The one who acted to their detriment in reasonable reliance may recover damages for the costs of his/her actions or demand performance.

—USLegal.com

so just one moment please—where was the Federal Housing Finance Agency then? All summer long, Paulson, Bernanke, and Lockhart of the FHFA kept repeating that the two agencies were well capitalized and federal supervision was in place. People relied on all of this to make securities transactions and now we are told that the Treasury's actions were taken because of accounting irregularities and lack of capital and the management of these two federally chartered agencies is being turned over to the same group that supervised them and told us everything was fine while we went out and bought their securities based on all of these assurances.

No, no, I can see the smoke; the plain truth as seen by me is that these people either lied to all of us, to the public, or they are incompetent and have no business being in their respective positions. I do not accept the scam that these people are trying to foster upon us. I do not accept the notion that there were new irregularities, when they oversaw and supervised both agencies the entire time. These three people and other people in various governmental positions must be held accountable for either their untruths or their statements of obvious fiction, and the people of the United States and the rest of the world cannot be punished for relying on their fictitious statements when buying the securities approved by the FHFA and GSE federal agencies touted by these men as being financially sound.

The current mess that has been caused by the government must find redress in the courts or Congress, or the theory of reliance and the laws that encompass this concept have no validity, especially—most especially—as these people occupy positions in the government of public trust. It is morally, ethically, and legally wrong to have public officials who supervise the two housing agencies represent the financial soundness of these agencies, thus causing people to buy their securities, relying on their pronouncements, only to be told later that dividends will not be paid because they are protecting the American people, to whom they have been lying this entire time; or, if not lying, then misleading us by their own incompetence either singularly or in collusion, as they were the people entrusted with the oversight by Congress.

What strikes me as incremental parts of the entire agency fiasco were the raising of the mortgage limits for both FNMA and Freddie and then the lowering of the surplus requirements shortly thereafter. "The lowering of the prudential cushion was appropriate in line with the company's progress and with the need to maintain safe and sound operations," said oversight director Lockhart. In fact, the FHFA has supervised and directed and approved all of the FNMA and Freddie Mac operations, and they must take at least partial responsibility for the deterioration of these two agencies; yet, in a feast of irrational thinking, the government has now put them in charge of management and oversight and maligned investors worldwide as a result of their unbelievable ineptitude.

You may think I am speaking harshly, but the facts are the facts here, and the supervisors must take responsibility for their charges. This strikes me as similar to the investment bank CEOs who fired everyone in the mortgage department when they had losses, to protect their own behinds. I say loudly and clearly to the Fed, the Treasury, and the FHFA: You were entrusted to supervise the housing agencies, you failed in your duties, you have failed in your prescription for fixing the problems by your poor choice of new management, and you have grievously hurt investors who relied on your characterizations to invest in these two companies.

One Moment, Please!

September 10, 2008

There is a commonality that exists for all children growing up in the United States. From Staten Island to Kansas City, and from Miami to the coast of Oregon, we are taught that America is a democracy and that the voice of a single citizen can make a meaningful difference. This morning, far past the age of my childhood, I shall put this long-held belief to the test.

Following is a letter that I have sent to the members of our Congress and Senate. For those of you who believe, as I do, that the owners of the preferred shares of FNMA and Freddie Mac have been grievously wronged by the actions of Secretary Paulson, I invite you to join with me and send your own letter to the elected officials of our country. Capricious dictates of a single man must not be allowed to injure the citizens of our country or the worldwide investors who relied on pronouncements of the current administration to make their financial determinations. The reputational damage that has been caused by the secretary of the Treasury must not stand.

September 10, 2008

Dear Sir or Madam,

My name is Mark J. Grant and I run the structured finance and the syndicate departments for a publically traded investment bank. During my thirty-four year tenure on Wall Street I have run capital markets and served on the board of directors of four investment banks. I have also been president and on the board of directors of a public company in telecom. I currently write a commentary on the financial markets, Out of the Box, *that is distributed to more than 5,500 financial institutions in forty-eight countries inclusive of being published by the eminent MTN-I out of London each day. In my entire life I have never written to Congress but today I am relying upon the tenet that we all learned as school children; that one single American Citizen can make a difference.*

I believe you are being misled by many people in the Administration when it comes to the shameful treatment received by the preferred shareholders in Secretary Paulson's recent takeover of FNMA and Freddie Mac. Many institutions and individuals alike relied upon the pronouncements of the government that these government-sponsored enterprises were financially sound when purchasing their shares. Preferred shares, as you know, do not represent ownership in a corporation but are merely a junior class of security to subordinated or senior debt. A very large amount of the American public are investors and for them to rely upon a federally chartered enterprise to receive dividends and then for them not to receive them as mandated by Secretary Paulson is an American injustice in my opinion and is wrong on moral, ethical and perhaps even legal grounds. These two housing agencies had federal oversight the entire time of their existence and if there were financial problems I ask why the Federal Housing Finance Agency allowed the GSE agencies to issue preferred stock to raise capital in December 2007 and then in May 2008?

In fact the FHFA approved the raising of the mortgage limits that the Agencies could purchase and lowered their capital ratios while Chairman Bernanke, Secretary Paulson, Director Lockhart and a slew of other people in government were assuring the American public that these agencies were on solid financial ground. Having a federal charter and having a government sponsorship is now meaningless if Congress does not stand up to the obligations of the agencies they have created and the dividends of the preferred stocks are just as much an obligation of these agencies as the classes of senior debt. One can make a valid argument, in my view, that separates the common stock from the other classes of securities but the line should have been drawn between the common stock and the other debts. To pay the subordinated and senior debt holders while leaving the preferred holder, who relied upon the government sponsorship and statements by many in the administration of financial health and an implicit government guarantee, to be without receipt of the stipulated dividends is equivalent to the U.S. government not paying its stated obligations. If you are unaware of the implications I can assure you that the American public and the world have been severely damaged by Secretary Paulson's actions as the price of the $25.00 securities are now trading around $3.00 and the owners are not receiving the income to which they were promised by the two agencies of the government.

What I ask for today is simple and straightforward; I am asking Congress to direct Secretary Paulson to pay the obligations of these two government agencies, all of the obligations, based upon federal charter, government sponsorship, federal oversight and the assurances made by those who knew, or clearly should have known, the financial soundness of these two housing agencies. The American public and other investors across the globe relied upon these pronouncements when purchasing the preferred shares and the information provided was, as we all know now, apparently inaccurate. These agencies were created by Congress, had supervision mandated by Congress, were allowed to issue securities under specified federal supervision of the FHFA and now in a capricious and executive dictate Secretary Paulson has violated the specific charters of these two government agencies that have been created by Congress. I take no issue with the overall rescue plan for FNMA and Freddie Mac but I find it inconceivable that Secretary Paulson has mandated a plan that does not pay all of the obligations of these two agencies that were specifically chartered by the American Congress. This is tantamount, in my view, to the United States of America not paying its debts and the reputational damage done to our country by the actions of Secretary Paulson is a travesty for our nation.

I thank you for your consideration of this matter.

Mark J. Grant

Freddie Mac and the Fairy Tale

March 12, 2009

You may have seen the announcement, but it may not have struck you quite in the manner that it did me, which is why you are reading this, after all. Freddie Mac announced yesterday that it would book a fourth quarter loss of $23.9 billion and that it would require $30.8 billion of new capital from the Treasury. Freddie Mac's new CEO resigned after six months at the helm just as the numbers were released. Now here is the rub: The new capital infusion will raise the government's position to $45.6 billion in preferred stock with an annual coupon of 10 percent, which equates to $4.6 billion and is more than it has earned in most previous years. This is at the same time that Congress is demanding the issuance of more mortgages at lower rates. This is akin to Paul robbing Peter and Peter having nothing but an expired Visa card. In other words, it's not working for Peter and it's not working for Paul, and there is no way, in present circumstances, that anyone can afford to buy bread.

I want to talk about political and economic fairy tales.

—Ronald Reagan,
40th U.S. President (1911–2004)

The simple truth is that Congress has created a fairy tale by putting the housing agencies in conservatorship and then demanding the impossible and expecting to get paid back for it. The situation is not only an untenable one but, at some point, the bricks have to hit the mortar and will hit the mortar. You know, sometimes there is just no way around the obvious regardless of everyone's desire to rush around proclaiming otherwise. The reality of this situation is that no Congress has ever been idiotic enough to bankrupt a federal agency before and then scramble around claiming some kind of ever-changing guarantee that the federal government will continue to pay the debts of two bankrupt agencies so they can continue to borrow. There is a point, and we are awfully close to it, I fear, when people will actually look at the coffee can and realize that it is empty; and let me assure you—it is empty.

With the demands put on FNMA and Freddie Mac for more lending at decreasing rates, these two agencies couldn't pay back the government if the preferred stock coupon were 1 percent and survive economically. You do not have to accept my reasoning alone here; just read what Freddie Mac itself stated yesterday: "The amounts we are obligated to pay in dividends on the senior preferred stock are substantial and will have an adverse impact on our financial position and net worth." On the issue of principal repayment, they said, "We may not be able to do so for the foreseeable future, if at all." There you go, in black and white, so please do not bury your head in the sand and look around like you didn't know what was happening.

Now you may think—and probably correctly so—that the government will be forced to do something, and I agree with that position, but just what they might do is a cause of concern to me. The right thing, of course, would be to just nationalize Freddie and FNMA and make their obligations direct obligations of the federal government, but they don't want the debt on the books, so this fantasy has continued until one day when the world realizes that the emperor has no clothes. Then, you will truly see some "shock and awe." All it would take is for China or Japan or even Bill Gross at Pimco to look at the balance sheets of these two agencies; realize that they were, in fact, bankrupt; and wonder aloud about the fuzzy guarantee, and the game would be up. This situation is not a joke, and each of you should start to ponder the outcome that may be forthcoming as a result of federal agencies that have become insolvent.

It may be that finally these agencies will get taken over and their obligations become direct obligations of the government like the Government National Mortgage Association (GNMA), as an example, but suppose that doesn't happen; now there is a frightening thought and one that must be considered. I had little faith in the government several years ago, and I can assure you that I feel no better about what they might or might not do at this point. What is absolutely clear to me is that the present situation cannot continue without severe consequences because at some point the children's game of the "pretend friend" is ended by their parents. Freddie and FNMA jointly guarantee about 50 percent of the mortgages in this country, and they are now controlled by the government, which has created a sinkhole for these two entities that just cannot continue, in my view. With no "direct guarantee" and very questionable definitions of some sort of guarantee, does not one have to look at the balance sheets of the agencies at some point? If you do not, then prudent judgment is not being exercised. I have made my thoughts well known enough about the mortgage securitizations and questioned the "political risk" of who is going to actually pay for the losses that will surely be taken in our collective desire to help homeowners, but there, at least, is some kind of collateral for the debt. But in the plain vanilla debt of these two entities, there is nothing but a "promise to pay" by two agencies that are bleeding red ink.

The very structure that is now in place will, without doubt, make it impossible for the agencies to repay their debt without more and more government

God defend me from that Welsh fairy,
Lest he transform me to a piece of cheese!

—William Shakespeare

loans that cannot be repaid, by Freddie's own admission, so these two companies are now trapped in a death spiral. The bet has now come down to only one thing: whether the government will take them over. If it does not, then someone will surely opt out of the current game of musical chairs!

Chapter 2

The Call on the 10-Year Treasury

Trying to predict the direction of interest rates is one of the most difficult and critical decisions that any money manager makes; it affects each and every market. Economists and strategists are paid large amounts of money to help with this issue because it is so critical for everyone's portfolios. To arrive at the point where I make this call and stick my neck squarely under the executioner's blade requires a lot of intense thought. For me it is a two-cigar problem, and it also requires lots of strong coffee. I provide advice daily to some 5,500 large financial institutions in approximately 48 countries, including central banks, sovereign wealth funds, insurance companies, mutual funds, and money managers of all descriptions. Consequently, when I indicate a change of direction, it is only after I am relatively certain that events coupled with market psychology, sometimes referred to as sentiment, has reached a critical juncture so that a turn is coming. This process also brings to bear another crucial decision that involves timing. To make the decision after the turn has come is of little value and a call in retrospect is hardly a useful exercise. You must be out in front of the change in direction, and this is not, I assure you, an easy task.

The temptation to form premature theories upon insufficient data is the bane of our profession.

—Sherlock Holmes

I quote "the world's most famous consulting detective" here because he is quite a useful fellow to assist you in getting the markets right. The methodology that he utilizes, exquisite deductive reasoning, is also applicable to financial reasoning. It is not technical charts or economic quantum mechanics or a host of other indicators that allow me to reach a final conclusion. I use many of these indicators along the way, no doubt, but in the end it is focused thinking and carefully calculated rational judgment that allows me to reach my conclusion and then to present it to my clients, who are all professional managers of money. My commentary, in fact, is not released to the general public at all, and so I wander in the bounds of other beasts of burden, who are quite ready to challenge me at any point after I have made my case and presented it to them. You may trust me here—this is not the shy and retiring crowd of academics and cloakroom postulators, but the guys that put the money down on the table and are held accountable for their bets. Consequently, if you are advising them how to bet and in what order, then you better know what you are doing and you had better be prepared for the consequences of providing your opinion. These people are an unforgiving lot, and like the rest of the decisions made in the financial markets, you are either right or you are not. On Wall Street, hell is not only paved with good intentions, to quote Dante, but hard work, diligent application, and the length of hours worked, when it all gets down to it, mean nothing—you either get the joke or the punch line has eluded you and you fall by the wayside. Here is one of the most difficult things to teach the young up-and-comers and the realization of it or the lack thereof often separates the men from the boys.

In the early summer of 2010, I went on record calling for the 10-year Treasury to head down to a range of 2.25 to 2.50 percent based on fears of deflation, the possibility of another economic downturn, the problems in Europe, and a plethora of indicators that I watch to help signal the direction of yields. I was, in fact, correct, and we broke through 2.50 percent, back and forth, for a number of days.

Then I reversed course. This was based on the forthcoming American elections, the probability that the Republicans would gain in power, the relative stability achieved in Europe, economic indicators suggesting that another downturn was not eminent, and the actions of the Federal

Reserve Bank. This was also a correct call, and yields have risen since then; in addition, the yield curve has steepened, which was also my prediction.

Now the people that manage money are a suspicious group, as well they should be in our profession. All kinds of touts are trying to get at us and all with their own agendas. When people first start to read my commentary, I am sure many of them credit my calls to luck and to being on the right side of the roll of the dice but 36 years on the Street and being out there each and every day finally have brought more than a few around to the opinion that I may know a thing or two and that providence does not allow for that much luck; then they begin to pay more attention to my musings. As the author of a commentary of this size, it makes me smile, and I proceed ahead with each new day bringing fresh data to the equation that fashions my thinking. I generally jump out of bed each morning at 4:00 A.M. enthusiastic about what may be coming and what might have happened in Europe and Asia overnight as I slept, and I cannot wait to reconnect with the world to see just what is going on. There is no video game that has been created or will be created that is better than Wall Street. I call it the Great Game, and I am as fascinated with it now as I was all those years ago when I first wandered into a trading room and stood amazingly still while I watched all of the antics of the people scurrying about. While I had no idea what they were doing, nor did I understand even half of what they were saying, I so wanted to join the crowd and engage in whatever it was that I return again and again to the playing field.

One of the best and brightest money managers in the world and a client of mine calls it his "great obsession," and I think that is right. It is a worldwide sandbox where the boys come to play—to engage in ritualized combat—and where, if you can somehow manage to win, you get to enjoy more fruits of your labor than you ever imagined possible.

The call on interest rates does just not influence the debt markets or yields on Treasuries by themselves, but affects each and every market in existence. Nothing on Wall Street lives in stasis, and each and every market is judged in a relative value to every other one. The level of the stock market or the level of the bond markets influence, in very real ways, the direction and the behavior of everything else. Like cousins at a family picnic, the gathering tumbles along in an intertwined fashion. Consequently, it is just not a call on yields that must be made, but also the consequences of the result if you are right. You must constantly ask the critical question, "What does this mean?" and then be prepared to answer the question. It is here, by the way, where most people stumble, as they may see the handwriting on the wall, but they do not under-

Advice is judged by results, not by intentions.

— Cicero

stand the implications of either what is written or who is reading it. To win at the Great Game requires skill sets not taught in any school, and it is only years of playing, regardless of your IQ, that may bring consistently positive results.

United States Treasuries are the baseline securities from which almost all other securities in the world are judged. This is true of sovereign debt, corporate debt, and almost any other market that you can consider. Then, in this arena, the most critical single maturity is the 10-year Treasury. Everything fluctuates from this focal point, including mortgage rates, securities tied to mortgages, and even the yield curve itself, which steepens or goes flat or inverted off of this critical mark. Imagine interest rates dancing one way and another all tethered to this point, and you will then understand why predicting the price and yield of this security is so critically important. Short rates are often determined by the Fed, but the 10-year is reflective of intrinsic value, meaning that it heads this way and that way dependent on future expectations. This is what makes the call here so important—you are peering out into the future and making an informed guess, but a guess nonetheless, and one that you better get right!

There Is No Blushing in Brussels

June 30, 2010

Surely, no government on the continent is the blushing bride this morning or even the virtuous young girl as speculation mounts that there were deals and back door affairs transacted to lessen the borrowing amount at the European Central Bank (ECB) today. The ECB reports that only $161 billion was borrowed, which was far less than the consensus view and far less than my estimate, but then all the cards may not be on the table and the joker remains in the deck. "Oh no," you say, "certainly not that"; but there is a reason that the French, unlike Americans, keep all hands on the table when the landed gentry dine in Avignon or Normandie. There is speculation that the sauerbraten was passed in Germany from one bank to another, which will find its way back to the ECB in due course, but not today. The same game is played out in the Spanish version of hiding the empanada, while the French have always played "Ring around the Roquefort" with great dexterity.

After the news that credit-default swaps (CDSs) tied to Greek bonds fell 32.5 basis points to 970.5 while contracts on Portugal declined 8.6 basis points to 322, it might be expected swaps on Spain dropped 1 basis point

> *One is never so dangerous when one has no shame, than when one has grown too old to blush.*
>
> —Marquis de Sade

> **Sir Percy:** *If we are to succeed, we must maintain our anonymity, mask our identities, even if it means suffering the mockery of others; being taken for fools, fops, nitwits, even cowards.*
> **Lord Timothy Hastings:** *That's the easy part. The hard part's not being able to boast about our exploits to the ladies.*
>
> — Baroness Emmuska Orczy,
> *The Scarlet Pimpernel*

Porthos: This sash was a gift to me, from the Queen of America.

D'Artagnan: There's no Queen of America!

Porthos: I beg to differ, infant. We're on quite intimate terms, unless you can prove otherwise.

— Alexandre Dumas,
The Three Musketeers

to 271.5, according to the CMA Data Vision. CDSs also declined for many of Europe's major banks after the ECB announcement, but the whole exercise just made me smile and nod and appreciate the joie de vivre of the European wink, and what else did we expect, anyway? Dollars to brioches the next round of financing, the weekly issuance, will show a higher amount, and the three-month facility will build in size over the next few weeks.

In the meantime, I would be preparing for a 10-year Treasury approaching 2.50 percent, and I would not be breathing too many sighs of relief. I must tell you, and I certainly admit that when I saw this morning's ECB announcement, I started laughing—not the right-from-the-gut, tears-in-your-eyes kind of laughing, but a good bout of chuckling nonetheless. I had a sneaking suspicion that the dandies on the Danube might do something like this, and I expressed this to an international client yesterday, whose response was, "As prudent men of some experience, would we expect anything less?"

Nothing less, of course, and thanks for the laugh!

Spasms of Fear

July 15, 2010

L et's take 10 steps back. Let's take a moment this morning to
examine the rest of the year and give some thought to setting up
for it. The biggest risk continues to be Europe and whether the
European Union (EU) muddles through in some form or fashion or
whether it comes apart at the seams. Regardless of your opinion of the
ultimate outcome, the risk is there, no doubt. My opinion is well known
and I'll stand there, but even if I am wrong, the potential risk is so
serious that I do not think anyone can ignore it without putting his or
her portfolio in serious peril. Europe is literally a make-or-break decision, and the best strategy has to be prepared for a breakup even if the
actuality does not take place. I am a big believer in safe over sorry.

I am fortunate this morning to have the head of investments of one
of the major U.S. insurance companies aboard my boat. He regards the
European situation as a continuing series of "spasms of fear." I think my
friend is right. You have to be prepared for these events and minimize
your risks, and at the same time you have to be prepared to have some
capital that can take advantage of the pending opportunities.

The next large concern has to be the forthcoming elections. I think
that the odds are that the Democrats will have much less power after the
balloting comes and goes in November, and it will just be a question of
the size of the change in power. This should be tucked into your minds
now, as the markets will react to this event, and to not begin to plan for
the elections would be misguided.

Next, I would point out the distinct possibility of the 10-year
Treasury going to somewhere between 2.25 and 2.50 percent. I think
this takes place as the overall economy does not meet expectations, as
Europe cavorts from one crisis to the next and as money continues to
flow into bonds and out of equities. The cash flows into bonds will

cause compression in and of themselves, while corporate bonds and other secondary securities will widen in the first instance and then play catch-up during the rest of the year. Ultimately, probably sometime in the first or second quarter of 2011, the Fed will begin to back off and yields will begin to rise, but that is not likely to happen anytime in 2010. The game changer here, however, remains the situation in Europe, which may well cause a financial upheaval and very low rates well into the next few years. This will be problematic for many of you, as finding yield in an arena of appropriate risk is going to be very difficult. All of us can participate in a flight to quality for a time, but eventually the search for return crowds back into the picture, and at current levels of interest rates, finding a reasonable return either from yield or appreciation is a very difficult task.

Here is the most difficult investment issue in my opinion: It is my odds-on viewpoint that America and the rest of the world are facing several years of very low interest rates and very low yields in investments. The opportunities, when they come, will be related to upheavals that can be taken advantage of, but I think the overall financial conditions are going to be one long slog through the mire.

One of These Days

August 1, 2010

In this life, one thing counts
In the bank, large amounts
I'm afraid these don't grow on trees.

—Fagin, *Oliver,* Charles Dickens

Truer words were never spoken. Given my viewpoint that the 10-year Treasury is on its way to 2.25 to 2.50 percent, it is going to get tricky to get much yield or appreciation out of anything. If you think it is tough now, well, me lads, it is going to get worse. There are various ways to play it, of course. Long-dated Treasuries for appreciation and liquidity or long corporate bonds, where additional yield may be found and so forth, but going right down the center of short-term or even medium-term securities is not going to get you much in the way of either besting your competition or beating some index, as the correlation coefficient is not much more than a few percent at this point

> **Annie:** *Who would want to kill Mr. Warbucks?*
> **Grace:** *The Bolsheviks, dear. He's living proof that the American system really works and the Bolsheviks don't want anyone to know about that.*
> **Annie:** *The Bolsheviks? Leapin' lizards!*
> —Carol Sobieski, *Annie*

in bonds. You should also start setting up for the American elections, some additional surprises from across the pond, more money coming into the debt markets, and the possibility of another slowdown in the U.S. economy.

For most of us it is not a "hard knocks life," but it is going to be a hard knocks time to find return. One sector that comes to mind, that has lagged and that through time is straightening itself out, is the insurance sector. Let's consider Lincoln National Corporation (LNC) first. They just reported out a quarterly profit of $255 million versus a loss last year of $161 million, and last month they paid off all of the preferred stock owned by the U.S. government. I have looked carefully at their financials, and the situation is definitely improving; I would take a look at their longer debt as a chance to capture both yield and compression. Insurance companies are generally a good bet as the cycle changes. Everyone runs from them when a credit crisis begins, and then they lag everything as things straighten out, and finally they catch up with the market as the situation improves and people realize that they are still around and kicking. This is mostly because investors are wary of what is in their portfolios when the crisis begins and people are afraid that they have some kind of nuclear holdings, but many of these companies have been around for generations and it is not their first rodeo, and they somehow make it through to the other side.

> *In here, life is beautiful. The girls are beautiful. Even the orchestra is beautiful!*
> —Joe Masteroff, *Cabaret*

It was approximately two years ago, shortly after the American credit crisis began, that I suggested exiting or reducing your exposure to the insurance sector. Today, I suggest it is time to reenter. During the crisis, some companies, American International Group (AIG) in particular, got so ridiculous in spread that I was a buyer for some clients with great frequency. I continue to like the credit currently and still find their yield attractive, but there are now other names to consider as well. Another name to now give some thought to is Liberty Mutual. Some of their longer-dated bonds now yield just shy of 9 percent, and I think, with falling yields and continuing compression, that value can be gained here. Some of the higher-rated credits, such as Teachers Insurance and Annuity Association (TIAA) or Massachusetts Mutual, also have good value, but the market has recognized that and the opportunity is no longer there except for core holdings.

The Offerings You See from My Group

As I have sailed up the East Coast and met with clients, it has become apparent to me that not everyone understands clearly how I operate, and I readily admit that it is not the standard model of dealing with institutional accounts. For the most part, Angela, Tara, and I operate as an independent and self-contained unit of our firm. We do the trading and interface with our clients, and no offering is made by any of us unless I personally think there is value in the offering. I take that responsibility head-on, and if I think something is mispriced or I do not like the credit or the sector, then we do not show it out—simple as that. The offering may not be for you or you may disagree with the premise, but my opinions are expressed not only in my daily commentary, but also in my choice of what we offer. It is a different model, no doubt, but it is one that works for me, as the decision is mine and not my firm's and I believe my clients appreciate that I personally stand up for what is put on the table in front of them.

During my 36 years on Wall Street I have never forgotten one of the great speeches in American theatre that was spoken by the immortal Sky Masterson in *Guys and Dolls*:

> *One of these days in your travels, a guy is going to show you a brand-new deck of cards on which the seal is not yet broken. Then this guy is going to offer to bet you that he can make the jack of spades jump out of this brand-new deck of cards and squirt cider in your ear. But, son, do not accept this bet, because as sure as you stand there, you're going to wind up with an ear full of cider.*

> —Jo Swerling and Abe Burrows

The Legacy Influences

August 19, 2010

Where we come from is one determinant of where we are going. This is an axiom with a lot of truth to it. To this you can add the notion of where we "recently" came from, as time either exacerbates or diminishes current market psychology and direction, including the volatility of the moves. I cite this today as a consideration of current economic conditions. Lately, I have seen a whole raft of commentary about the Dow having yields higher than the 10-year Treasury and also speculation that we are currently in some sort of bond bubble. Both discussions want to make projections as if we are in some kind of normal range of events, and right there, at that point, is where I think both discussions begin their erroneous presentation and hence calculations made from both assertions are wrong in the first instance.

Factually, the Dow's yield was higher than 10-year Treasuries from 1920 through 1957 and then went negative until 2008–2009, when it spiked and then went negative again, and has recently broken to the upside once again. That is the truth of it, and you can make a lot of noise about the occurrence, but I do not place much stock in its value. Then you can add in the conversation about a "bond bubble," but I place no inherent value in that notion, either. It is not a question for me of some new game plan or some new way of visualizing the markets—it is just a question of the correct interpretation of the facts.

In the first place, if there is a bubble that was in occurrence for many years and has now been broken, I think it is that equities will outperform bonds over a given period of time. This notion has held sway for decades and has only recently been pinpricked with the hard slap of very cold water. It just is not so, and coupled with that has been the recognition that equities are at the bottom of the capital structure and the further recognition of the implications of this reality when times get tough.

Dividends and preferred dividends can be waved aside by the flick of some board of directors' late afternoon yawn while the debt must get paid or the company goes into bankruptcy and the management loses their jobs. In fact, the comparison of yield from debt against the yield from common dividends is a comparison of apples and pomegranates. The first "must" get paid or there is no company, while the second "may" get paid if the suits in the boardroom decide to do it. Our recent financial calamity drove this last point home to investors, and that is clearly demonstrated by $562 billion into bonds funds and $240 billion out of equity funds. You can argue all you like, but there it is: Investors of all stripes woke up and got the joke. Now money moves markets, and if anything has changed, it is that corporates and other assets are going to trade tighter to Treasuries as a consequence of the change in the public's asset allocation.

The next reality is that short yields are at nano spreads to absolute zero. Zero is the floor, my friends—nowhere to go from there. Except for a few silly moments, no one is going to pay the government for holding their money. Consequently, when yields are at this point as manipulated by the Fed and market conditions, there is going to be a continuous compression of both secondary assets against Treasuries and of the yield curve against the absolute floor until both the Fed and economic conditions take a radical turn. This is not rocket science; it is just common sense.

Next, you throw in an economy that is sputtering along—and that may be the best that can be said—and add in a dash of financial travails and uncertainty across the pond and you have now defined our present reality. In my opinion, there are no bubbles at present, no conditions that do not reasonably reflect the facts, and certainly no uncertainty in my mind about why we are exactly where we are at this point in time. My view is the 10-year Treasury going reasonably soon to 2.25 to 2.50 percent, continuing compression in corporate bonds and all other bonds against Treasuries, yield as coupled with safety getting harder and harder to find, a stock market going either down or

> *Facts are stubborn things; and whatever may be our wishes, our inclinations, or the dictates of our passions, they cannot alter the state of the facts and evidence.*
> —John Adams

nowhere, and leverage as being the best way to achieve some decent results until the moment comes where the Fed stops their game and when the economy turns up once again, which I think is several years out. No consultation with the Wizard is required here. The facts speak for themselves; all you have to do is listen.

Highway to the Danger Zone

August 20, 2010

There are a number of technical indicators that are flashing red. The first and foremost are to be found in the bond markets. Yes, I projected a 2.25 to 2.50 percent yield on the 10-year Treasury some time ago, and yes, it looks like I will be right on the money shortly, but the velocity of the move is startling. For the most part in my commentary, I give you the conclusions and do not waste your time as to how I got there, but I do wish to point out today that certain velocity indicators are giving me some concern. Rather than regarding this as some form of bubble, which I discussed yesterday, I think we are getting a strong signal that the economy has stopped sputtering and is spiraling downward once again, no credit crisis this time, just part two of the recession as all of the stimulus—some well spent and some not—has provided some respite but no cure. The Fed apparently holds a similar view, as they are reinvesting their money and not shrinking the balance sheet—a sure sign of their opinion. This does not bode well for the equity markets, and overall I advise caution in stocks.

I think we are bordering right on the brink of deflation, and the increase in unemployment claims and several major indexes are painting a picture that, at least to me, bears no resemblance to pretty. Further evidence of this can be found not only in yields cycling down all across the curve but in the few areas of relative value that were left, such as BBB Build America Bonds (BABs), that have tightened up like a bolt being ratcheted down by the big monetary wrench. For investors in fixed income products, value is at a scarcity premium, both relative and absolute, and the compression to Treasuries is just unrelenting. The scenario is now like being in a very crowded parking lot; you can park the money, but you aren't driving anywhere. What is worse, I suppose, is that I don't see our current environment getting any better for several years.

The flip side of the equation, though, brightens up things to some extent. It is a great time to add leverage at current rates, a wonderful time to be a borrower or an issuer as money is desperately seeking good homes, and the low rates coupled with the consistent demand means that refinancing of all types will continue, which is very helpful for high-yield credits in particular. For those of you with a more aggressive nature, I would try longer bonds trading at a discount that are currently callable or have calls upcoming, as I think we will see a number of issues called and the debt rolled over into current rates. Here, I would look at hybrids or trust preferred securities (TruPSs) as particular examples, though there are a number of bonds that fit my criteria, and I can show you some examples if desired.

Peering across the Pond

I have consistently said several things during the European crisis; it is not good here, but it is worse there. If the break comes, nationalism will be gone, and the situation will continue to deteriorate. CDS spreads for the weaker sovereign credits in Europe have gaped out almost 4 percent in the past few days, and the newest data from Greece shows an economy in a virtual death spiral. In the first five months of 2010, the banking institutions have lost 8 percent of their deposit base, and this is the absolute worst rate of attrition since the figures were first tracked in 2001. Unemployment is now higher than 60 percent in some areas of the country, while the Greek banks borrowed approximately $123 billion from the ECB in July; I wonder just how much collateral is left in their banking system. I would be keeping an eye on all of this; we may not be quite at the end, but, in my view, we are nearing an inflection point once again. Also watch the euro; it will be back under 1.20/dollar soon.

The "First-Class Indicator"

September 7, 2010

I f you could peek into the Wizard's sleeves, which will not be happening anytime soon, you would note that he stores a number of tricks up those willowy bits of cloth that cover his arms. The old conjuror is not as without artifice as he appears. The fact that you get the conclusions does not mean that he does not have some methodologies for arriving at the point of embarkation. However, it is tough to get these out of him; he is closed-mouthed that way, and it is rare that the nuances of the trade are discussed.

He has been poring over some dusty manuscript lately, with formulas and ruins that looked like some grand spell having to do with dragons and ogres, but it might have been something to do with finance. It was tough to tell, and when I tried to peer over his shoulder, he closed the thing right up, but then, as if feeling somewhat badly, threw me an olive branch and asked me if I had ever heard of the "first-class indicator." Now the Wizard is a first-class fellow, and I thought this was going to be something about his character or a continuation of his "always take the high road" dictum, but it was not that at all. At first, I thought it more trivial, but now I think perhaps not.

The old boy claims that during the beginning and well into the middle of a recession, all of the articles in the press are about cutting back, getting the cheapest seat or the cheapest anything, and that the concern of everyone is how to cut back, save, pare costs, and so forth. Then he claims—very unscientifically, of course—that when the turn comes and the economy is verging on getting better, you will see the press beginning to talk about the advantages of first class. He tells me that over the weekend, in the *New York Times, Departures* magazine (vacations for wizards and sorcerers, I think), and the *Wall Street Journal,* there were articles on the advantages of first class. I did see him say "aha," but then, at the time, I had no idea what he was talking about. Now I know, and I wonder if he is not onto something here; I generally find that when I take the other side of his pronouncements I am on the losing team, so I will consider this with some care. Anyone his age must have learned something!

So if the old codger is right, then what? I gave you a range of where I thought the 10-year Treasury would go to—2.25 to 2.50 percent—and I am

All that is gold does not glitter,
Not all those who wander are lost;
The old that is strong does not wither,
deep roots are not reached by the frost.
From the ashes a fire shall be woken,
A light from the shadows shall spring;
Renewed shall be blade that was broken,
The crownless again shall be king.
—J. R. R. Tolkien,
The Lord of the Rings

on the record there, and that is where we went and we have now backed up. Short of some further calamity, which is always possible, such as counterparty fallout from the winding down of the Anglo Irish Bank, new data showing the EU bank stress tests were not accurate, or some further disaster in the EU or America, it would now appear as if yields are set once again to back up and for the yield curve to steepen once again as a better economy may be in the offing. It may also be that the stock market is about to shoot up, and my bet there would be on the financials, especially the large American banks, as having a good way to run as earnings and are likely to surprise on the upside.

Of course, the "first-class indicator" is not the Hindenburg Omen or the Piper Cub Oscillator or even the Goodyear Blimp Verbatim— nothing as good as that, I am sure. Heck, the darn thing doesn't even come with mathematical symbols or a valid equation or even authorship of some professor at MIT or Cambridge. Don't you just hate it when common sense is applied and there is no higher validation by the high and mighty? Or it may be that the mighty are just high—I am never quite sure how the phrase actually goes. It is a funny thing about life; when we are born, we get our dose of intelligence, one shot of it, and that is all that we ever get, but it is hard-won experience that fine-tunes how we use it, if used at all.

The commanding general of the U.S. armed forces got his initial infusion like all the rest of us, and his intelligence as a plebe or a buck private has not varied in his career from then to the top, but what he achieved through experience got him to his lofty position, and for that we recognize achievement. In our world, on Wall Street, it is not your family's name nor the schools that you went to that have allowed you to gain success.

Those things may have helped you get in the front door, but that is it. It is you, who on your own two feet stood up and utilized what God gave to you that has marked your ascent. We owe no apologies to anyone, Republican or Democrat, for having been honorable and moral and ethical and having made money, and I wish to state that loudly and clearly today with as much emphasis as I can muster. To be sure, if someone does not follow the high road, then they are accountable; but for the vast majority of people that I have known in all the varied positions that the Great Game offers, most have been real guys who have tried to do the right thing while they clawed their way up the very complicated ladder of becoming a somebody and having made money for the betterment of themselves and their family.

With that in mind, the turn here will come for several reasons. The Republicans are about to, at the least, get some counterbalance to the procedures implemented by the current administration, and the markets, looking forward, will begin to anticipate this upcoming reality. It may just be that both small and large businesses sense that they might not continue to face the lash and the whip quite so often, as we may no longer have to be badgered into being ashamed that we make money or operate at a profit. In my own heart, I have always believed that our country operates on the hope that you can make it to a higher ground and that the majority of Americans were not looking for a handout but just wanted the chance to be on the playing field and compete. It is here, at this precise point, where I think many of our politicians have failed in their leadership; they somehow lost one of the founding principles of our country that has driven America, a land where our ancestors fled for a wide variety of reasons so that they could have an opportunity for a better life. I will tell you this: Having worked all of my life to achieve some success and having gained some of it, I will damn well not let the holier-than-thou politicians try to make me feel guilty for what I have achieved.

It is here where I stand and where I am able to make a call that some of you will listen to and perhaps be rewarded for your listening. This is what we do—we call the ball and we take our responsibilities seriously, and we consistently face the consequences of our decisions. This does not mean that one has to lack a sense of humor or lack a smile in the process; there is nothing in the playbook of the Great Game that states that! Today's commentary has gone far past where I thought it would end, but I am delighted to have reached this point as we all stand on the time-honored ground of actually creating value or we do not stand at all.

This Morning in Europe

The finance ministers of the EU are in session today, and something seems amiss. The euro has dropped markedly against the dollar from Friday's close, and the sovereign debt of Greece, Ireland, and Portugal are gapping out. The Anglo Irish Bank issues are now on the table, and there is a lot of concern about counterparty fallout here both with the other Irish banks and also with other major European institutions. I suspect that part of the fallout today is also a result of an article in this morning's *Wall Street Journal* that very politely—divergent data, they call it—suggests that the EU cooked the books on the stress tests. The article is well worth reading. Certain banks netted their sovereign risk exposure (longs minus shorts equals total exposure) or didn't report the exposure in their subs and others, and suddenly when they report their financials, voila—much bigger positions and exposure than had been previously reported and with almost every institution claiming that they only reported the numbers as directed by the EU. Here, I fear, is what many of us have long suspected— a sham as promulgated by the European Union and the European Central Bank designed to mislead investors one more time. Now it is very ungentlemanly to call someone a liar, so, bearing that in mind, I will give you my honest opinion of what the European Union did with the bank stress tests: They lied.

Chapter 3

The Importance of the Euro

E urope represents the single caveat that is now in existence for all of the world's markets. It is the singular thing that could derail every projection, every strategy, and every bet laid down on the table and could cause a reversal in course for the world's economy. This turn, I am afraid, would be swift, and it would be similar to the angel of death entering a room with his scimitar, swinging his sword with wild abandon as he wreaked havoc on all of the financial markets without exception. The issues here are the European Union (EU) and the European Central Bank (ECB), and the construction of a grand experiment where Europe tries to become a political entity and not just a geographical reference.

This grand design can be traced back to its roots in 1951 with the formation of the European Coal and Steel Community. This organization grew over the years to become the European Economic Community, and then, in 1999, the European Union was formalized. As of September 2010, it is composed of 27 nations with 16 utilizing a common currency known as the euro, which is the U.S. dollar's major competition for the world's reserve currency. The EU is an incredibly complex structure at this point, and to fully appreciate its makeup, you have to come at it from a number of different angles. Each of these different perspectives must be considered to fully understand the paradigm of a political Europe, and each must be remembered when considering the actions of the EU and the ECB and their substantial influence on all of the world's financial markets.

At one level, it is a group of nations with a long history of tribal warfare and strife that is trying to form some kind of amalgamation where conflicts are settled by common agreement and not by bloodshed and the loss of life. This is the noble viewpoint and the one that these countries would like us all to accept prima facie, but there is much more to this union than this lofty notion. At another level, it is a demonstration of power where Germany in the first instance and France in the second is trying to dominate the continent by the use of capital and economic prowess as the substitution for guns and ammunition.

During the past 100 years, Germany has tried twice to take over Europe, and it has failed twice; but now, with their position within the EU, they are having great success mandating just how Europe should be run.

They have used Brussels, Belgium, as their focal point of power, which is a clever ruse where a non-German city is ruled by Berlin. To be clear, Germany does not win every skirmish, nor do the other countries always allow them to have their way, but they win often enough with the use of their special carrot and stick so that it can be accurately stated that Germany is in virtual control of the EU, with France tagging along for good measure. Germany is the leading economic power in Europe, as it has been in times past, but they have learned their lessons and they now try to govern Europe by the strategic use of their money as the carrot and the refusal to let other countries in Europe have access to their money as the stick.

In a recent demonstration of power, the EU, prodded by Germany, took over the regulation of the financial markets in London as Britain just rolled over in submission in a very similar fashion to a small dog when a big dog enters the room. It was quite pathetic, and I had visions of Mr. Churchill retching somewhere, but it was also a clear demonstration of who holds the power and that the consequences of not giving in to the demands of the EU are so compelling that nations just acquiesce. These consequences are tied directly to the construction of the EU: Either you are a member of this club or you are not.

If you are a card-carrying member, then you have access to their central bank, the ECB; your citizens can not only travel freely between countries, but they can work in the country of their choice; they can use the euro as their currency if they so desire, providing a common cost of goods and services to their country; and they can be backstopped by the EU if they get into financial trouble, exemplified by Greece, where loans from the EU were provided and where the ECB bought the debt of Greece for their own account to help shore up the rather perilous situation. The ECB can also allow other nations and European banks to buy the debt of Greece or any other country in trouble and pledge the debt as collateral at the same rate as, say, Germany, so that, in fact, the countries of Europe and their citizens' money helps to pay for some nations' lack of fiscal constraint. These are but a few examples of what the EU and the ECB provide if you belong to the club, but these same advantages, clearly, also represent what you do not get if you are not a member. Imagine a nation trying to sell their goods and services to other nations that are members of the European Club and being constantly shunted aside because they stand alone and you can get some idea of the measure of the power that the EU now holds over the rest of the continent. It is obvious that many nations will take the honey rather than being left with the vinegar, and this is precisely the situation that now exists in Europe.

Now the common currency of the EU is the euro, and it is the one major competitor with the American dollar for dominance in all of the world's markets, both in financial and nonfinancial transactions. Its relative value to the dollar has recently swung quite wildly this way and that way as the consideration of the EU has come under the microscope. There are other major currencies, no doubt, such as the Japanese yen and the Swiss franc, and there may be a time when the currency of China becomes a player on the world's stage, but, for the moment, the dollar and the euro wrestle for control of where nations and large international corporations are going to put their money. Currency trading for the public at large is mostly speculative and is a game for the very nimble, but for nations and major companies it is a different thing altogether.

The wealth of the world is generally governed by the central banks, such as our Federal Reserve Bank, which control the flow of funds of a nation. They square up the capital that is available in their country, often using quite complicated mathematical formulas that are unnecessary to go into here, which regulate the globe's financial marketplace.

These central banks report to their country's politicians, of course, and everyone has different standards and a different political agenda, but with the great European experiment, the ECB reports to everyone in the EU in a quite different fashion than any other place on Earth. Here again, one may easily surmise that the German voice is much louder than the desires of Luxembourg, for example, and you begin to get the idea. This all goes along in a normalized fashion unless two things begin to coalesce. For instance, the ECB decides that it is an independent operation and Germany or some other country gets aggravated enough that nationalism rears its ugly head; or some nation is having financial issues, and here we can point to Greece, Spain, Portugal, Italy, and Ireland so that internal problems within the EU begin to arise. These issues do not exist in a vacuum—of that you can be assured—so when problems bubble up to the surface, it is the currency of Europe, the euro, that comes under extreme scrutiny as countries and other major investors push and pull on its relative value, which is the only value, unlike bonds, that exists in currency trading.

There is nothing absolute about the worth of any currency, and the judgments are all based on how one currency stacks up to another one. Significant influences can be the cost of oil and energy, the price of the metals and other commodities, the political stability of a country or now of Europe, the price of foodstuffs in the world's markets, and even the costs of labor. There is just a giant amount of data that goes into the valuing of a currency, and each country can also deleverage its currency by selling it, exemplified by Japan recently, or by supporting it by purchasing it in the open market. You soon get an idea of the complexity and importance of getting the call on a currency correct. If this all sounds daunting and overly difficult to understand, then consider this: The cost of a $30 steak at your local restaurant is for you just that, $30. But for the English guy sitting next to you, if he pays in pounds, it is $19.20; for the lady from Paris, in euros, it is $23.40; and for the family from Sydney, in Australian dollars, it is $28.50. It is not just the cost but the currency that determines the real price of anything on this planet, and consequently the relative value of the euro becomes critically important as to whether to buy bonds denominated in dollars or euros or whether to import wheat or export wheat in what currency, and I think you begin to get the drift.

In my world, the world of the major financial managers of money, the issue of the value of the euro holds a special place of prominence. It is an economic issue, a political issue, and an issue that could, in a crisis, have a material effect on each and every thing that there is to invest in. Consider a major war where who is winning or losing causes the currency markets to reverberate with each battle—so it is with the euro at present. If the construct were to somehow become unhinged so that a country left the EU for any reason at all, then the value of the euro would depreciate rapidly. I will discuss all of this in more detail, but whether it is a country that withdrew because of the imposed austerity measures or where one of the major funding countries such as Germany or France withdrew because they no longer wished to foot the bill, or where Britain decided that it no longer wished to be subservient to the political authority of a greater Europe, the fallout would be severe. There are a tremendous number of what I call "inflection points" that are continually at risk, far more than what takes place in a single country such as the United States. Consequently, the companies and the nations that are my clients pay close attention to what is happening in Europe and to the euro, as any serious misstep could severely damage any market that you could possibly imagine.

Dolphins/Pelicans—Things that Matter

March 4, 2009

The New Stimulus Plan

Countless verbiage will be written about the government's new plan, and it will concentrate on what is presented and not generally upon the implications of what is proposed, which is where the real importance lies. Several things come to mind when considering the new proposal. First and foremost for those of us in fixed income is that we may have deflation now, but inflation is coming and it will be quite significant unless the entire scheme fails, and then it won't matter much anyway. So, based on the assumption that we make it through our current run of the gauntlet alive, maturities and duration should be kept short, and I would not be swinging past three years in maturity. When the "printer of money" not only has the capacity to do so but outlines the basics of just how much he is going to print, and this is compared against the gross domestic product (GDP) of the American economy, then serious inflation just cannot be avoided. It is actually more than that if you consider the financial crisis carefully, but no central banker is going to stand up and admit it; the one and only way out of the morass is to reinflate, and every senior person at the Fed and the Treasury knows that, I would guess, and will do whatever it takes to cause the reignition. Assets must rise

Of Dolphins and Pelicans and things that really matter
Of Hats full of Cats and playful Dogs and joyous clamor
Of Family and close Friends and wild outbursts of Laughter
Of Chapters of our Lives and wondering what comes After
Of Dreams and clever Schemes and avoiding the Disasters
Here is the Stuff of Life; and all the rest but idle Chatter.

—The Wizard

in price, real estate must inflate, commodities must appreciate, and the first indicative sign of this will be when Treasuries begin to lose their luster and rise in yield. When the populace of the United States and the world begins to see some signs of hope and stops buying Treasuries/Federal Deposit Insurance Corporation (FDIC) debt and certificates of deposit, then you will get the first and best sign that it is time to enter other markets. Here, if you will, is the "sign" that will mark the turning point, and since we are all enamored with prophecies that predict future events, this is the prophecy of the Wizard for when to head back into the bar and drink up.

The New Housing Plan

Today, the government is supposed to announce its new plan to help homeowners. This is all fine and good, but for many of us with exposure to the mortgage market, the take is considerably different. For those of us who manage money, today will be the day when we ascertain if the mortgage securitizations that sit in our portfolios are going to get slammed by the deferrals, defrayments, extensions, and the like in residential mortgages. We will find out today, perhaps, if the government is absorbing all of the loss in some fashion or whether the mortgage securitizations will bear some of the losses from helping homeowners. Today is the day when the "political risk" that I have long spoken about regarding these holdings will be unveiled and revealed in the light of day of the Fed's construction. If, in fact, the mortgage securitizations are going to be modified by the new plan, and the scheme allows some way around the "material change" and other provisions of the securitizations, then I would suggest an immediate lessening of exposure to this class of assets; as in hurry up, you can't get it done too soon. It is my opinion that if the terms of these securitizations are changed by Congress, then they will no longer trade to an "average life" but to maturity, and that there will be no way to accurately evaluate these securities because who knows how and when the underlying assets, the mortgages themselves, could be modified. All you may well know, in fact, is that the value of the asset that you perceived is no longer the real value, and there is only one way to go and that is down. I advise you to never own assets that have only one way to go when the direction is "down!" Today will be a red-letter day in this regard, and we will collectively hold our breaths and watch.

The Euro

Now just cents of its November lows. Watch for the breakdown through 125/dollar, and then hold on to your hats.

FNMA and Freddie Mac

If the administration is living up to its claims, and I mean this quite sincerely, if they are making proclamations about full disclosure and not hiding behind various financial constructs then I say to them: Nationalize the Federal National Mortgage Association (FNMA) and Freddie Mac; put them on the U.S. balance sheet and guarantee the debt and be done with it. I say clearly: Either do that or stop making the frivolous claims about doing business in a new and open fashion. That is my view!

> *The democracy will cease to exist when you take away from those who are willing to work and give to those who would not.*
>
> —President Thomas Jefferson

Manna from Heaven

April 17, 2009

The Euro

I have been generally bearish on the euro for quite some time now. I have generally been right about the direction of the euro for quite some time now. It is at 130.81/dollar as I write my commentary this morning. I expect it to head back to 125 or so, find a lot of resistance, and then eventually to break toward 118.50. It is my opinion that the economies on the continent just cannot sustain the current level as America begins to show signs of life, while national interests in Europe overtake regional considerations. One indication of the difficulties, and a historically interesting one, is the world's oldest sovereign wealth fund, which resides in France. It was started after the Napoleonic wars in 1816 and is named Caisse des Dépôts et Consignations. For 193 years they have never had a loss, but this longest of economic records perhaps has broken the chain and is reporting a loss for all of 2008. Now I am heading to Saint Tropez toward the end of July for two weeks, where I have taken a flat in the port. In this town of the ridiculously expensive, I am hopeful that it is somewhat more affordable than in times past, and I have my doubts whether the bubbly will be flowing with as much gusto as in prior years.

The MTN-I conference in Miami, April 22–24

Mike Tims, the publisher of MTN-I, has graciously allowed me to invite my clients to attend this conference for free. There will be a host of significant people on different panels, and last year's event was well attended and full of visionary folks. The Wizard will be speaking on several subjects, and I would personally enjoy meeting many of you that I have never had the opportunity to visit with in person. I am sending out a formal invitation in a separate email today; the kickoff event is Wednesday night, April 22, with a beach barbecue at the Mandarin Oriental Hotel. Let me caution you—do not attend if you do not enjoy being with bright people, being in warm weather, hate watching scantily clad people wander around on white sand, or might be offended by yours truly with a cigar in hand and a Grand Marnier close by. The event could be a game changer for many of you, and you may actually remember what it is like to smile once again.

> *If you're not using your smile, you're like a man with a million dollars in the bank and no checkbook.*
>
> —Les Giblin

> *The Democrats seem to be basically nicer people, but they have demonstrated time and again that they have the management skills of celery. They're the kind of people who'd stop to help you change a flat, but would somehow manage to set your car on fire. I would be reluctant to entrust them with a Cuisinart, let alone the economy. The Republicans, on the other hand, would know how to fix your tire, but they wouldn't bother to stop because they'd want to be on time for Ugly Pants Night at the country club.*
>
> —Dave Barry

A Poignant Quip

I read this morning, with some interest, that our president made $2.7 million recently from the sales of his book. Now the American taxpayer is paying his salary and even providing him a nice white house. I read everything I could find on the subject this morning, and nowhere did I see Senator Dodd or Congressman Frank yelling in anguish about protecting the public and the $500 million cap on income. This horse looks pretty much like the other horse to me and calling it a "horse of a different color" just doesn't change the reality of the horse.

Some Bonds I Bought for Clients Yesterday

C (SUB) 5.625 8/27/12 $76.50 14.76% +1351/3YR 172967BP5

Now these bonds are subordinated notes of Citigroup and senior to the U.S. government's holdings in Citigroup. In thinking about this purchase, it has occurred to me that either we are all going straight to hell in a handbasket again or that the brighter minds on Wall Street have fled to Estonia to escape the cap on their income. No other explanation makes sense to me when I consider the maturity and the yield that is available in this bond. Perhaps there is some other rational explanation for this, but I have not come up with it. I can tell you this: If my brethren on Wall Street are now offering manna from heaven, then I am happy to step up and buy it!

Greek Downgrades— The Fallout

February 25, 2010

Writing today's commentary is difficult—not because there is not plenty to consider, but because it is blowing 28 knots at Sampson Cay, and while we are tied up at the marina typing is a serious challenge. For those of you not familiar with boating, suffice it to say that we are being blown this way and that way with wild abandon while the seas are more than two meters in height. I only imbibe coffee in the early morning hours and yet walking in the boat is truly akin to the late night antics of the proverbial drunken sailor. Here is a time when I envy the two Sages, as the use of four legs is certainly a better option than only having two. It is disconcerting, I can tell you, to try and type a letter on the keyboard and get only about one in three keys that you aim for hit correctly. I will have to have the patience of a saint to get this sent out to you, but I shall endeavor to get it done as the swing on the lines must be the revenge of some Greek god who has read my recent missives.

As light dawns in the Bahamas, and I walk to the stern of my vessel and gaze out on the frothy sea, I am reminded of the events cascading across the continent so reminiscent of the ocean that surrounds "Wishes Granted." The country of Greece is paralyzed by strikes, their politicians lashing out at the other EU countries, the value of their debt plummeting as first Standard & Poor's (S&P) and now Moody's threaten downgrades by possible notches. Pierre Cailleteau, managing director of sovereign risk at Moody's, said in Tokyo that the agency could downgrade Greece two notches. Now there is a serious problem here beyond the ratings: Greece has more of its debt pledged as collateral with the ECB than any other EU nation, and if it loses its A rating, then their debt will no longer be eligible for collateral, which will have severe implications not only for Greece but for other countries and EU banks that have pledged Greek debt. Be especially mindful of the German banks here that have utilized a carry trade using Greek debt as an offset to German debt, as there is now quite a real possibility that this whole trade could be forced to unwind to the detriment of the German banks.

I read the article on Spain in the *Wall Street Journal* this morning and see that the light is dawning on other men besides the author of this commentary. The winds of change are heavy on the continent of Europe and the gods that be are whipping up a storm that does not bode well for the currency, the countries, or the people who inhabit that realm. Virtually all of the equities of the European banks took it on the chin in Europe overnight, and I continue to warn about their debt as a group. The spreads of this sector do not justify the risk that is present, and I am particularly concerned, as I have said before, about the Spanish banks as their exposure to real estate and their contracting economy may well hold some nasty surprises in the months ahead.

The euro is hovering around 134.90/dollar this morning, and I believe it will continue to head lower. I have been calling for a 125/dollar number for some months now, and my opinion has not changed. The problems in the Eurozone are real and growing worse, and I just do not see the euro sustainable at even these lower levels from where I first made my call. America and Asia have weathered the world's financial crisis in better shape than the Eurozone, and national issues coupled with the poor construction of the EU will continue to batter their collective debt and their currency.

Not Much to Like But . . .

One segment of the American debt markets does hold some interest for me at present and it is the regional banks. I will start out by saying that I think Citigroup and Bank of America will tighten some from current levels as their financial conditions improve, but the best shot now is in the regional American banks, whose spreads still represent value as the risk declines. I would be considering Zions, Regions Financial (RF), and Marshall & Ilsley (M&I) in particular. The yield curve and the Fed are currently their friends, and as their real estate exposure and their securitizations improve, I think better financials are on the way. The spreads in these credits are still rather wide on a relative basis, and I think some additional compression in these names is to be had over the next year. America is certainly not doing great, but by comparison to our European cousins, we are looking good.

It Is Not All Greek to Me

March 24, 2010

Sometimes when you write a commentary that goes to thousands of financial institutions in so many countries, you forget an important lesson that I have learned and relearned over the years; what is obvious to me is not obvious to everyone else, and for this I apologize to all of you. It is not your fault; it is my fault that I have not spelled out things in a clearer fashion, and I will try to rectify that this morning.

It is not that I am fascinated with Greece; I have been there any number of times and like Mykonos and a number of the Greek islands and find Athens little more than a passing historical interest, but this is not why I have been focused in on it lately. Neither is it that the relatively small country of Greece is particularly relevant on the world's financial scene, because it is not. It is that Greece, in its unfortunate circumstances, partially brought to bear by its own reckless abandon of financial honesty, has shifted and is shifting the balance of power all across the globe. The unfolding story of Greece and the response by the European Union is not just "a story"—it is "the story" that may well change the importance of Europe for decades to come.

The short version is that America, her financial system, and her culture—or lack thereof, as some would argue—has dominated the world since World War II. Even during the Cold War as Russia pressed its case, there was never any real doubt about who held the sickle and the hammer. That standoff was a proposition in military power, while the European Union was conceived as a challenge to America's financial power, as different parts of the world—as is a normal part of the human experience—want to take their rightful place in the hierarchy. There is no cause for complaint in any of this; it is just the way of life, as many Europeans wanted a mechanism to stand toe-to-toe with the rather brash American cowboy. Not only that, but how did it happen that all of the miscreants, who left Europe either because they were persecuted or to find a better life that they could not find on the continent, come to rule their former masters? One does not speak about this generally, as it is not polite dinner conversation, but if you don't think many Europeans were galled then by the situation and are galled now, you are mistaken. So we come to the EU and a history I have delineated before and a challenging set of circumstances that will redefine the financial world, and I am not, in any manner, over-stating the case.

Much can be said and has been said about the similarities of Europe and the United States, and there is a treatise in that discussion, which I am not going to write today. Where there is a clear and marked disassociation, however, is in the "plight of the common man," and this definitive point earmarks the United States as a rather singular entity among the nation states. It is my viewpoint that a single word defines America in so many ways: *hope*. The country was founded by those that left distant shores in the hope of a better life for themselves and their families, and it continues to thrive on that principle to this day. In Europe, one generally must be from the right family and attend the right school and have a long familial history to become a "somebody." In America, this is patently not the case. You can show up from Austria or Denmark or Korea or China and, with a little luck, a great idea, a lot of hard work, or a skill set brought with you, establish yourself as a success. It was never that America had streets paved in gold; it was always that you could come here and pave your own street with gold for yourself and your family. Sure, we have had some prominent families, the Roosevelts and the Kennedys and others, and we have our prominent universities such as Harvard and Yale; but look around you and you will find that virtually all of the people running our financial institutions or our major corporations or the whiz-bangs connected to the Internet are just normal guys, common folks, and good old boys from Missouri or Iowa. Make note here that they are not from rural Mississippi but once came from Germany because in America, whatever your roots in some other country, no one cares a whit—the tribe is American, and that is all that needs to be said.

In any event, while our ancestral cousins on the continent may not have liked our lack of civility or our Wild West attitude, they did have to confront our financial success, and so they did. Then, with the passing of years, the money achieved from Middle Eastern oil, the rise of China, and the importance of the Asian contingent, others poured in to help support Europe's counterbalance against the United States for their own reasons. We have witnessed changes in power before, and I mention in particular Britain and its loss of empire, but this is a different situation. The European Union is the continent's economic structure to offset America, but the real problem is that there are any number of structural flaws that Greece is highlighting in a very dramatic fashion, and hence the importance of the unfolding events.

While the euro today is at a 10-month low against the dollar, it is at an all-time low against the Swiss franc. Think about this for a moment and you may realize that any number of financial institutions in Europe, the Middle East, and Asia are piling in trying to stop the precipitous decline of the euro as national and international forces are lined up, each with their own reasons, trying to stem the tide; if you think I am wrong, let me assure you that I am not. Not only is the currency issue coming to the fore; economically, the euro should be at less than parity with the dollar now, but the very structure of a European Union with 16 or 27 different tribes and cultural histories, depending on how you wish to slice it up, is under extreme pressure. I have made the prediction before and will make it again today: the European Union with its present structure will not stand.

You will note that I am not attacking the concept of the EU; I get it and I fully understand the reasons for Europe to try to unite in some fashion, but they just did not get it right. Many of the mechanisms are flawed, as is clearly demonstrated by the Greek debacle. You just cannot have so many national interests, each with some sort of veto power, each with very different traditions and culture, and expect to succeed under the present construct of the European Union. It is all well and good to have the pretense that everyone is European, but much more basic is that everyone is a Greek or a German or a Frenchman with a different language and a different national interest, and the real politics that elect everyone are back at home so that being a European is a secondary— much more secondary—concern.

What we are in fact witnessing, what Greece has brought to the fore, is a power struggle. This is a major power struggle in Europe that will affect the United States in the way it is resolved and affect all of the rest of the world's nations by its contagion. For those of us on Wall Street the most surface issue is how we regard each nation's sovereign debt, while the much more important issue is how we regard the sovereignty of the EU and the finances of each European country.

I suggested you consider exiting credits denominated in euros at around 148/dollar, and I suggest it again today at 133/dollar; when I suggest it again around 125/dollar, I hope it will be no longer relevant for you!

Self-Determination Becomes an Issue

May 14, 2010

O ccasionally, it is useful to sit in a hard-backed chair and make every attempt to stare at reality in its multifaceted face. One should approach these moments with some trepidation, as the reflection is not often attractive and the conclusions that are forced on you by this experience are generally not the ones whose intrusions are welcomed. No matter; the world must be squared up with some frequency if you are going to be a winner in the Great Game.

An error does not become truth by reason of multiplied propagation, nor does truth become error because nobody sees it.

—Mahatma Gandhi

America

We are not doing great. We have been through Credit Crisis, Part I, and we are surviving and beginning to have some prosperity again, but it has been a costly experience. We took on national debt out of necessity, which was a better option, no doubt, than the country's reaction to the Great Depression. A large segment of our citizens are angry, which, interestingly enough, is not just because of the usual of the policies of the Democrats or the Republicans but reflects a national unhappiness with the way the country is being run by any/all of the politicians, and there is a growing cry just to throw all of them out at our next national elections to get that point across. Having said this, however, and drawing the distinction between the absolute and the relative, I think it can also be said accurately that it is now better here than over there, which would include not only Europe but most of Asia and certainly Japan.

Europe

After the campaign of "shock and awe" wears away and the initial euphoria fades into stark contrast, the bitter sting of nations living beyond their means for years has settled in on the landscape. When I speak of the euro's declining to levels not seen in years against the dollar, it is not because I see the United States as stalwart or in great shape economically; rather, it is because I see Europe in much worse shape. The EU, by its very construct and then again as measured by its evolution, imposes complex strictures on the individual countries of Europe that are impossible to ignore. If I consider the austerity measures in Greece, Portugal, and Spain, as examples, there are just no good options to come from these cutbacks for the people of these countries in any but the longest of time frames. I note that this morning in the *Financial Times* I saw for the first time speculation that there may be social unrest in Spain as their unions have called for national strikes. The EU and the ECB are now setting regional policies that have trumped national interests, and I truly wonder if that will succeed. The options here are (1) acceptance in all 26, (2) new governments that reject the measures and withdraw from the Union based on national interests, or (3) social unrest that overthrows some government in the streets. There is not only an economic shift taking place in Europe but a power shift from the individual nations to a ruling coalition where none of the politicians are responsible to any particular citizenry. I am not sure—no one can be sure—if a very long history of national pride and directing your own destiny can be led to the sacrificial altar of a European Union without rejection or revolt as a matter of losing your national independence.

In the old Europe, each country elected its own government and the politicians were answerable to their citizens in the election process. In the new Europe, there is now a disconnect. Governments are elected and then other politicians appointed to the European ruling councils so that the people running the EU are accountable to no one and everyone de facto and de juris, as there are no European elections, just national ones. This is a very real new distribution of power and one that I think cannot hold.

When I first called for the decline in the euro at 1.48/dollar and said it was going to 1.25/dollar, I took a lot of flak for the call, but at 1.2454/ dollar as I write my commentary this morning, the call was obviously correct. This is a decline in a very short time of almost 16 percent and far overshadows any coupon that you may have owned to offset the loss in the currency. I did not make the call to offer advice about currency speculation but to offer advice about owning bonds denominated in euros. In my view, the risk factor present in the EU—present in its very construction—places too many possibilities for some kind of implosion squarely in the not-too-distant future, which are risks not inherent in the construct of the United States. I reiterate: It is not great here, but it is better than there or, put in other words for investors, it is safer to own bonds in the United States and denominated in dollars than to own either sovereign credits or especially bank credits or any bonds denominated in euros at the present time.

To be a prudent investor certainly involves reflection on past events, but more importantly, it involves deductive reasoning to be able to correctly assess future events. The past lights the way, but it is your ability to deduce the future based on the events unfolding around you that is the single most important ability that you must learn and relearn if you are to achieve success.

As bombs explode in Greece at courthouses and prisons in the past 24 hours and Spain reports the first bout of deflation in 24 years; additional stress fractures become apparent in the Eurozone. It is not a leap into the improbable that that the austerity measures under way in Greece, Ireland, Spain, and Portugal will cause further economic decline and deflation. It is not a jump into the unlikely that governmental opposition in a number of countries will stand for national independence at any cost, as opposed to resignation and bended knee to European council dictates. My best reasoning abilities, as a matter of Holmesian logic, indicate that the next set of events to come will be nation states beset by political parties calling for national independence and national self-determination, and it will be here that the European Union finally faces collapse or realignment.

Proceed ahead we must, but proceed with great caution, is the advice of the Wizard.

If You Know How to Work It

July 28, 2010

I have forever in my memory referred to what we all do for a living as the "Great Game." There are Bond Kings and Wizards and Doctors Doom and Gloom. There are television evangelists of the Game exhorting us all into heaven and their brethren that shout from the on-air pulpit that we are all going straight to monetary hell. There are "Masters of the Universe" and the crowd on the rise and the Ego that gets demolished and fortunes made and lost and the swindlers and the pirates and all manner of people trying to grab power as fast as they can stick it in their pockets, and politicians of every stripe holding us all out to be the most foul of villains as they rant at the populace in the stadium. There are the demigods and the godless and those of us that have become wizened as we peer around every corner like Captain Hook looking for the crocodile. Barnum and Bailey got it wrong; this is the greatest show on earth and each day for my 36 years of doing it I have taken delight in playing.

> *You have to learn the rules of the game. And then you have to play better than anyone else.*
>
> —Albert Einstein

> *A hot dog at the game beats roast beef at the Ritz.*
>
> —Humphrey Bogart

Not every moment, of course, has been delightful. I have had more than my share of painful winces where the spears of the enemy were thrust directly in my direction. Interestingly enough, it was not generally the markets that were the cause of the pain but the poor gamesmanship of people that disappointed me most often. After running capital markets at four investment banks, I now just shake my head as I am buttressed by long experience, but in my youth there were some anguishing experiences. Now, however, I have ascended to a different role; I only manage

*After a certain point, money is mean-
ingless. It ceases to be the goal. The
game is what counts.*

—Aristotle Onassis

myself and my team and I leave the rest
to others who still enjoy the joust, while
I am quite content to peer at the world
this morning from the back of my boat
in Newport, Rhode Island, and spend my
time pondering the next twist in the road
to come and how to get there before the jostling crowd arrives and ruins
the pleasure of getting there first.

Europe

What we are currently experiencing is the oft repeated "relief rally."
The damned thing didn't come apart for the moment and the markets are uttering a collective sigh. You can almost hear the whoosh of
exhaled breath in the euro, the European banks, and many troubled
sovereign credits. Nothing has really changed except that the construct is
still there, but then I am not at all surprised by that. The next phase, and
it always comes, will be to relook at the fundamentals and take note that
the incest continues, and things will widen out once again. It is my opinion that to step away from the situation when I first suggested it, when
the Euro was around 1.48/dollar, was absolutely the correct decision,
and now some are thinking of reengaging. I continue to advise caution.
If the EU breaks, I think it will come from a major bank's getting into
serious trouble or from the opposition party in some country gaining
power by campaigning against austerity measures or paying for a foreign
government to continue or, in the case of Britain, unwillingness to give
up its sovereignty to the French and Germans to manage. We shall see,
but the risks remain, way more risk than remaining in American credits
at present, and being the cautious fellow that I am, I prefer to remain on
the sidelines until the footing is safer.

CIT

The short story is $0.71 for the quarter versus $0.49 last quarter. Revenues
better than expected and non–generally accepted accounting principles (GAAP) up 27.7 percent while net income was up 46 percent as
Tier I capital now stands at 17.2 percent; compare that to some of our
major banks. All of this being said, however, I think the best story is
in their 7 percent series of bonds. Some of these bonds have yields to

maturity of around 8 percent, and the calls, which take place on 9/10/10, have yields to call over 90 percent. Do you think it is possible that CIT might now do a shorter-dated maturity and pay down the outstanding bonds and you get 8 percent or so if they do not but a home run if they do. For those of you who can transact in bonds with less than an investment grade (IG) rating, I think there is opportunity here that can be taken advantage of before the horde rushes in and compresses the credit back toward the IG universe.

One and one is two, and two and two is four, and five will get you ten if you know how to work it.

—Mae West

With an Eye on Europe Once Again

August 12, 2010

Today is the last day of my great adventure, and tomorrow the Sages and I return home to Fort Lauderdale. Many thanks to all of you who came aboard, broke bread, shared an adult libation or two, and partook of a little something in the humidor. Three months out is a long time, and I am ready to return home to my bed, Internet connections that work, phones that do not have a voice lag, and Bloomberg speeds that are faster than molasses running down some tree trunk in the dead of winter. I wish to publicly thank my crew, Captain Eddie, Chef Amy, and Stewardess Nicki, for their unfaltering great service and their positive attitude.

> *A tramp, a gentleman, a poet, a dreamer, a lonely fellow, always hopeful of romance and adventure.*
> —Charlie Chaplin

The Next Empanada

There were two significant events that took place in Europe yesterday. The first was the country of Slovakia's rejecting the aid package and voting 69 to 1 with 14 abstentions that they were not going to pay their share of the bill. While it may appear to be of little importance on its face, that is not my view. The EU is now left with three distinct options. They can change the size of the bailout package, which would require them to go back to the International Monetary Fund (IMF) and each member state for approval. They could reallocate each nation's costs, which would require each member nation to go back to their own Parliament for approval and face the possibility of some other country rejecting the change. Finally, they could ask some larger country, such as Germany, to cover the loss of revenue that was attributed to Slovakia, but here, once again, national politics may not play out as hoped. In other words, one way or another, the can of worms has been reopened and the risk factor has been increased.

The euro had bounced off its low of 1.1963/dollar on June 7 and then run up to 1.3280/dollar on the hope and prayer than the EU crisis had abated. This morning it is at 1.2826/dollar and it is coming under pressure once again. My call here is down and down to under 1.20/dollar and in the not-too-distant future. The upcoming grand event is the EU's trying to impose taxes on each individual nation and Great Britain's rejecting that plan, which I think hits the fan this September. The upcoming realization event will be the dawning notion for investors of just how bad the economic situation is in Spain.

The focus has been on the national debt of Spain, and the inspection has stopped there—but one moment please. Spain is not set up like most countries in Europe and certainly not like the United States. Spanish debt is not just the national debt but also the regional debt which, by law, the national government cannot back stop in case of an emergency. The regional governments account for literally one half of all public workers in Spain, and they have twice as much debt as the national government and while they used to be able to borrow at approximately the same rates as the country prior to the crisis, they now are mostly shut out of the debt markets with significant amounts of money to roll over in the next few years. As examples, Catalonia's borrowing costs have tripled in the last year and are now on par with Peru while Galicia has asked the central government to freeze its payments to the federal government, which was refused by the prime minister on July 27. Fitch now has now put all 10 regional governments in Spain on notice for possible downgrades while Madrid recently withdrew a bond issuance citing "market conditions." Also upcoming in September is a planned national general strike over the imposition of austerity measures where, unlike Greece, there has not been such a strike staged in over a decade. It is my opinion that Spain will soon return to the public limelight and that you should prepare your portfolios for another round of pain.

One Strategy

I return to an idea that I have expressed before. In the corporate bond markets, there is a gradual increase in yield as you head down the chain of credit quality. This is not the case in the Build America Bonds

(BABs) market and the abyss that exists between A-rated credits and BBB-rated credits can be exploited for your gain. I suspect that this has to do with the composition of the municipal market and the traditions built into it, where a BBB name might be investment grade, but it was deemed not suitable for many investors. I would stay with the larger liquid names and do your homework in credit but where you are comfortable with ownership; the yield distinction for BBB BABs is very favorable for the debt owner. In a time where relatively safe yields are tough to find, here is my single best idea at present.

Chapter 4

Turmoil in Greece

Greece, often thought to be the birthplace of modern civilization, may also go down as the birthplace of the demise of the European Union (EU). History will eventually determine the truth of this, but it remains a quite real possibility at this point in the fall of 2010. Here was a country, along with Bulgaria, that falsified its records to gain admission to the EU, and it is the opinion of many, including me, that the Europeans knew all about it but looked the other way during the mad dash to get as many countries as possible under the common umbrella. Here is a socialist country that lived far beyond its means, that had a national conscience that encouraged tax evasion, that had rolls of friends and political comrades that lived off the government largesse and rarely reported to work, and finally, that had social programs that provided very generous pensions that could not be afforded for all of those working for the government. Greece, as a country, also engaged in unsound financial transactions where it used derivatives to make its current cash position look better than it was as it moved liabilities, money it owed, from the present into the future and then roundly ignored what was to come. This all worked until the world entered a financial crisis—and then it didn't.

In retrospect, there are many aspects to the Greek calamity that significantly changed a number of aspects of investing. The first was a recognition, by many Americans and American institutions, that the majority of European countries are, in fact, socialist and that they do not operate in the same way as we do in the United States. Their value system is different than ours—significantly different—and their politicians do not behave in the same manner as the ones in our country. The American politicians, in general, spin things and manipulate data and may try to convince the populace of this and that, but there always seems to remain a kernel of truth somewhere in their proclamations. In Greece, and much of Europe, this is not the case—they lie. Now this is not the little white lie or the half-truth; this is the big untruth that they are fully aware of, and they take justification in the protection of their country as the reason that telling lies is acceptable. It has been my observation, during the entire process of the difficulties with the EU, that there is a very different social fabric in Europe that allows for not telling the truth as a matter of course.

We need no bilateral loans, we have never asked for bilateral loans.

—George Papandreou, the prime minister of Greece

This all turned out to be untrue days later, but it was the bluff that was fostered on investors as Greece sold bonds into the marketplace. The head of the European Central Bank (ECB) also was roundly denying that the EU was going to bail out Greece, and the charade lasted until Greece ran out of money and went cap in hand to the EU and the International Monetary Fund (IMF) as investors got the drift of things and refused to fund. What Greece and the EU wanted, of course, was for bond buyers to keep funding so that they wouldn't have to, but there does come a critical moment, as Greece and the EU learned, when professional money managers see the writing on the wall and say, "Enough." You see how democratic Wall Street is after all; we vote all of the time—it is just not with ballots, but with money.

Greece also changed the economic landscape in a number of other ways. Not only did they falsify their financial records to gain access to the EU, but they kept on doing it well past the point of admission and, as a matter of record, they have kept doing it right up to this moment. While the European authorities have repeatedly asked for the information about all of their derivative contracts, they have not delivered it, and the actual financial situation of the country remains unknown. This continues to cause consternation for investors, as it dawned on everyone that Greece may not be the only country that has cooked its books. In the case of a corporation in Europe, they answer to many regulations, penalties, and fines that are similar to the United States, but if you are a nation, a sovereign credit, then we have learned that some nations who make the laws and consider themselves above their laws may not be giving us accurate information. This has caused a marked change in investor sentiment, as many no longer blindly accept the data provided by the countries in Europe.

Germany and Britain may provide realistic data, but some other of the 27 countries that make up the EU may be engaging in their own cover-ups. To be forthright, it is not only Greece, but Portugal, Italy, and Spain that I am not convinced are providing us with real numbers. There are derivative contracts in all of these nations that I do not believe have been totally exposed. I do not know their counterparty obligations and I am not sure if some of their other data is accurate. I am not alone in my doubt, and the spreads of their debt to either U.S. Treasuries or German bonds have now widened out to spreads never before seen since 1999 and the inception of the EU.

Greece opened the proverbial Pandora's box for sovereign credits, and the lid won't be closing anytime soon. It seems only fitting that Pandora is a part of classic Greek mythology as the ancient story and its lessons come reverberating up through time. The data provided by nations will no longer be viewed in the same light. The assumptions about the safety of national debt have been eradicated and asset allocation models have been radically changed as a result.

The financial system always was and remains a matter of trust, and if that trust gets broken, there are always profound implications that are caused by the breakage.

Greece also shook the EU to its core, and the Union had to readjust its thinking and its regulations as a result of what the Greeks unleashed upon them. The flurry of activity and of new laws continues to this day as the European construct struggles to adjust to the new reality that Greece brought into the world. It began as Greek tragedy and has grown into a Greek farce, and it remains an open question of whether the construct continues or whether the Greek act of the European play brings the curtain down upon the audience in a manner reminiscent of the fury of some Greek god.

It is a curious thing that god learned Greek when he wished to turn author— and that he did not learn it better.

—Friedrich Nietzsche

The Greek Tragedy Becomes Farce

January 13, 2010

Tragedy, then, is an imitation of a noble and complete action, having the proper magnitude; it employs language that has been artistically enhanced . . .; it is presented in dramatic, not narrative form, and achieves, through the representation of pitiable and fearful incidents, the catharsis of such incidents.

—Aristotle, *Poetics,* 330 b.c.

It may be said this morning that they are still at it, carrying on the art form though they have risen to new heights as even the country's financial condition is "artistically enhanced." Of course, in the classic tradition, the current Greek regime claims it wasn't them, it was the prior government, and finger pointing is the stuff of Euripides, Act III. The EU presented a number of revelations yesterday in their report on Greece, including the somewhat startling fact that Greece achieved entrance into the EU in 2001 utilizing fictitious financial data. This point was hurried over in the report, but I was rather taken with the notion, and I have taken some time to mull it about in my mind.

If the financials for Greece were fraudulent nine years ago and are still fraudulent today, and if the ratings for Greece are based on numbers supplied by the Greek government, then what is staring us in the face? You may look that way and this way and hide behind the EU curtain in a state of denial, but that does not change reality. The actual truth is that we have been taken, are being taken, and I would exit the sovereign credit and other Greek credits with all due haste. The current spreads are indicative of financial weakness and not fraudulent behavior, and I suspect that as more of this comes to light the situation will only worsen and possibly worsen to such an extent that default may become unavoidable.

Grant's Rule 12 states that if a company is under federal investigation for fraud, then the credit should be sold. I see no reason why my dictum here should not include a sovereign credit being called out by its governing body even though the EU at this point, I am sure, would like to sweep it all under the steps of the Parthenon. The fallout here would be any number of German banks, hedge funds, and other money managers in the EU that are using the Greek credit as an arbitrage play against the stronger EU credits. This situation is just rank with risk, and the exit door beckons.

The *Financial Times* reports this morning that an IMF team arrived in Athens yesterday, and one wonders just what that could mean—nothing good, I am sure. The EU Commission report listed categories in which, it said, Greece had deliberately misreported financial data, including revenues from abolished extrabudgetary accounts, swaps write-offs, adjustment for interest payments, EU financial grants, and hospital liabilities. One cannot foretell how this play will end, but my advice is not to be in the audience for the final act.

> *History repeats itself, first as tragedy, second as farce.*
>
> —Karl Marx

A Couple of Comments that Are Not Greek to Me

Any large Treasury rally, such as yesterday, is a great opportunity to sell into it either as a trade or a strategic maneuver; I do not think current rates hold.

Keep a weathered eye on the Commodity Research Bureau (CRB) Index; the first hints of inflation should show up in the pricing of basic commodities.

Many corporate spreads are just out-and-out overdone and being driven by capital inflows, and some profit taking is in order. Try using fixed-to-float securities, step-ups, Build America Bonds (BABs) and the few lagging credits left as places to redeploy.

Pay particular attention to bonds in your portfolios that are now at large premiums and take some money off the table; yields are going to back up, and those bonds will mature at par, and one Greek tragedy is quite enough.

Greece on the Skids

January 29, 2010

T here is no joy in this Greek tragedy; that much can be said for certain, as the effects of a possible Greek default or, perhaps worse, an EU bailout or an IMF bailout continue to loom on the horizon. Listening to the prime minister of Greece and the political leaders in Germany and France reverberates of the famous statement in *The Wizard of Oz:* "Pay no attention to that man behind the curtain." "What else can be said?" one may ask, but the consistent denials of formulated plans by anyone about anything concerning the situation in Greece only lead to more worries in the markets exacerbated by the denials. This morning we face a German 2-year at 1.13 percent and a Greek 2-year at 5.29 percent for a +416 bps differential, and in the 10-year sector the spread has widened out to +370 bps. I believe there is an Aussie phrase, "having a run on the country," which is something akin to a walkabout in the bush, but the current "having a run on the country" is a matter of a different sort.

The Street, both here and in Europe, is just rife with rumors of some sort of pending implosion, and while the press hints around about it, some of the tales are eye opening as the euro continues to slide and is now under 140 to the dollar. Just this morning the British chancellor, Alistair Darling, publicly stated that they were not going to bail out Greece, and I have not seen so many denials since Queen Cleopatra ruled the State of da Nile. One wonders, if no one is doing anything or worrying about anything, why everyone is so public in their pronouncements! Now rumors are just that. They are not facts, but there does seem to be truth in some things I have heard whispered around: There were some inquiries made to the Chinese and some sovereign wealth funds concerning purchasing Greek debt; there has been a heightened pace of discussion about issuing Eurozone bonds; conversations have taken place in Germany and France about lending Greece some money in one fashion or another; there is apparently some very real institutional anger that the book runners for the last Greek deal did not report accurately on the order book, prompting a lot of finger pointing as quite real losses have now been taken; and finally, the financials of Greece, as far as anyone can make them out, bear little resemblance to the actualities, which is causing quite real angst in a number of European capitals. Now these are all rumors, as I have stated, but for a country that needs to refinance to the tune of 53 billion euros this year, this is a serious business.

What is actually happening, in my opinion, is something we have seen before but not on this scale. Sovereign debt is usually a matter of yield consideration and not credit consideration in the general sense. Now, however, as in the Latin American crisis of some years back or the Argentinean default, investors are first concerned with the credit of Greece but even more worried that the financials may be a fantasy dreamed up in Athens. It just never goes down well when one pays up to buy a diamond and it turns out, under closer examination, that the stone is a piece of quartz. Then, of course, there are the ratings agencies, which could also direct their anger toward Greece if it turns out that the numbers they were provided were a construction of something less accurate than a Pythagorean Theorem. Finally, there is the notion being worried about by some quite large money managers that if the ruse is up in Greece, the financials of Portugal or Spain and others may also be in question. It is precisely this concern, in my opinion, that is unsettling the broader debt markets and has also reached the shores of the stock markets in many countries. Here is a quite real example of when faith is lost, there is hell to pay.

Hell is a place where the motorists are French, the policemen are German, the chefs are English and the accountants are Greek.

—The Wizard

Watch the Money; Consider the Consequences

The Investment Company Institute reports that in December $3.86 billion was pulled from stock funds while $26.13 billion went into bond funds. Now consider that bonds funds took in $374.64 billion in 2009 as compared with $27.1 billion in 2008. This number is 166 percent above the previous record set in 2002. Next, think about that in 2009 equity funds had a total outflow of $8.84 billion, which is only the fourth time there has been a negative number since 1984, the year when the Institute began to accumulate data, and add that to the outflow from stock funds in 2008 of $233.8 billion, which adds up to $242.64 billion out of equity funds.

My conclusion is that there is a quite real shift under way for American investors, and while I chided the press the other day for not giving the consequences of this enough attention, I would add professional money managers and the banks/investment banks to the mix. It has long been my contention that one should buy bonds for income and that equities should be bought for appreciation. I have stated often enough that index funds or buying equities for dividends was a poor decision for the most part and our recent financial crisis has vetted my view. What has not changed, however, is the lack of various bond strategies for investors in the debt funds. Certainly, we have funds delineated by maturity and some by the type of bonds to be included in the fund, but the options in bonds funds and exchange-traded funds (ETFs) are limited and should be enlarged. Given the yields currently available in fixed-to-float securities, it would be nice to see more emphasis put in this area of the fixed income markets. Yields here are calculated based on the current London Interbank Offered Rate (LIBOR) for the most part and the yields be will quite different in the upcoming months if my view is correct that yields will be rising first as a matter of investors demanding higher and higher yields to participate, then as the Fed finally begins to raise rates, and finally as a matter of the inflationary impact of the monetary policies of the Fed, the Treasury, and the big government social schemes of the current administration.

The investment schematic for institutions and the public alike has been changed for at least a generation, and we should respond better to this reality. There is no doubt in my mind that this influx of money is one of the key factors in the continuing compression of all bonds across the spectrum and in even holding down Treasury yields. It seems to me that those institutions that broaden their offering plates will be winners in the game of attracting money for the next several years.

Go forth and proliferate!

The Shutdown in Greece

February 11, 2010

Allow me to pose a question to begin the morning:

If in the United States yesterday the majority of the civil servants just walked out on their jobs; virtually all of the schools across the nation were closed; the court system totally shut down, as well as almost all public offices; the railroads stopped operating; and all of the airports and airlines closed shop so that there were no flights in or out of the country, how would America be responding?

It is a simple question, not too complicated; and I believe that the answer would lie somewhere between panic and extreme nightmares of social unrest. So please pay attention when I tell you that this is exactly what happened in Greece yesterday—exactly. The unions in Greece just shut the country down, and I mean just stopped it cold. Here is what is on the web site of their largest public union:

> *No to the reduction in salaries. No to the downgrading of social rights. No to the downgrading of social security, the reduction in pensions and the increase in retirement ages.*

I marvel this morning that many people in the financial world are doing some kind of happy dance that Germany and France may provide some kind of assistance to Greece. The operative word here, of course, is *may*. It also *may* come as some kind of epiphany to you that it *may* make little difference what the other members of the EU may or may not do if the populace in Greece is not in support of the EU mandates. It is not default in Greece or Portugal or Spain that overly concerns me at this point; it is the public's refusal to adhere to proclamations issued from Brussels, and it is at this point where I think that the rubber meets the road.

If the Greeks close down their country and the Portuguese Parliament increases their budget deficit in absolute defiance of their ruling party and of the EU guidelines, then what part of the joke are we missing? Greek bonds have run up in price, and the euro has strengthened on the back of a hope and a prayer from France and Germany. I am here to tell you that unless there is a dynamic shift in attitude in the citizenry of the three troubled countries, Humpy Dumpty is right on the edge of falling off the wall. It may not happen, of course, and I am not wishing that it happens, but my Kansas City mind works quite well and I am telling you that whether the fall comes or not is going to be a damn close proposition.

By Way of Contagion

Consider that the Greek banks are one of the major financiers to the Balkan countries using the ECB for funding by pledging Greek sovereign debt and that this financing will dry up with the implementation of the EU mandates causing difficulties in that part of the world.

Consider that the German Landesbanks are reported to have major exposure to the Greek credit-default swap (CDS) contracts, which do not need to go into default just to erode in price to cause serious problems for these institutions.

Consider that French and Swiss institutions, according to the IMF, are the largest creditors of Greece and that the Swiss exposure is approximately 12 percent of their gross domestic product (GDP).

The Point of Consideration

There is but one element of government, and that is the people. From this element spring all governments.

—President John Adams

It is my view that the financial world, in general, is missing the critical issue. The question is not whether the EU nations in some form or fashion will help out Greece, but whether the people of Greece will accept the shackles that will be appended to any EU assistance.

Greek Austerity and Other Fairy Tales

February 12, 2010

> Bah! Humbug!
>
> —Ebenezer Scrooge

One of the most enduring quotes from Charles Dickens sums up my reaction to the EU's plan to help Greece. The text can be read in German or French or English, but the meaning is the same, "If you don't need the help, then we will give it to you." When you cut through the political jargon and meaningless metaphors and get down to the facts, that is just about what the EU's pronouncement says right there in black and white. The first reaction, as the EU hoped, I am sure, was to run up the euro based on the fact that the EU opined, but the second reaction, as is evident this morning, was for people to actually read what they put in print and now the euro is falling backwards once again.

The EU nations promised "determined and coordinated action if needed to safeguard stability" and that all sounds well and good but there is no rack whatsoever to hang your hat upon. There are several realities here in my view: Germany, which just reported out a flat GDP for the quarter, is unlikely to actually do more than provide lip service because the German public wants none of it. France, who might offer up a few cases of champagne or some decent bordeaux for any further meetings does not have the financial capacity to start bailing out anyone by themselves no matter what size sword they may wave in the breeze. Consequently, the whole plan relies on some sort of fantasy that all of the EU countries would somehow come together and stand as a bloc to bail out Greece or Portugal or Spain if it came to that and that kind of political fluff cannot be taken seriously by any rational person involved in the financial markets.

If you actually thought that the EU's proclamations were substantive then let me outline for you what you are betting on:

- That the current political leaders in Greece, Portugal, and Spain can actually deliver on their promises of austerity, that they will remain in power to deliver them and that the citizens of each country will not throw out their elected officials in one form or another.
- That the member countries of the EU will vote to change the rules of the Union to allow for bailouts of individual countries.
- That the EU will vote to provide funds to troubled and that the citizens of the financially stronger nations will allow their elected officials to utilize public monies to help out countries that contrived their financial data, over spent their resources and provide social programs that their countries cannot afford.

The race may not always be to the swift nor the victory to the strong, but that's how you bet.

—Damon Runyon

Greece's economy contracted more sharply than expected, by 0.8 percent in the fourth quarter, and official data on Friday showed downward revisions for the previous three quarters too, spelling a deepening recession. . . .

—ATHENS, Feb 12 (Reuters)

That would be your bet and in my opinion, and there is no other way to politely state this; that would be a really dumb bet.

Just Out as I Write My Commentary

There you have it. So much for the Greek forecasts, so much for the EU forecasts, and so much for the fantasyland vision of a 10 percent rise in Greek GDP accompanied by a 10 percent rise in Greek tax revenues; all the stuff of dreams and Easter bunnies and Zeus descending from Mount Olympus. In fact, the Greek economy shrank by 2.6 percent on a year–over–year basis, and I would make no bet at this point that all of the horses and all of the king's men could put Humpty Dumpty back together again!

A German and a Frenchman met in a bar after work for a drink and were watching the 6 o'clock news on TV. A man was shown threatening to jump from the Brooklyn Bridge. The German bet the Parisian $50 that he wouldn't jump, and the Frenchman replied, "I'll take that bet!" Anyway, sure enough, he jumped, so the Berliner gave the Frenchman the $50. The Parisian said, "I can't take this, you're my friend." The German said, "No, a bet's a bet." So the Frenchman said, "Listen, I have to admit, I saw this on TV on the 5 o'clock news, so I can't take your money."

"Well, so did I, but I never thought he'd jump again!"

The Fifth Labor of Hercules

February 22, 2010

The fifth of the Twelve Labors set to Heracles (or Hercules) was to clean the Augean stables in a single day. This assignment was intended to be both humiliating (rather than impressive, as had the previous labors) and impossible, since the livestock were divinely healthy (immortal) and therefore produced an enormous quantity of dung. These stables had not been cleaned in over 30 years. However, Heracles succeeded by rerouting the rivers Alpheus and Peneus to wash out the filth.

Greece was given until February 19 to send a memo to the EU outlining the derivatives contracts that it had undertaken. Greece assured the EU and the world that they would provide a comprehensive and full report of these transactions on time. Whatever else that can be said, this was not the case. Amadeu Altafaj, the EU spokesman for economic issues, announced this morning, "We have received some information, but not all the relevant information." He further went on to state that the Greek government had blamed the lack of providing the data on the strikes in Greece.

Now there are those, I am sure, who believe in little green fairies and large white rabbit Pookas and elves and gnomes and other denizens of the forest, but it is a tough row to hoe claiming that unionized strikes are preventing the obtainment of the derivatives contracts. Here, the muck of the Augean stables smells like rose water by comparison. Here, the Greek government not only stinks, so to speak, on providing the truth, but they also fall on the sword of Odysseus in believable creativity. One truly wonders what kind of people are running the Greek government if they provide this kind of total nonsense to the European Union.

According to Desmond Lachman of the American Enterprise Institute, the EU mandates would require Greece to cut 10 percent of their

GDP, which would result in a savage depression, resulting in massive unemployment, already at 10 percent. Even preliminary hints of this are creating strikes and demonstrations in the streets, resulting in serious repercussions, including government employees stopping work, no goods being taken or shipped at the major Greek ports, and petrol being in short supply as a result of all of this. With Greek 10-year debt standing at 6.41 percent this morning or +313 bps to the German 10-year the price talk on a new 10-year Greek issuance is 7.25 to 7.50 percent and even that, I would guess, would have to be accompanied by full disclosure of all of the outstanding swaps.

The situation with Greece, in my opinion, is like standing at the entrance to the Netherworld while Cerberus, the three-headed dog that guards the gates, is snapping at the Hellenic state with bestial ferocity. It is getting down to a reality of where there are not only no good answers but a series of bad choices that all will be negative for Greece, the euro, and the European Union.

A number of international banks and, of course, the countries themselves, have protested the use of the acronym PIIGS (Portugal, Italy, Ireland, Greece, Spain). I can understand this—the saying is not exactly kosher. This morning I propose a new term that seems kinder and targets the most troubled countries, which I call "ALMs" and is a term resplendent in asking for help to survive. My construct refers to Athens, Lisbon, and Madrid. Feel free to use the term at your leisure.

What is clear now is that Greece will have to release, in detail, all of its swaps at some point and that Spain and Portugal will have to follow suit. This will not only be a matter of EU regulation, but I think it will now be demanded by the investment community to make any new purchases of sovereign debt. The old way of tactfully looking the other way and not being fully apprised of realistic financials will no longer be tolerated. One may surmise, with some assurance, that whatever the actualities are here, they will not bode well for these countries and that further declines in sovereign debt prices are on the horizon. As for me, I would not be buying any country's debt until I knew all of the facts no matter how much nonsense was heaped upon the stable's floor and how many assurances were strewn upon the pile that was already present. Each and every country may well object and claim all kinds of matters of privacy, but I would remain steadfast until all of these derivatives contracts were brought fully into the light for examination.

Why Greece Matters

March 21, 2010

No nation has friends; only interests.

—Charles de Gaulle

You may note in this quote that the author is "Charles of Gaulle," which is the European tribe to which his ancestors belonged, to which he belonged, and to which his descendents belong. This is of critical importance to understand when fully appreciating the present difficulties in the EU. Today, I am going to try to answer the fundamental question of why the small nation of Greece is so important to today's financial markets and why the consequences of the outcome here will shape the way many professional investors view the economic world and, in particular, the safety of sovereign credits.

Some historical background is needed to fully understand the present day psychological implications of what is taking place in the EU. Going back before the time of Christ, Greece was a great civilization that dominated the known world in many respects, but that time is long gone and they have never returned to power. After that, as we all know, we had the Romans, but they imploded with their own corruption and the challenges of other Northern tribes. In fact, Europe is made up of a set of tribes that have been warring on and off with each other for millennia. Over the course of history, these tribes crystallized into nation states and then coalesced even more as one given tribe or amalgamation of tribes won out over their neighbors. This is the history of Europe, and there are long and quite serious prejudices and strong ancestral feelings that are a very real part of the psyche of the people in each country. While the news media spend no time exploring this deeper reality as

they exert all of their efforts on the events of the moment, this kind
of historical perspective is a very important part of comprehending the
actualities of trying to forge a number of very different tribes into a
European Union.

Forging ahead, we have the Great
Wars and the economic ruination of
many nations in Europe along with
spilled blood and the loss of many lives.
There are bitter memories and tales of
horror, which are imprinted into the

History is past politics, and politics is present history.

—E. K. Freeman, 1886

collective souls of the European nations because of all this, and this is
a kind of pain not easily forgotten when sovereign difficulties arise. My
family came to America from Austria in 1840, and it has been long
enough for me and many of us in the United States to have forgotten
what must have been harsh realities that would cause our ancestors to
leave their homelands. With the exception of Native Americans that
is the history of our country and we just do not have the conflictual
imprints held by many of our friends across the pond. It is with this in
mind that I make some observations about Europe that play a vital part
in understanding the present difficulties.

What I am about to comment on is all my own personal speculations,
of course, and this must be said, but I have traveled enough in the world
to have some viability in my observations. Let us consider the two largest countries in the EU; my consideration of the difference between the
way the French view the Greek issue and the way the Germans look
at the same problem is one of tribal history. The French, said with no
disrespect, have a long history of fooling their own government about
taxes and their incomes to the point that it is almost a national sport, so
they have a very different view of the Greeks cooking the books to gain
admission to the EU or of their continuing inventive accounting than
the Germans. The Germans—a very proud tribe, if nothing else—have
been severely humbled in the last 100 years by being the losers in two
great wars and humbled even further by the atrocities that were committed in the name of the German people. The Deutsche, therefore, are "by
the book," and there will be no crossing over any lines and if a person
does or a nation does then, "Es gibt keine Hilfe" (there will be no help).
Two very different views of the world and hence two very different
reactions to the Greeks and what they have done and what they are presently doing. You will note that if some historical perspective is brought

to the issues at hand, then the situation begins to make sense and is not just the idle speculation of the uninformed.

Now let us move forward to the creation of the European Union on November 1, 1993. At the time, the Europeans created this committee of tribal oversight in hope of competing with the Americans on one hand and the Japanese on the other. Please recall that the Western world was afraid of the Japanese economically at the time, though now they have denigrated themselves through overreaching into a deflationary country that is no longer a financial threat to anyone. This was the basis of the EU, in my opinion, as they have 500 million people and are a larger population base than the United States and Japan, with effective international industries. The idea was creative, of course, but it did not take into accurate account that America, as an example, is a nation of just one tribe—a new one, of course, and mostly European outcasts, but still one with no reverence to anyone's former homeland. In Europe, however, the psychological implications are quite different as each member state has one vote in the EU and that vote is solely dependent on the tribal customs and history of each separate country. All of this actually began with the European Coal and Steel Community founded by six nations in 1951 and then the Treaty of Rome founded in 1957 by the same states. This then brings us to the present day, where there are 16 nations that use the euro as their currency, and all of which, if it is an EU decision, by mandate, must agree on the terms and conditions to help Greece. So what do you say—16 tribes with 16 different histories and prejudices that are going to agree on the specific points that it will take to provide Greece financial assistance? I say, "Not—just not going to happen."

We are asking the nations of Europe between whom rivers of blood have flowed to forget the feuds of a thousand years.

—Winston Churchill

This then brings us to the IMF, controlled at least in part by the United States, which will set very stringent controls and conditions to help out Greece and will probably cause an even more severe recession than at present or social unrest, which might change the government if implemented, but there is really little other in the way of choices. Greece has just too much of a shortfall in financing upcoming just around the corner, and Spain is not that far off either with $20 billion needed to be raised in the short term. The outcome here, no matter how you slice and dice the problem, is just not going to be good for Greece or the EU or the euro as a currency.

This brings us then to the second major problem; how to correctly appraise sovereign debt. Some bright people have raised the issue of whether a corporate credit in a given country could be safer than the nation's debt, but I believe this is a very secondary issue. The more pressing problem is whether the financials of a sovereign credit are, indeed, accurate. We know that, in the case of Greece, they cooked the books for entrance into the EU but at the same time, in the same fashion, they cooked the books for the ratings agencies and for us as investors, and hence we bought bonds based on falsified figures. I am of the camp that the first mistake is on me, but the second mistake will not be made so quickly. I now look askance at sovereign debt and wonder what I might really be buying. I will not suggest these credits at current spreads and without knowing all of their derivatives exposure, and if I do not think the figures are accurate or if I don't know what their CDS exposure is, then I am not interested; frankly, at current spreads, in my view, there is way more risk than reward. We have a long tradition of blindly accepting the sovereign numbers that are given to us, but for me no longer, and neither do I trust the decisions of the agencies that rate these bonds. They didn't get it when Greece falsified the numbers in the first place and why should I trust them now? I do not! J. P. Morgan (the person, not the bank) said the following:

> Asked: "Is not commercial credit based primarily upon money or property?"
>
> "No sir," replied Morgan. "The first thing is character."
>
> "Before money or property?"
>
> "Before money or anything else. Money cannot buy it. . . . Because a man I do not trust could not get money from me on all the bonds in Christendom."

I am with Mr. Morgan here, and if Greece provided knowingly inaccurate data to the EU and to the rating agencies, then the problem is endemic and I will not excuse them on the basis that some other political party was in power. No sir, I will not.

The old thinking was that sovereign numbers were real and that sovereigns should trade tighter than corporate credits. I no longer accept that viewpoint, and I suspect that institutional investors are reluctantly coming around

Who do I call if I want to call Europe?
—Henry Kissinger

to that opinion. As a matter of sad reality, it is easier for a government to concoct numbers than a corporation residing in a given country as the nation regulates a corporation, but who, I ask, regulates a sovereign nation; the plain answer is no one but their national conscience, which is obviously not good enough.

Greece matters because she has exposed the flaws of the European Union and the Euro.

Greece matters because she has exposed the risks of sovereign debt.

Greece matters because she has exposed the flaws of the ratings agencies.

Greece matters because she is forcing us to reassess how we value sovereign debt.

Greece for Dummies

March 23, 2010

You have to imagine a family discussion where everyone has a veto over where to go for Sunday dinner. You are sitting there with 16 members of your family, such as Bubba and A. J. and cousin Bertha, and trying to decide where you want to go to eat. The family rules are that no one can go anywhere until everyone agrees. Uncle Jake is on a strict diet and can't eat fatty foods, and Aunt Amelia is as round as a Jimmy Dean pork sausage and is craving fried chicken, and Mama only wants a small salad with the dressing on the side, please—and now you are getting the drift about what is happening in the EU. Sixteen yokels hanging out in Brussels and Grandpa Franz, the one with the most money and who everybody had hoped was buying dinner, just ain't having none of it. You see, Franz knows that if he opens his wallet and picks up the tab, when he gets home, his wife, Gertrude, is just gonna wallop him across the backside. He has been there before, and he just ain't gonna go there again. Moreover, Franz wants a Braunschweiger sausage, and he sure don't want nothing to do with that nouvelle cuisine stuff that Cousin Pierre keeps suggesting—who knows what is drizzled on the food; it could be anything at all underneath that drizzle, and Franz knows he has to keep a watchful eye on Pierre under any circumstances.

Then there is the problem of Cousin Tony, who is about to lose his Greek diner and who wants a handout before everyone tries to make a decision about dinner, and then, of course, he wants to eat for free. Tony is "poor mouthing" and wanders back and forth between saying he doesn't need the money and then sobbing if anyone agrees, and then reminding Grandpa Franz that he whipped his butt when he was younger and he is trying to lay the piety of Greek guilt on his sauerbraten. Tony has even brought a picture of the delicious seafood dinner that he could give to everyone at his restaurant, if he gets the handout, but Franz is no dummy and has noted that it looks suspiciously like an American hot dog. Of course, if you listen long enough to Tony, you begin to believe that he is so darn poor that he can't even afford to pay attention.

We, of course, not being members of this dysfunctional family, all get to sit quietly at home while we get Twitter reports from various people sitting at nearby tables to the EU table, now renamed "Eggplant United," that are observing this event. One of the most comical things about all of this is that the Eggplant family hails from different countries, and you can find yourself quite amused by the nuances of their conversations. It was reported that Pierre was talking about "loading the dishwasher" and Franz thought he was speaking about getting his wife drunk. All of the family got quite concerned, I am told, when Tony was complaining loudly about the stock market until everyone realized that he was speaking about a place for cows with a fence. Then there was the cousin from Belgium who said that he was going to pick his teeth so that everyone looked away and then he opened up a dental catalog from Luxembourg. It is no wonder, you see, that this is all so difficult to understand as they have a hard time communicating in plain old English.

In any event, Tony, known as my big fat Greek ★&^%$ (censored by compliance) is causing a hubbub at the table, and the entire family has just about had enough of it. The situation is so ludicrous that the cousin from the Netherlands orders a Jack Daniels while he is waiting and Pierre wonders aloud when he will show up. This is while Giuseppe orders some Dom Perignon and Tony thinks this is some guy from the Italian Mafia who is going to join them for dinner. Now I am not joking here; if you pay close enough attention to what is going on in Belgium, I think my version is an excellent explanation of just what is happening.

So you watch all of this and then they want you to take their marker? No, no, not happening, and heck, the paper money they are trying to hand us ain't even green. Not a chance; not lending them my hard-earned money and not investing in any Greek diners, thank you. You may want to own a piece of "gyros on a spit," but I'll put my money with Colonel Sanders, thank you!

ΑΦΗΣΤΕ ΤΑ ΠΑΙΧΝΙΔΙΑ ΝΑ ΑΡΧΙΣΟΥΝ

April 9, 2010

Soon—very soon, in my opinion—Greece is going to ask the IMF and the European Union for aid. The issue is no longer funding but has now become one of solvency and the iron curtain has descended once again across Europe. Everything up until that moment will have been the prelude, and then the real show will begin. There will be more drivel spewed from the mouths of the politicians in Europe than the refuse in the barn that Hercules was directed to clean. There will be more lies, half-truths, and utter fantasy proclaimed as truth than we can yet possibly imagine. Octopuses do not have enough tentacles for the finger pointing that is about to take place. Political comments made in one country will have little relation to comments made in a politician's home country and denials and faulty translations will be the lament of the day. Calls for European unity will be wailed into the empty night sky, as nothing is more important to these people than being reelected back home. Three-card Monty will morph into 16-nation Monty, and the spectacle will be a show beyond belief and would be just great fun if the consequences weren't so severe.

> *The Greatest Show on Earth*
> —P.T. Barnum

> *Cass Mastern lived for a few years and in that time he learned that the world is all of one piece. He learned that the world is like an enormous spider web and if you touch it, however lightly, at any point, the vibration ripples to the remotest perimeter and the drowsy spider feels the tingle and is drowsy no more but springs out to fling the gossamer coils about you who have touched the web and then inject the black, numbing poison under your hide.*
> —Robert Penn Warren,
> *All the King's Men*

Pull up your comfy armchairs and grab the popcorn; one of the great farces of your lifetime is about to begin!

The last time there was a grand event of such magnitude was at the end of World War II when America, Britain, and Russia held the keys to the kingdom. This time, in an achievement that the Germans have found wanting for almost 100 years, they will get to call the game. A smaller arena, to be certain, no loss of life, just fiscal livelihoods—but still, they are finally Masters of the Universe in their own domain. The French will chime in, no doubt, and bitterly complain about everything, and the United Kingdom, as part of the larger group, will have a polite word or two, but the Reich will rule. Past prejudices will come roiling to the surface, tribal prejudices of 1,000 years will be exposed one more time, and the anguish of each nation's hand as it brushes across the boiling water will be echoed in homelands seething with mistrust and rancor. The evasive politic will cede to the Beast, and Germany will declare the victor. We now all await the famous Greek pronouncement, "Let the Games Begin."

The Greek Orthodoxy have become the Antichrist, and the shroud of Turin was torn with the Greek falsification. The Lords of the Manor have been disgraced and the Dukes of the Rhineland do not take insult lightly. Two timeless sins have been committed: lying about what is in the Treasury and then not being able to repay what has been lost. Everyone may not be a Berliner, but, *achtung*, everyone will be held to that standard, everyone accountable.

All treaties between great states cease to be binding when they come in conflict with the struggle for existence.
— Otto Von Bismarck

If there are any sure bets in this situation, there are three, and I will enumerate them for you:

1. Dislocation
2. Vindication
3. Punishment

This is where you place the money. The EU will not emerge from all of this where it started. The euro will no longer be the same kind of contender with the dollar. Bonds denominated in euros are likely in trouble, and a default does *not* have to be the answer that causes rupture. Greece, one way or another, is going down, and the logbooks of Hades will mark the passage in history. The ECB, for all of the grandiose design, will not come through this crisis intact. Germany will be the Maker of Rules or withdraw, leaving its brethren to wallow with the PIIGS, and this will be made abundantly clear. The great design, as currently constructed, cannot and will not stand.

Just be patient. Trichet and the ECB will strew palm leaves upon your path and assure you that all is right with the world. The Greek bonds will march this way and that in grand procession as various politicians come and go from the stage. The press will run from corner to corner as the actors enter stage left and stage right. Everyone and anyone will postulate if the curtain will or will not go up and just push back with a broad smile upon

Never believe anything in politics until it has been officially denied.

— Otto Von Bismarck

your face as the grand event gets under way. Also keep this in mind: As the situation worsens and people find themselves somewhat further down the path, it could well be that institutions cast a weathered eye on the exposure of Germany and France and their banks to Greece or perhaps other countries that fall into the abyss. Their bonds could also begin to back up, and if the whole Union actually starts showing signs of fragility, then the debt of no country in the EU is safe, which is why I have advised backing up from each and all of them.

I Am Not Backing Down

April 14, 2010

I have noticed in my life that when it comes to truth, nations often mask it and hide behind the illusions of it that they present to the world as fact when, in actuality, they are falsehoods created for their own purposes. I suppose this is the way of politics on a grand scale, but regardless of the proffered illusion of the masquerade, there is truth hiding behind the slings and arrows of untruth, and to make an accurate assessment of the best possible use of the money entrusted to us, we must find it. The large amounts of money handed to the public relations firms cannot hide it, and the fees paid to the ratings agencies cannot disguise it, and even the slant secured in the press by national influence does not change the truth, even though some would like it hidden from public view.

We are wiser than that; we are better than that, and blind acceptance is not the way of the standards we impose upon ourselves when looking reality dead in the eye and drawing conclusions. I, for one, will not wilt or take the path of least resistance or be bullied by others with questionable agendas. I am disposed to consider anyone's opinion about the truth, but I am wholly and absolutely in defiance of anyone that makes up a politician's tale and entitles it the truth.

Sixteen European finance ministers who use the euro as their currency have agreed to a plan to provide money to Greece. There is the truth. Sixteen legislatures have not yet approved it, and the money for the financial assistance package is not yet available, may not be available, and that is also the truth. Greece did raise money utilizing Greek Treasury bills mostly bought by Greek financial institutions; it was not a bond issuance, as was widely reported, and that is also the truth. Since the bill issuance, Greek debt has backed up considerably, and that is also the truth:

As of 6:28 A.M. EST on April 14, 2010:

The Greek 2-year yields:	6.44% (+547 bps to the German 2-year)
The Greek 5-year yields:	6.95% (+475 bps to the German 5-year)
The Greek 10-year yields:	7.02% (+396 bps to the German 10-year)

In just two examples of 16, the Dutch Parliament will take up the proposal tomorrow, and to fund they would have to not only approve the proposed bailout, but also pass a supplementary piece of legislation to distribute the funds, while the German Finance Ministry just announced this morning that the German Parliament would likely have to vote on any assistance for Greece. At present, the EU has a proposal, and it is nothing more or less than that and I will be damned if I will allow various members of the EU or the ECB to stand up in the press and declare that the deal is done because, quite plainly, it is not. Even the Greek prime minister has called present funding levels "unsustainable," which they certainly are if Greece is to avoid outright default, while Fitch yesterday said that a downgrade to a level below investment grade was possible if Greece could not implement its budget plan.

After my examination of what I believe to be the truth, I have reached some conclusions:

- The Euro is overvalued and will decline from present levels.
- The Greek economy cannot sustain the present levels of debt, and while the endgame may get delayed, it is virtually impossible to thwart.
- Bonds denominated in euros may well have a currency risk in 2010 that overtakes the coupon interest.
- Portugal and Spain are also both under the gun and to ignore their plights will be a mistake.

The EU Scenarios for Greece

April 29, 2010

T his morning, I am going to try to map out the most likely scenarios of what will happen with the EU and Greece so that you can take defensive action, if necessary. I will chart the most likely paths and the ramifications of each so that you can fully consider how to position your portfolios as a result of what may happen. In each and every case, except for the last, in my mind, the consequences are negative for the EU, but in what way and in what manner is where there are distinct differences. The play has begun, the curtain has opened, and we are nearing the next act. Let's begin.

Scenario One

The EU package for Greece is the amount originally proposed or close to it as the $10 billion extra that the IMF first proposed makes very little difference. Here, I would contend that the institutional investors now better understand the problem and that the euro and bonds denominated in euros will be punished, as it is clearly not enough money to heal the wound. In this case, default or restructure would not take place in May, but it will be coming and European credits will continue to be hit as the inevitable will be a known factor. This solution, in my opinion, would be a complete failure.

Scenario Two

The EU and the IMF come up with a plan that is close to the $161 billion that the IMF first suggested would be enough for Greece to stave off bankruptcy. There would be a brief relief rally in Greek debt, of course, and in the Euro, but then it would dawn upon people that this is a large amount of cash that has to get paid by someone. Not only would

Germany have to cough up somewhere around 40 billion euros, possibly damaging their credit, but the weakest of the European countries— Portugal, Ireland, Spain, Italy, and others—will also have to come up with their share, and it would be quite likely that they could have difficulties with the capital raise or be downgraded for taking on this extra debt. While in the first go-round the politicians of each of the 26 EU nations said they would come up with the cash, something we may never know for sure, there may be several countries that could refuse to put up this amount of money, and there is no mechanism currently in place for one country to pay for another's share, and more than that, under prior agreement, each and every country has a veto over the entire package. This scenario has hazard written all over its face.

Scenario Three

One can reasonably infer that if the amount is to be around $161 billion, then the terms and conditions for the loan will be more severe than for the smaller amount. These could be so stringent, in fact, that Greece cannot accept them because it would cause the government to fall, and they reject the terms and conditions and withdraw from the EU. This may well be the ploy that Germany has in mind so that when all of the political rhetoric is exhausted, they can claim that Greece voluntarily withdrew. Subset two here would be that Greece rejects the terms and conditions but does not leave the EU and defaults, which causes the EU to vote to evict Greece. No good results here, though Greece voluntarily withdrawing from the EU may, in fact, be the best solution for the EU.

Scenario Four

It is now April 29, 2010. Prior to the due date for the Greek debt rollover on May 16, each and every nation in the EU, all 26 countries, accept the terms and conditions of the IMF/EU aid package. Each country, in a little over two weeks, passes legislation in time for their share of the Greek aid money and sends it to the ECB; no one is late. Greece staves off default just in time; the ratings agencies do not care about the additional debt taken on to bail out Greece for Portugal, Spain, Ireland, and all the rest and there are no downgrades; the Greek economy picks up so that its debt payments to the EU are current; the economies in the other troubled nations also improve, so there is no need for financial assistance; and the euro rises and the EU returns back to its former glory. The number of variables that have to work exactly right, precisely right, here are just overwhelming, so much so in fact that the odds against all of this happening on time are incalculably poor. You may wish to make this bet—I do not.

What No One in the European Union Wants to Discuss

First and foremost is what the additional debt for Greece could do to the ratings of the other European countries or even whether the economies in the other weaker nations would be able to support their share of the Greek debt. Next is the social unrest not only possible in Greece for undertaking the EU austerity measures but the possible social unrest or change of governments in other nations who are angry that they have to bailout Greece. Then there are the upcoming German elections, where the ruling coalition could well be turned out by the prospect of a huge amount of aid for Greece and the new coalition in Germany gives the whole Greek package a thumbs down just days before the outstanding Greek debt must be rolled over. Finally, there is this: If the whole thing actually blows up and the EU is dissolved, who pays for all of the bonds denominated in euros? Think about this: Not only sovereign debt denominated in euros, but the debt of IBM or Siemens or whoever—how would it all be settled in a currency that no longer exists? While you may have once thought of this as an outlier event in the extreme and while it still may be not that likely, it is likely enough to give this question due consideration.

Chapter 5

The Crisis in Europe

Imagine, if you will, sitting high atop the Island of Gibraltar and gazing out across the watery expanse at Europe. You are sitting comfortably with your elbows propped up on your knees and you are gazing at the continent wondering in your own unique fashion just what is found now in front of you. What it was certainly is not what it is now, and as you focus your stare, you try for clarity to make an accurate assessment—all of those nations, all of those different tribes, all of the pain and suffering built into the social fabric of their history, and a grand unfolding design to shape them into some kind of a unified political and economic union. The attempt at the building of a complex utopian dream careens off the political walls that separate the countries, and their prejudices, as the momentum of the implementation of change acts like ever-breaking waves that alter the shape of the beach.

It can be said with accuracy that during the early formative years, when the world's economy thrived, the building process of Europe's pyramid went on mostly unabated until overspending, grand social programs, and the downturn of the Great Recession arrived. Now the winds of monetary decline batter the structure with such force that prudent people of all beliefs wonder if the grand construct can survive. I take no note of words spewed for the masses nor the many inaccurate statements made by the politicians

It was already one in the morning; the rain pattered dismally against the panes, and my candle was nearly burnt out, when, by the glimmer of the half-extinguished light, I saw the dull yellow eye of the creature open . . .

—Mary Shelley

But I am a blasted tree; the bolt has entered my soul; and I felt then that I should survive to exhibit what I shall soon cease to be—a miserable spectacle of wrecked humanity, pitiable to others and intolerable to myself.

—Mary Shelley, *Frankenstein*

in Europe as I attempt to gaze directly into the maw of the beast, and I make no apology for my effort, as I am more than well aware that this European creation can seriously hurt us all.

It is rather like living in the shadow of Mordor and wondering just who and what might come pouring out of her gates with the further question of when it might happen firmly affixed in your mind. If you recall *The Lord of the Rings*, it was Tolkien's description that the castle was surrounded by several mountain ranges that served a dual purpose: protecting Mordor from attack and also keeping the people who lived there from venturing forth. The very real political waves that continuously batter the European Union (EU) are a result of the design flaws that are part of its initial construction to gain general agreement to build the thing and then to continue to build it, as the master plan is consistently modified by the political directives of both the individual countries and now, well along in the process, by the beast itself.

With each crisis, there have been several now, and I am quite certain there will be more. We live in a realistic fear that the creation, if axed at any of several vital limbs, could cause mayhem for the world's financial markets. The hemorrhage that could be caused by some debtor nation's withdrawing under political pressure based on their own national interests or by some funding nation no longer wishing to provide the monetary blood to keep the being alive is a quite realistic fear and one not to be minimalized. It was Greece first and then Portugal and Ireland that experienced the viral pain of austerity and bloated social programs

My master, Sauron the Great, bids thee welcome.

—J. R. R. Tolkien,
The Lord of the Rings

to feed their citizens as we all wait and wonder if the invention can survive the onslaught of some nation buckling under the demands of those not wishing to provide more of life's sustenance. It is a question of how much pain can be borne at the top and then at the bottom that will answer the question of survival.

What is also abundantly clear is that the beast is now alive. The EU answers to many masters, some more powerful than others, but it must also be remarked that the varlet now dances, as much as it can, to its own tune regardless of the music played by those in attendance. We sit and wait, watch and wonder because this demigod is ever present and he is now quite large enough to bring the venom of a living hell spewing down upon us all if he is not properly guided and instructed by the sirens that are singing the ancient song.

> *Surety you crave! Sauron gives none! If you sue for his clemency then you must do his bidding!*
> —The Mouth of Sauron, J. R. R. Tolkien, *The Return of the King, Lord of the Rings*

The PIIGS of Europe

December 16, 2009

They are being called the PIIGS in Europe: Portugal, Ireland, Italy, Greece, Spain.

It is like the "Dogs of the Dow" has morphed into the "Hogs and the Sow" of the Eurozone. It all seems fairly distant, except that with the recent rise in yields internationally and the real economic problems facing these countries, this is serious stuff. With the euro at 145.50 to the dollar this morning, it is abundantly clear that there is real concern about some of these nations as people recall that it is now impossible to devalue the currency of any EU member. The safety valve has been permanently shut, if you will, by the treaties now in place, and there is language that prohibits the EU or a specific member of the EU from bailing out a given country, which leaves the IMF and its rather strict controls as the lender of last resort and, if used, could exacerbate the problems greatly. There is speculation, of course, that some way could be found around the EU rules, but I fear that any such moves would weaken the entire continent even further. We also open this morning with the European Central Bank (ECB) virtually forcing the nationalization of the sixth-largest Austrian bank that was heavily tied to loans made in eastern Europe.

In a rather surprising announcement, Norbert Barthle, budget spokesman for the ruling Christian Democratic Union of Germany, declared today that Greece was "just the tip of the iceberg," which sent shudders through the European markets this morning. The Greek markets saw another sell-off on Tuesday. Greek stocks fell 2.1 per cent, while yields on two-year government bonds rose 23 bp to 3.30 percent. Yields have jumped 150 bps in the past week. That kind of jump in yield is just bone shattering in that time frame, and it puts further pressure on an already shaky Greek economy. While this may all sound far afield to some of you, it is my opinion that this is no longer an outlier, and the possibility of some real cracks in the EU must now be considered in earnest.

Yields

The 10-year Treasury's yield has increased 9 since November 30 while the Producer Price Index (PPI) yesterday jumped 1.8% increasing fears about the Consumer Price Index (CPI) to be reported today. The backdrop is several large institutions taking profits, shortening up on duration, and preparing for what could be a difficult 2010. I am reminded of the Moody Blues and their famous song, "Go Now."

The long bond, during the same time frame, has fared no better, jumping some 9.2 percent in yield, and I fear that we are only beginning the journey to higher levels. If you have not taken some profits, I encourage you to move quickly before the bond behemoths make sure that there are none to take!

The Volker Rule—A Call for Action

January 24, 2010

Sovereign Credits

I continue to think this is one of the most overvalued segments of the fixed income markets. It is not that I am suggesting default; it is that I am suggesting that reality returns. Many of these credits, which are trading just basis points back of Treasuries, have no business trading at those spreads, and as more becomes known, Greece will not be the only national debt trading at more realistic yields. Tuesday is the day when Portugal reports to the EU, and if you have exposure there, I would be exiting or paring back prior to the announcement. Their deficit is estimated to be about 8 percent of gross domestic product (GDP), and if it comes out behind that—or worse, if their numbers do not seem believable—you could see a major widening in this name. The spread between Portuguese debt and their German counterpart stood at 1.008 percent as of Friday, and I do not think this number holds. Greek debt, in the meantime, continues to gap out to new record spreads, and their 10-year is now 3.18 percent over the German 10-year. What is particularly interesting is that Greece has announced that it is going to do a five-year benchmark at these record spreads, which only indicates to me the severity of their problems. I have been warning about sovereign debt for some time now, and the problems have been and are playing out as I expected; I think we will all see more serious issues in the months ahead.

As the EU begins to examine the accuracy of the data provided by Greece, Spain, Portugal, Italy, and Ireland in particular and does not take the figures provided at face value; even more problems could arise. The effect here, in forthcoming months, in my opinion, will be to cause questions about the entire Eurozone and to have a negative impact on the euro. Further, I suspect that Moody's and Standard & Poor's (S&P) will be forced to cast a more jaundiced eye at the euro credits and not be so accepting of that data or benign in their judgments. Moreover, as one projects out past the present to a time when the Fed and the ECB begin to raise rates, then the cost of borrowing increases for everyone, which only adds to the strain for the EU-mandated 3 percent of GDP limits. Here is a sector of the fixed income markets thought by many to be a safe haven, and, in my view, it is not nearly as safe as spreads would indicate.

> *There is only one duty, only one safe course, and that is to try to be right.*
> —Winston Churchill

The Issue

The American government's desire to defend against systemic failure in the United States' financial system.

The Volcker Rule

I have noted, in my 36 years on Wall Street, that the more a solution is presented that is complex and difficult to define, the greater chance of failure. In my opinion, the Volcker Rule is every bit of that, as proprietary trading is often not separable from trading for clients. I would also make the point that our government's proposed scheme is an unnecessary intrusion into private enterprise, to the detriment of both the debt and equity holders of each and every major bank in our country. If the battle cry is the prevention of systemic financial risk, then the solution offered by the administration is worse than the problem. It seems to me that in a political rush to enrage the public by stirring up the pot against the evil denizens of Wall Street once again after the Senate debacle and after the decline in support for the health care bill by proposing a plan that has been around and ignored for almost a year is little more than political demagoguery. The so-called Volcker Rule, in fact, does not solve the problem—it only makes matters worse!

There are times to stand up and be counted.

The Grant Plan

1. All assets and liabilities must be fully recognizable on any bank's balance sheet.
2. There will be no assets of any kind off the balance sheet.

3. A bank's Tier I capital will be assessed by the Fed, and leverage will be limited by strict criteria based on the Tier I ratio.
4. Risk components will be defined by the Fed so that a bank may only have so much of its capital in separable and clearly defined classes of assets.
5. As long as a bank is owned by its shareholders and not the government, then the rules of capitalism apply and the bank should endeavor to maximize profits for its shareholders, which are its owners.

Achtung, Absolument, and Being There

March 9, 2010

> It is incumbent on every generation to pay its own debts as it goes. A principle which if acted on would save one-half the wars of the world.
>
> — Thomas Jefferson

It seems as if the world is not presently following President Jefferson's sage advice. Not that this is any surprise, of course, as we are all realists and we know that sage advice is to be nodded at with a very serious look on one's face, which is quite different from following it. In proper context, then, you begin to see the logic of what is going on around us. Everyone is nodding and bowing and swaying, and the countenances are most serious. Offers of support are heaped upon the funeral pyre of the sublime and the ridiculous, and those of us in the know stand outside the gates and get to have a good laugh once again.

The only problem is, of course, that we have our money or money entrusted to us down on the betting table on all of this, which seriously ups our countenance (Grant's great English) as we bet on each move in the dance. So now join me in rotating 360 degrees and we see Iceland, Greece, Portugal, Spain, the Emirates, and a few more on the periphery dancing badly. The problem is that if there is just one poor dancer, we can judiciously step around them, but if the floor becomes crowded with the high and mighty dancing badly, then one rebounds into another and participants can ricochet around the floor, causing all kinds of unpleasantries. Now it is at this point that things become interesting, and this is the subject of my commentary this morning.

We have recently come from a time when money sloshed around the globe and nations tossed it up into the air and spread it around in a fashion that was none too judicious, and then the gods of the financial marketplace laughed once again at our antics and turned off the spigot. Then, in a rush to get what one still could, nations started the careening process; then came the finger pointing, the browbeating, and the infamous "it is everyone else's fault but mine," which leads us to the circumstances of the present day. So there you have my take on all of this, and then we have to figure out just how these overjuiced countries will behave and what we must do about it.

First and foremost, don't believe any of the nonsense that comes spewing out of their mouths. The best line of the moment is the "offer of support." Now, in American English, this is akin to "I am there for you"—stuff and nonsense and hot air and whipped cream poured all over the ice cream sundae. In any major city in the world when a fellow stands there with his hat outstretched or his palm outstretched, we all know what it means: "Please give me some money because I need it." So, recently, we have gotten to watch the Greek prime minister, hat in hand, rush around to Berlin, not asking for money, of course, as it isn't polite, while the palm is outstretched and the bear intones, "Achtung, you have my support," though no coins are dropped. Then Greece heads off to France, where no coins are forthcoming, but there is the "Absolument, you have my support." Then it is off to the United States, where no money will be forthcoming either, and it will be "Cowboy, I am there for you."

Now in Iceland, the dancing is even worse. Not only have they screwed themselves up, but they have ricocheted off both the United Kingdom and the Netherlands and, in doing so, spilled their $5 billion drink and then refused to pay the dry cleaning bill. This is not the polite thing to do, of course, and it could be "back to the fishing nets, Sven." Now here is the clear and present danger, as they recognize the bill but don't want to pay it. There is a lesson here, which is that national interests forever trump regional interests or paying Winston or Hans when it has to come from Soren's pocket.

- Do not believe all of the gibberish in the press.
- Do not accept the financials from any country on a prima facie basis.

- Buy nothing until all of the numbers are on the table, including all derivatives.
- Worry about the risk now; the reward will come if you assess it properly.
- Any austerity measure not based on real numbers in the present tense is worthless, as projections for improved revenues are the stuff of Easter bunnies.
- The coins in your pocket will buy you dinner; the ones that you might get tomorrow will not!

The Fire Is Out of Control

April 8, 2010

Pay Attention Here

When I am writing about Greece, I am not just addressing the cancer that has invaded the body of the general politic; I am writing about Europe. Greece is a relatively unimportant country with an economy that is not worth more than a secondary glance on the world scene, but what I am addressing and what I continue to address is a grand scheme designed to compete with and then overtake the American financial system, and we are watching it unravel or perhaps implode in the worst of circumstances. We are all watching an amalgamation of nations that had hoped to compete with the United States by banding together and are now failing mostly, in my view, because all of the political leaders are elected nation by nation and not by region so that national interests must first and foremost trump the so-called European interests. They had hoped to create a "band of brothers," but the circumstances of their cartel that is of their own making gave them a "band of cousins," all with different families, interests, and designs.

> *It is the gravity of the situation, Mark, and never suppose, even for one instant, that just because people are wandering around on the Earth and subject to the laws of gravity, they have any notion of the laws that govern them.*
>
> — The Wizard

The Europeans thought and think that America had just become too powerful after World War II and they realized that the only strategy left open to them was to form a European Union where they had a larger population base, a bigger GDP, and more civilized societies. I am quite capable of identifying the great white shark, and there you have it. I am going to continue being forthright here and name what is not often discussed: The Asians were happy to help, as they were tired of being pushed around by the Americans, and the oil-producing countries in the Middle East were delighted to be supportive of the European effort as well—all in an attempt to corral the American cowboys and put them in their place. This is just the way of nations and global politics and the push and shove of life, and it might have all worked if constructed properly, but the Europeans just "screwed up"! Here, you may read royally and parliamentary "screwed up," and there is just no other way of stating it.

Most of the world reads about Greece and wonders why there is so much fuss. The financial press gets some of it, I think, but not all of it, as the EU is about to hit critical mass, which will be a defining moment for America, Europe, and the entire world that will have financial consequences for generations. This is at the epicenter of what most people do not get—the importance of the unfolding events, which will redefine the economics and the politics and the balance of power in the world for the rest of our lifetimes. Strong stuff, strong words, but that is exactly my take on what is under way, and Greece is the trigger just as the death of the Archduke Ferdinand in Sarajevo was the catalyst that set off World War I. It is that "this leads to that" and that a single domino at the beginning of the line can cause havoc for dominos strewn down the line and that there is a reason that certain scientific events are called *nuclear reactions*. What we are all witnessing is an event—a significant event where nations are set to collide and Mount Olympus has risen to prominence once again, but in a manner hardly envisioned by the Greek gods of old.

6:09 A.M. EST, April 8, 2010

Greek 2-year yields:	7.75%
Greek 5-year yields:	7.41%
Greek 10-year yields:	7.50%

The match was the new government in Greece which revealed that the former government had falsified the numbers for admission to the EU, and the fire has not stopped burning. Now we don't know what sovereign nation has what numbers as sovereign debt, unlike corporate debt, as an example, is unregulated except by any nation's own designs; we don't know, once again, what the ratings agencies are doing, as they obviously missed the boat; and we don't know for how long and how far this fire is going to burn. But I can tell you with certainty that the raging blaze is now out of control. Here, allow me to quantify it for you—if you own Greek debt, debt denominated in euros, or have exposure to the euro, your risk/reward ratio is about 90 percent risk and 10 percent reward, which would only and singularly be a return to a stabilized situation. In other words, there is absolutely no upside.

What we have learned from nuclear explosions is that there will be fallout, and this situation is so rife with danger that I am now convinced that we are just at the brink. Let me ask some questions so you may ponder them for yourself:

- What if the terms and conditions of the IMF are so strict that Greece balks, or any of the 16 nations with a veto for aid to Greece balks, so that no aid is forthcoming?
- What if Germany, given its political situation at home, decides that it has had enough and decides to go it alone and withdraws from the EU? Who picks up the tab?
- What if Greece, finding no real support, withdraws from the EU and the euro? Who then pays the Greek portion of bonds denominated in the euro? And what if Portugal or Spain or both follow suit?
- What if the countries in the Middle East or Asia or China specifically decide that the risk is just too great and start withdrawing money en masse from the euro or selling sovereign and corporate debt denominated in euros so that the 125/dollar that I predicted long ago is breached and then parity is breached and the financial centers of the world just no longer have any faith in the currency or the bonds of the EU? Please tell me then who is going to pay the bills?
- What would actually happen if the EU just could not agree and the whole scheme dissolved? A perhaps almost unthinkable question some months ago, but you had better begin to ask yourself this question now.

You may think that Grant has wandered far afield, but then you may have wondered six weeks ago why you had to pay any attention to Greece. I may not be a great and powerful Wizard, but I have spoken, and time will bear out the result.

The European Union in Stress

April 21, 2010

I did not get to write yesterday's commentary as I suffered an episode and found myself spending the day at the emergency room in the hospital. Not a great way to spend the day, I can assure you. I had a scare and underwent any number of heart tests only to find out that I might make it a few more days. Actually, everything was just fine and all blood tests, nuclear stress tests, and x-rays were as good as they are going to get since my heart attack some five years ago. Still, a scary day and one that I hope I do not have to repeat anytime soon. So the good news is that here is today's *Out of the Box*; the bad news is that you will have to put up with me for some longer period of time. Today, I am speaking at the MTN-I conference in Miami, but Angela and Tara will be minding the store, so you will be in good hands. My thanks for your understanding; it gets tough as Wizards approach 600.

The EU

Under assault once again as the Greek 10-year hits a 7.87 percent, +477 to their German counterparts, as we watch Portugal's 10-year yield widen once again. For all of the protestations by the Greek prime minister and finance minister that no new terms or conditions would be required by the IMF or the EU for financial assistance; that is the main subject of today's discussions. The fantasy that the Greek government has tried to promulgate upon investors is slowly giving way to reality, as one wonders why they thought that spreading new Greek myths was going to be a winning strategy. Not that they have been that much different than Germany or France or certain officials of the European Union, but with each fictional denial or positive assertion, we find ourselves having less and less faith in their statements and hence the accuracy of their financials.

The IMF yesterday released their Global Financial Stability Report, where they roundly criticized several EU countries for not providing "credible" plans for their debt. The head of capital markets for the IMF called Greece a "wake-up call" on Tuesday, and it should well be one for those of us that manage money for a living. In fact, it is a large, gaping hole now when looking at sovereign credits as to accuracy, and once again I will tell you that the majority of spreads in these names continue to be nowhere near the risk assumed. With the failure of the ratings agencies to prove sovereign numbers as credible, there is just no way, at this point, to know what you are actually buying, and with devaluation no longer an option for the 16 nations that use the euro as their currency, the risk factor has exponentially increased.

I continue to believe that this whole extravaganza is not going to play out well—not for Greece, not for Portugal, not for the euro, not for the EU. We will all watch the story unfold, but status quos will not remain, and the "new reality" will be a painful one for many of our brethren across the pond. That has been my call for some months now. I believe I have been on the right track, and I believe I am still there. In addition to this, there have now been calls from the ECB to approve a nation's budget before it has been released to its public—bureaucracy at its best. Privately, I have heard from friends of mine in Germany and France that if some ECB technocrat from Luxembourg thinks that the EU is going to approve their country's budget, they can take a shimmy up the church rope, or other, more artistic, words to that effect. As long as each nation's politicians are elected by a country and not by Europe, it will be that Europe is little more than a geographic location. The construct for the EU is just inherently flawed in a number of ways, and the stress fractures are increasing and will continue to increase.

Caveat emptor!

The European Union in Crisis

April 26, 2010

O ne of life's more poignant quotes:

Blaming speculators as a response to financial crisis goes back at least to the Greeks. It's almost always the wrong response.

—Larry Summers

I have said it often enough: This is an EU crisis, with Greece only the trigger event. If there were any doubt before, there should be none now; with the IMF and the EU working on a plan for Greece, the markets are just macerating Greek debt all across the board. The Greek 2-year Treasury hit 14+ percent, and their credit-default swap (CDS) rose to +674 this morning in London, while the debt of other imperiled EU countries is also coming under pressure. Both the Portugal and Irish 2-year are down over a point, while the Spanish 2-year is back one half a point. It seems that it has finally dawned on a significant number of investors that there are quite real solvency issues with Greece and perhaps some other countries, and that the money currently being discussed to aid Greece will not fix the problem but only delay the inevitable restructuring or that the EU will have to come up with another 100 billion euros to address the rest of the problem in the not-too-distant future—the latter an event that I do not think will come to pass.

It apparently has also dawned on the Germans that this is the case and their political leaders are coming under severe pressure back at home to consider not providing money for Greece as it will be lost in the eventual debt rescheduling shuffle. It has also come to the market's attention that the other countries with difficulties will also have to put up money for Greece, which they can hardly afford and will further exacerbate their own problems. Portugal would have to put up 774 million euros and Ireland 491 million euros while Spain would have to hand over 3.7 billion euros, and this would all be just for round one. When I first started writing about Greece, the idea that they would ever ask the EU for money was an outlier, and here we are this morning with restructuring being the majority bet. The deductive logic of Kansas City has prevailed, the play has now begun and the rest of the ride is going to get really ugly.

Besides the Greek debacle and the EU/Greek ploy that has cost both of them severe credibility, there now comes the question of Portugal. They have total debt of 300 percent of GDP, a current account deficit of 11.2 percent and a budget deficit of 9.4 percent. Their prime minister has said that they have no need and will not make any further cuts in spending. Next, we have Ireland and Spain and the European banking system, which could come under real pressure from marks-to-markets in all of this plus actual eventual losses.

I have iterated before and will reiterate again my views here:

- Do not have exposure to Greek, Portuguese, Spanish, and possibly Irish sovereign debt, though I will say that Ireland has done the best job on austerity to date.
- Do not have exposure to their equity markets as the risk is quite real for very painful falls in these markets.
- While I am not concerned about German or French sovereign debt, I would not have exposure to their banks, as they just own way too much of Greek and the other mentioned countries' debt, and I would also carefully monitor any counterparty exposure to these credits.
- It is now quite possible that Germany, in a carefully worded statement, will orchestrate a situation where they will not lend Greece money for a variety of reasons having little to do with actuality but that will be the outcome. Here is where things may get incredibly unpleasant for Greece and for the EU so much so that the outcome could be catastrophic for the EU.
- I would not be exposed to Greek, Spanish, or Portuguese banks, and there is now a real possibility that Greece could face a run on its banks.
- I would not be exposed to the euro or debt denominated in euros, as the currency itself will be under exceptional pressure for quite

some time with past supporters, notably the Middle East and the Asian markets' unwinding positions.

- The sovereign debt of a whole host of countries is now in question, and the spreads for sovereign credits are vastly overvalued by points, which in my view should be avoided.
- It is no longer a black swan that the entire EU could come undone, and preparation must be made for this eventuality even if it does not come to pass. You just cannot afford to bury your head in the sand now even though you may wish you could!

As I reflect back on the last several months and my concentration on the crisis in the EU, my warnings have not been for nothing, nor, as I know in several cases, did they fall on deaf ears and for that, this morning, I am profoundly thankful. I have been fearful during this entire time, and today those fears are becoming realized and, I am afraid, will continue to be realized in the coming days. Pride and prejudices may well overcome logic as the crisis intensifies, and this must be taken into consideration when preparing for unfolding events. I hope

Greece isn't the only country with debt problems and there is a risk that fiscal strains in the Euro region will be more dramatic than they now appear. . . . Other countries also have major problems and in a worst-case scenario, this could develop into a debt crisis in several countries, which also affects the bank system.

—Swedish Central Bank
First Deputy Governor
Svante Oeberg, April 26, 2010

that rational thought and pragmatic minds will prevail, but there is no guarantee of this as 16 nations with 16 different political agendas fight it out on the international stage. Real blood may well get spilled, and serious harm may get done, and the methodology to evaluate sovereign debt, EU credits, and the strength of Europe's banking system could all take hits that change the Great Game for a generation. This crisis is history in the making, make no mistake about it, and I predict a painful lesson in history has been set upon us.

A Matter of Perspective

May 4, 2010

nvesting, of course, is a matter of perspective. We can all look at the facts and reach different conclusions. As the audience for my commentary is wonderfully diverse, I get feedback from around the globe that gives me some sense of a consensus view that is tempered by those of you that speculate for a living and those of you that are longer-term investors. Sitting where I do, I am able to get a picture of what people are doing, which is sometimes invaluable. I can report to all of you this morning that the general viewpoint remains avoidance of risk and that the crisis in the EU is thought of as a quite real risk. I can report to you that a major international supra is fleeing from the euro and bonds denominated in euros as well as several non-European sovereign wealth funds and non-European central banks. The reasons for this are clearly not all the same but the gist of it is risk avoidance. I have spent some time pondering this, and I think a lot of it just gets down to variables and there are just too many of them to make people feel confident that they have a good grasp of the situation with the EU and Greece.

I will also comment that the European politicians have brought some of this upon themselves. When facts are presented, then people can make an honest appraisal, but when there are obvious misstatements and obvious attempts to mislead investors, then suspicion begins to breed contempt. Let me be specific: To this date, on May 4, 2010, there is no deal yet to bail out Greece; there might be one, no doubt, and a proposal has been made, but there is no hard-and-fast agreement yet as the deadline for Greece to roll over their debt is a scant 15 days away. If you doubt that I am correct, I point to two realities: Not all of the 26 nations have agreed to the proposal or passed legislation to that effect, and no nation has yet sent one euro to the ECB to pay for their share of the bailout. To date, it can accurately be said that there is no money yet available to give to Greece. The press talks about this as a done deal, the EU speaks of it as a done deal, and the ECB presents it all as a done deal, but the truth is clear—it is not.

Then there is the variable of Slovakia. Now many Americans would not be quite be sure where Slovakia is, and I admit that with some sense of embarrassment. However, those of us who invest for a living realize that they are part of the EU, regardless of the size of their country, and that they have a vote. Their prime minister stated yesterday, in very clear terms, that they have to change their legislation to approve the Greek bailout, that they cannot approve it now under their Constitution and that they will not have any money available, if they do pass the legislation, until probably sometime after June 9. I have not seen one, not one, mention of this in the press anywhere, and yet it is a salient fact. Germany set up the Greek bailout process explicitly so that any country—Germany was thinking of themselves, of course—could veto the pending legislation, and if Slovakia cannot approve the Greek bailout and cannot fund on time, then any rational person must ask where that leads. I won't even draw a conclusion except to state the obvious; it is a fly in the ointment, and it seems that no one but me recognizes the issue. Now I don't mind standing out in the cold alone—I have certainly been there before—but you would think that someone or another would ask some pertinent questions.

Another quite real variable in this whole situation is the populace in several countries. In Germany, it is the pending election that may leave the current coalition with the votes to get the Greek bailout package approved, but maybe not. In Greece, the population is engaging in social protest. Last night, a teachers union took over a television station and broadcast their grievances to the country and today a group has taken over the Acropolis—all of this before larger protests get under way that will most likely shut down the country for several days, if not worse. It has been more than 40 years since serious unrest took place in America, which occurred over civil rights, but I was around to witness it, and I can tell you it is a quite unpleasant business with an outcome that is anybody's guess.

Another variable is the EU's proposal for Greece. The proposal calls for about $146 billion for Greece to be paid over three years if Greece satisfies certain requirements that will be monitored on a quarterly basis. To be quite candid, regardless of good intentions, I am not sure at all if the adherence to the EU/IMF mandates are economically possible.

You may not have realized this but the $146 billion represents 44.5 per of the current GDP for Greece, and with the GDP now projected to decrease by 4 percent in this year alone, by the time the three-year time frame concludes and utilizing the IMF projections then the bailout comes in at almost 55 percent of the Greek GDP. This is during the same time horizon when Greek debt will hit 149.1 percent of GDP, and I ask calmly just how the payback to current Greek bondholders and the EU countries that may put up money for Greece is going to be accomplished? It may well be that Greece gets the money somehow to cover their May debt payment, but past that I just do not see how Greece has the resources to pay its debts. Here, if you are smart, you will peer out a little further on the horizon with foreign institutions owning about 80 percent of Greek debt, which will increase if the EU proposal comes to fruition. The majority of the outstanding debt is held by the German and French banks, and if you reach the same conclusion that I have, then you need to protect your assets now before future hits are taken and reduce your exposure to these entities. There is also the issue of sovereign exposure. If the bailout package goes through, you not only have to be concerned about the additional debt taken on by Portugal, Spain, Ireland, Italy, and others and what that might do to their financials and their ratings, but also ask what happens if Greece cannot make the payments and defaults at a later date so that each EU country that has contributed is left with a worthless asset. Not fun to consider and not a pretty picture, but it is a real possibility none the less.

This morning, as the euro declines to 1.3130 and Greek CDS widens again to +675 and their 2-year widens back out to 10.57 percent at 5:12 A.M. EST, Fort Lauderdale, Florida, it seems as if the initial euphoria is turning into a more somber reality. If the American stock markets rose yesterday, as some postulated, buoyed by the possible Greek bailout, then I am afraid that disappointment may be forthcoming. As a matter of candor, I think that the equity markets are in for some unpleasantness, that volatility is going to increase, and that spreads in the bond

> *Look now how mortals are blaming the gods, for they say that evils come from us, but in fact they themselves have woes beyond their share because of their own follies.*
>
> —Homer, *The Odyssey*

markets are going to gap in the very near future, especially those of sovereign credits, which have widened some but which I think are in for a shellacking along with a number of European bank credits.

I Make the Call—The Credit Crisis, Part II

May 7, 2010

A s we open the day and the Greek 2-year is trading at 19.31 percent, I am musing about what actually caused us to get to this point. I think a lot of it, honestly, has been caused by the European politicians who tried in almost every manner possible to mislead the markets. Chancellor Merkel has been quite vehement about blaming the speculators and the hedge funds, but I am afraid that she has been ill advised. Those two groups may be part of the issue, but they pale in size beside the real guys—the serious money, the real investors—and it is my opinion that the long-term investors no longer have much faith in what the elected officials in Europe are proclaiming as fact. I speak with a large number of institutions in various parts of the world, and this sentiment keeps getting expressed and with vehemence. The financial markets function based on trust, and when the trust has been broken, it is not necessarily that people are shorting something; rather, it is that people refuse to play—will not fund—which is exactly what I think is happening.

I'm not upset that you lied to me, I'm upset that from now on I can't believe you.

—Friedrich Nietzsche

I believe the decline in the equities markets actually began yesterday morning in the bond markets; by mid-morning there were virtually no bids. Everyone all across the Street was backing up and stepping away. What bids could be found were gapping back from the offerings, and trucks could once again be driven through the hole that separated them. Traders were doing everything and anything to sell their inventory, and it was quite reminiscent of the Credit Crisis, Part I. Then, as the day wore on and senior managers smelled the stench in bonds, they started reining in their equities people and cutting positions; you can trust me here; I know enough guys. This was going on, and then as it dawned on people that the debacle in the EU was really going to affect the American markets after all, the pin pricked the equities world. To be straight up, we are now, once again, in a mess, and we have entered a second period of instability. For America, it is good news and bad news. The good news is that "it ain't us." The United States and its banks and other financial institutions have very little exposure to Greece, Portugal, Spain, Ireland, and the rest, and while our banks have some counterparty risk to the European banks, this is a controllable problem. The bad news is that Europe does not have a central bank that is adequately structured to deal with many of the serious issues that confront it. The next round of credit issues is centered squarely in Europe with sovereign debt issues laid upon over spending and bloated national deficits based on social and governmental programs that can no longer be afforded and a socialist mentality that makes cutting back on expenditures extremely difficult. I believe I can say this and not too many of you would disagree. I was out early on Greece and the serious problems in the EU, and today I am going to move out early once again and make the call: Credit Crisis, Part II, is upon us.

So let us begin. The Greek issue will be solved, but only momentarily, as they get the money for their May debt payment somehow or another, and this will be all trumped up by the Europeans, but pay no attention to the man behind the screen. The IMF and the EU will monitor them and they will not be found to be in compliance in either quarter one or quarter two at the latest, and the funding will be cut off and Greece will be expelled from the EU. This is the most likely scenario now. In the meantime, the European banks will have hedged, sold, and covered to a great extent their Greek debt and Greek bank exposure, and there will be pain but not the kind of pain that would take place if this cauterization had to be done tomorrow. Portugal, Ireland, Spain, and perhaps Italy will also have serious issues, and the Germans and the EU will relent on some of the austerity measures citing extreme financial conditions; it will all get played out but at a slower pace. In the American credit crisis, we had the very real question of the solvency of many banks and financial institutions, but here, I am afraid, we will have worse issues, which will be not only the solvency of many European banks but the solvency of nations, and not just one of them as we enter uncharted territory where an economic union with a single currency for 16 countries begins to fall apart. I make the comment that no one on this planet knows anything about this beyond very speculative theory, and that makes this condition even more dangerous.

There is a good possibility, during all of this, that we will see further social unrest such as we have seen recently in Greece. I was speaking on Bloomberg radio with a rather august group yesterday and I mentioned this. Everyone asked me if I wasn't a little far out on the limb. I don't think so. It is just that people are not looking far enough through the foliage. When you impose strict measures of austerity on a government, it is not the government that suffers; it is the citizens. Somehow, the officials in the EU have forgotten about this, and if you push too hard on the people, this is the reaction you are bound to get. To avoid this, the EU has to relax the austerity measures and play out the game over a longer period of time. I hope they figure this out.

It is no longer a question of whether Portugal, Spain, Ireland, and perhaps others are going to get dragged in; they already are in and the perimeter has been breached. It is now a question of consensus recognition and then what to do about it. To be honest, what I initially thought was a two-cigar problem has branched out to a more cigars than I have in my house problem, and a lot of consideration over the next few weeks will have to be given to these issues. Fortunately, I will soon be on my boat, and I tend to think better in the salt air, so I actually may come up with a few useful thoughts. In the meantime, however, you should be cutting your exposure to Europe wherever you can. This includes the sovereign credits and especially the banks domiciled in the weaker nations that will get hammered or worse during the European downdraft. You should be cutting back on your counterparty exposure wherever you can to operations headquartered in Europe, and you ought to begin to prepare your portfolios not for inflation or the easing of rates but for a sustained period of low interest rates and Treasury yields that will continue to be miserly as everyone flees to the dollar and to American debt. I make the further comment that in stage one, many will head into German debt as the strongest of the EU countries, but in stage two, institutions will even begin backing away from German sovereign debt as the contagion will affect the entire EU as the construct unwinds in some way that I cannot yet fathom.

Grant's Rules 1 through 10: Preserve your capital.

Stopped at the English Channel

May 19, 2010

We have decided to follow the example
of the prophets and the fathers of the church and
write German hymns for the German people.

—Martin Luther

This philosophy, first proposed so many generations ago, does not seem to have been lost in the fine print of history. It appears, from yesterday's events, that the Wehrmacht was on the move once again as the directives from Berlin sought to establish order and imprint the rest of Europe with the will of the German people. It appears as if the notion of a united front has now been cast aside and that the Germans will make the rules and, achtung, the rest of the nations in the EU will be expected to follow them.

"The lack of rules and limits can make behavior in financial markets driven purely by the profit motive destructive and lead to an existential threat to financial stability in Europe and even the world," Chancellor Merkel stated in her speech to German lawmakers last night. This is serious rhetoric, as Germany bans short selling of European sovereign debt, one-sided short CDS contracts and the short-selling of a number of German financial institutions. This is a blatant attempt at financial control, where the German state is trying quash not just speculators, as they claim, but investors who are not putting up their money in lockstep with the directives of the German Republic. Germany has further declared that it expects other European governments to fall in line behind it as it seeks to singularly control the EU now by its dominant financial position.

If you think I am being overly rigorous in my examination of the German position or that I am overstating the push for European control by Germany, then let us consider the other directives being issued from Berlin. According to the *Wall Street Journal,* the German government has now stated that if its lower House is to approve the bailout bill, there must be a European tax, not just a German tax, on banks—a tax on financial transactions—to help pay for the EU bailout legislation. Chancellor Merkel also stated that Germany will lobby other European governments for ratings companies to come under European supervision so governments regain "primacy" over the financial markets. Further, Germany wants rigid controls set for hedge funds and private equity funds not only in Germany but across the entire EU. Then there is the issue of budgetary regulation. The EU has formulated a plan, at Germany's behest, that all 26 members of the EU should submit their national budgets first to the EU for approval before going to their national legislatures. I cannot imagine this happening, to be honest, and it may be at the English Channel where the tide is stopped once again. All of these missives, when taken singularly, represent some foreboding, but when considered together clearly indicate a German push for control and dominance on the continent.

The Stage Is Set for Battle

In the early morning hours, and not seen in the headlines of the press, several northern European countries, the Netherlands, and Finland, have now stated that they will not go along with the German directives. Finance Minister Christine Lagarde said France doesn't plan to ban use of contracts to speculate on European sovereign debt as Germany has insisted. Battle lines are now being drawn, and one can only guess as to the ultimate outcome. I had thought previously and have stated many times in my commentary that the EU would not survive and that the first possible breakpoints would be at one end or the other of the spectrum, but now my vision has evolved. Until today, it was my belief that the break would either come with the troubled nations, Greece or Portugal or Spain, either being forced from the EU due to lack of financial controls or leaving on their own desires based on national pride and not wishing to be subject to the EU-imposed austerity measures. At the other end, I thought perhaps that Germany might opt out of the Union based on their own national politics, which did not want to support a "Transference Union" of German capital to the weaker countries in the EU. Today, my view has widened.

I make the rather interesting point—even interesting to me as I ponder it—that the first country to secede from the European Union may well be Great Britain. The world has two financial centers at present: New York in the United States, and London in the United Kingdom. London, for a time during Credit Crisis, Part I, thought that it was the leading contender, and it may have been for a moment during the darkest of the American days. But that has receded once again, as Credit Crisis, Part II, is centered in Europe. Certainly, for the continent, London has been and remains the financial center, and I do not think it will be transferring any moment soon to Berlin or Paris regardless of the desires of these other countries. London has already stated its opposition to the short-selling rules and to the imposition of a transaction tax and to the controls desired by the Germans for hedge funds and the like. Now it may be possible for some compromise solution to be found here, but where I cannot imagine any compromise at all is that Great Britain would submit its national budget to the Germans and the French for their approval before being approved by the English Parliament. Mr. Churchill would turn over in his grave and the fabled heroes of Westminster Abbey would rise up and revolt and the stiff upper lip of Blimey would fall on the floor in abject horror. No, not happening. And it is here where Britain, already refusing to pay its share of the "shock and awe bailout" will stand its ground and withdraw from the Union. The British, after all, did not fight two world wars so they could turn over the governance of their country to the French and Germans for their approval.

I remain convinced that the EU will not survive, and I suggest once again making tracks in the opposite direction and getting out of the euro, bonds denominated in euros, all European sovereign debt including Germany, all European bank debt, and anything with the taint of contagion before the infection becomes a mortal danger.

An Easy Choice

June 2, 2010

Iran is reported to be selling its euros and buying dollars. This reportedly represents some $55 billion that is going to be sold/bought in three tranches and marked shift for this Middle Eastern nation. Without naming other countries or institutions specifically, I can tell you that Iran is not alone in this enterprise. I make note of this because I think we are seeing a global movement out of euros and into dollars that will only increase the pressure on the price of the euro and bonds denominated in euros, as clearly a flight to safety is under way.

As a number of institutions have changed or are considering changing their asset/allocation models because of the risk represented now by sovereign debt and European banks, I am often asked where else I think is safe besides U.S. Treasuries. One of my answers would be Canadian credits. In the financial sector, I am comfortable with TD Bank and with the Royal Bank of Canada (RBC) as having enough securities in the market so that liquidity is available besides credit quality. Higher up on the food chain are the Canadian Provincial bonds, which, while not cheap, do give you some extra yields over U.S. government bonds and provide some diversification. My boat will be in Washington, D.C., in the next few days, and I am having a dinner on board with several notable Canadians as well as the treasurer of one of the supras to discuss other potential investment opportunities in our neighbor to the north. I will keep you all posted.

I make note of two other items connected with the flight from the Eurozone: (1) Treasuries are likely to keep rising in price during this process, especially in the longer maturities, and (2) the Fed is likely to be quite restrained in raising rates now as the unfolding story in Europe plays out. I expect these two events to be the continuing story during the summer. Another safe bet, in my view, will be on volatility as events in Europe ratchet the markets in the direction of safe havens and preservation of capital. I continue to expect, at the least, some very stormy confrontations on the continent both between nations and between opposing parties in many nations where brinkmanship may well become the order of the day. There is a long history of tribal prejudices and angry feelings that have just begun to surface in Europe, once again, that may be one of the contending factors in how the future of the EU eventually plays out.

I would also like to point out, once again, that in times of a financial crisis you must go up in the capital structure. I think we are currently in the midst, though at the beginning, of the European credit crisis, or we could refer to it as Credit Crisis, Part II—Europe. I speculate, and we may all speculate, as to how it plays out and where it will end. But if things go badly, as I suspect, it will hold nothing good for equities of any stripe or design. If I am wrong, which is always possible, you will have lost some yield. If I am right, you will have preserved your capital to be utilized as later opportunities arise. Make a little less or keep your money—a fairly easy choice in my opinion!

Record Deposits at the ECB

June 3, 2010

In a continuing signal of the European credit crisis in progress, the ECB continues to log record amounts of overnight bank deposits. For the past five days, deposits have been in excess of 300 billion euros at the central bank. Yesterday, the number hit another new all-time record at $394 billion, as the European banks clearly do not know what problems or credit exposure one bank or another may have and have seriously cut back on lending and counterparty risk and are parking their money in the safest of depositories available to them. You may have one opinion or another about the reasons for all of this, but the number speaks for itself; European banks do not want to lend as I remind you of the beginnings of the American credit crisis that began in the same manner. This number, in fact, is a higher figure than during the height of the Lehman debacle and a quite worrisome indicator for the financial markets. While there is no absolute data on the American banks yet, the prudent assumption is that they have also cut back and in some cases probably way back on their exposure to the European banks as the credit markets appear to be grinding down to a snail's pace once again.

In a related announcement this morning in Europe, retail sales, whose consensus call was for up 0.1 percent, actually declined 1.2 percent, which is the largest decline since October 2008. The consumer confidence number in Europe hit a seven-month low as the continent faces unsettling politics, high unemployment, and new austerity measures. This does not bode well for the projections of economic growth, quite overly optimistic in my view to begin with, as the data begins to portray another story, which will exacerbate the issues with debt to GDP in many nations and cause further tension in the EU.

The Financial Sector

I am quite cautious here at present for two reasons: equity and debt. The first reason is the pending legislation in Congress. There is a lot of speculation as to how this will play out and what the final outcome will be as the House version and the Senate version get merged into one acceptable bill that will pass both legislatures. It would appear, at present, that in almost any scenario the final outcome for the earnings of American banks will come under pressure. Some possibilities will have a relatively minor impact, but some options will seriously hurt both revenues and profits. I think it is prudent to wait here and see what the final outcome brings to the table. In the second instance, I am concerned about the investigations going on related to fraud at the major dealers. Maybe something will come of it, but maybe not, and I would rather stand to the side until we all have some sense of what may come from these investigations. I am not advocating selling positions at this point, but I would not be adding to them now either. Prudence dictates caution.

Counterparty Risk

I had hoped that we were past the time when this subject needed to be at the forefront of our thinking. Sadly, this is not the case, as indicated by the number of deposits at the ECB. I would be especially mindful of your obligations and outstanding commitments with the European banks, including those with large facilities in the United States. In Germany, the banks have been politically motivated to take on or not sell sovereign credits or the debt of other banks. In other countries, such as France, the selling of European sovereigns and other bank debt has been strongly discouraged by the government. There is certainly added risk to the balance sheets of these institutions, of which none of us are aware in specific, but which are present nonetheless. In particular, I would point to the Banco Bilbao Vizcaya Argentaria (BBVA) and the Spanish banks as institutions with credit issues that may well be more than are reflected in their financials given their marks-to-market and assumptions about their real estate holdings. Further, I would make note that while the decline in the euro may be a positive for exports in Europe, it is certainly a negative for bonds denominated in euros, which adversely reflects on the balance sheets of the European banks and insurance companies. This is not a case of absolute value, of course, unless the whole construct implodes, but it is certainly a case of relative value versus bonds denominated in dollars or yen.

Nationalism Is the Trump Card

June 23, 2010

Sunrises on the water are wonderful times to sit and consider the state of affairs in the world. I recommend them with absolute confidence for those of you who make decisions about your investment portfolios. A strong cup of coffee, some juice or coconut water, and an honest appraisal of just what is going on will tide you through the most difficult of decisions with remarkable clarity. Before the investment committee meets and before the agendas of the talking heads cloud your vision, sit peacefully on the water or near it and stare out into the open sky. The serenity of these moments will go a long way to provide you a placid platform firmly ensconced in your mind for considering the events that swirl around us.

With America wanting to spend its way out of its financial crisis and Europe wanting to impose austerity measures as her reaction; one must ask which is the right course and which is to be ultimately successful. There are answers here but not "yes" or "no" ones. You would think that with the American government pouring out billions of dollars, the citizens would be happy to get "money for nothing and chicks for free," but this is not the case, as exemplified by recent state elections. Americans, without doubt, are angry and it is just not the policies of either party that are setting the tone but how business is conducted in our nation's capitol that is rankling both conservatives and liberals to the point where the famous axiom of the baseball field is once again shouted from the stands: "Throw the bums out!"

If you have a moment I invite you to watch the famous scene from the movie *Network* that seems to encapsulate the American feeling of the moment: www.youtube.com/watch?v=QMBZDwf9dok.

Consequently, as we approach the November elections, just a few months away now, one must give some thought as to how things will play out, as most of the bonds we buy have durations miles past this fall's decisions. I raise this issue now as very little has been said concerning it in the media, and I think one must begin to consider the elections in earnest when making prudent investment choices. In a broader sense, this is the "nationalist card" for American investing, and the same card must also be given consideration in Europe except there are 27 of these cards in the EU construct—a rather large deck to be shuffled. In Europe, the single largest risk for the breakup of the EU is centered at the nationalism of individual countries. Politicians, being what they are, represent people trying to obtain power for their own self-interests. The recent imposition of austerity measure are going to give the opposition parties all across Europe the ace of hearts trump card, which I think will come to the fore in Germany or Britain first, and it will be that the identity and pride of the country and its citizens will not allow for European integration past the point of its borders or, put another way, will not allow for submission to some grander ideal.

In a funny way, both the American and European experiences are similar. Europe has been living past its means for years now and is trying to impose economic restrictions as the bills have come home to be paid, while America just started this process during the recent credit crisis. Recall that "austerity measures" is not some sterilized concept but very real and painful downsizing of incomes, health care benefits, and pensions for each country's citizens. What has not been given is not painful to lose, but once given and then minimized or taken away can cause radical shifts in political power or social unrest or worse. Inflation and deflation may be economic notions to be considered, but it is raw national politics that I think will be the deciding card for both America and the success or failure of the EU.

The Wizard's Stress Test Primer

July 19, 2010

I have spent the last number of months listening to the proclamations of the politicians in Europe. I have found most either to be quite amusing or directly in the camp of the disingenuous. We have politicians who are in the same

It is my belief that you cannot deal with the most serious things in the world unless you understand the most amusing.

—Winston Churchill

camp, no doubt, in America, but it is rare that some Senator from Iowa will say one thing to the paper in Des Moines and another totally opposite thing to the national press. It must be that European politicians come late to the notion that other people out of their own countries speak their language or that there are translators at various media outposts, so they make the assumption that local blather and international blather can be two different statements and no one will know. How grand it must be to have a face with two sides, and how inconvenient it must be to try to hide them both.

We actually do not know much about the stress tests at this point. We know they will be announced on July 23, and we know that the haircuts for two countries, Greece and Spain, are not even close to the projected haircuts in the CDS markets. We also know that 91 banks in Europe are being examined, but not much else. One can look and see that the largest American banks'

If I were two faced, would I be wearing this one?

—Abraham Lincoln

CDS spreads are about 114 bps and that the largest European banks have spreads of about 244 bps. We know the American banks tightened up significantly after the release of the stress tests in the United States, but

I would not make that bet on Europe. I have spoken with the Wizard, and here is how he thinks it plays out: In the first instance some tightening as investors look at the results, but in the second instance widening and spreads wider than at present as people carefully examine the construction of the stress tests. It will be here, in the makeup of the stress tests, where the Europeans will concoct the carefully designed artifices to make one more attempt to dupe the madding crowd. The problem is that investors are not so accepting at present, not quite so ready to blindly believe the jargon that is presented to us as truth. We have all watched the European sleight of hand and the grizzled fellows behind the curtain, and I expect some serious examination of what we are all presented by those that truly matter.

The baseline to begin is the S&P 500 Financials Index down about 6 percent this year while the corresponding Bloomberg Index for Europe is down approximately 14 percent. The major U.S. banks now trade at a premium to book value, while the large European banks trade at a discount. The major American banks trade at a 10 percent premium to the net value of their assets, while their European counterparts trade at a 10 percent discount to the same, which is a 20 percent spread in value. This is where we begin the show, with those in Europe, I am sure, hoping the spreads narrow. But I am not a believer, so I express my serious reservations this morning.

One of the major looming issues is capital. After the U.S. tests, the American banks, in one fashion or another, raised $74.6 billion in new capital, some provided by the American government and some by private sources. Here, we look at 27 different countries, which are a mishmash of financial conditions, and wonder whether some nations have the wherewithal and the ability to raise money to provide capital to their major banks; I note specifically the countries of Greece, Spain, and Portugal. Perhaps we are in for another round of musical chairs as one bank buys the debt of another bank or one sovereign credit buys their bank's debt and then issues sovereign debt to other nations and lenders. Perhaps we will have the ECB providing capital and then issuing some form of ECB debt all in the continuation of the European Ponzi scheme that is already in place as the collateralized debt obligation cubed (CDO-cubed) of Europe grows larger and larger and the band plays on.

Now Europe's total banking system was $31.7 trillion at the end of 2009 and is significantly larger than the U.S. banking system. Bear in mind that under current plans, American banks will have written down

7 percent of their assets by the end of this year, while Europe is far behind at 3 percent. There is also another game being played in Europe that is significant in its design: the reclassification of assets. Utilizing accounting rule changes made in October 2008, the banks in Europe were allowed to "reclassify" unless there was a significant risk of default. It is my belief that a lot of funny business has taken place at the crossroads of what may or may not default. The German Deutsche Bank used the new standards to change about 38 billion euros of assets, including commercial real estate and leveraged finance, onto its loan books from the third quarter of 2008 to the first quarter of 2009, saving them a net 3.2 billion euros in markdowns based on valuation gains and losses through the first quarter of 2010 as these debts were reclassified as current. ING, the biggest Dutch financial-services company, reclassified 24.4 billion euros and Société Générale shifted 25.3 billion euros in assets, escaping about 2.8 billion euros in losses—all very legitimate, of course, but all somewhat misleading, as I have the suspicion that many sovereign nations turned their eyes in another direction when there was any actual discussion of a potential default.

I mistrust the judgment of every man in a case in which his own wishes are concerned.

—Daniel Webster

Questions I will be looking to answer:

- Are the numbers, the data, believable or were they concocted?
- Is the construction of the stress tests uniform across all countries?
- Does the actual makeup of the stress tests fall within reasonable guidelines, or is the construct of the stress tests a sham by design that masks reality?
- Does a given country where a bank is domiciled have sufficient resources to provide capital to a bank that fails the tests?
- Have questionable assets been removed from any bank and relocated to a sovereign nation or to the ECB in an attempt to hide serious difficulties?
- Are the haircuts for sovereign debt reasonable, or are they hopes and prayers of a given nation or the ECB?
- How much bank debt of another bank does a bank hold, and are the haircuts in line with standard operating ratios?
- Are bad debts and real estate exposure in line with reality, or are they assets being carried at inflated valuations to default risk?

- Are the macroeconomic assumptions of projected growth and revenues for a nation in line with reasonable expectations?
- Are the assumptions about the cost of the $1.7 trillion of European bank debt that must be rolled over in the next 18 months in line with probable yields?
- Do the stress tests accurately take into account the default of a sovereign credit?
- Do the stress tests have adequate provisions for the results of a major bank failure in Europe?

The 800-Pound Gorilla in the Room

The financial crisis in Europe remains the barbarian at the gate. Call it right and there is literally no other call to make. Call it wrong and someone is likely to make the call on you; for you, I make the point that whichever way the European crisis goes, it is a matter of politics much more than it is a question of economics. I make the further point that if things go badly, they will go very badly, which is why I have advised all of you to clean up your portfolios and avoid the possibility of a major blow-up. If things do not go badly, you have made somewhat less money, perhaps, but you have prudently avoided a potential disaster. If the situation in Europe does become a calamity, you will be doing the happy dance while others weep around you. We may all surmise about European politics and make rational guesses, but that is the best we can do, and investing should never be a reliance on luck. When luck is the determinant of whether you win or lose the Great Game, then you have strayed from the arena of prudence. Unless you are being paid to speculate, as in roll the dice, then the best and only decision is to curtail your exposure to the sovereign and bank credits in Europe until we have a clear picture of what is actually there and not assume that political statements that emanate from the continent have any basis in fact. Politicians have their own game, and it is power and control and being reelected. And, like lawyers, they will say and do most anything to protect their position. It is there that I rest my case.

Who Espied the Beggar's Leap?

July 26, 2010

Who espied the beggar's leap, and who now takes the last hurrah? I think it can be said with some polite certainty that the European bank stress tests were "light." One could use other words, of course, and perhaps pinpoint the situation in a more accurate manner, but general civility is usually the high road and the one I will take this morning. To allow for certain bonds to be placed in a "held-to-maturity" basket, which were then exempted from being stressed, is a concocted scheme arranged to produce a certain result. What else did we all expect anyway? There is nothing new under the sun for the EU. After the results of the tests were released, each and every nation in the EU had its politicians in the press proclaiming the solvency of the banks in their country. It may also be speculated, with some reason, that certain pockets of money were opened to support the euro after the release of the data and that this was a helpful response, no doubt, to steady that table in the first instance for the Europeans.

Now we shall all see how the results are taken by the marketplace. Will lending free up certain sovereign credits and their banks, or will the sense of caution continue? As Greece is expected to get its second tranche of EU lending shortly, some $11.5 billion, I pause to consider what we have learned of late. All the huffing and puffing aside, we have watched the EU and the ECB amble or bumble, depending on your perspective, down the path. Real risks remain in many credits, and a substantial part of the risk is not economic but political in nature. I have speculated before and I will again this morning that the greatest risk in the EU is a breakup that occurs because of nationalism. I define this as an opposition party that is trying to get elected that wins some national election based on leaving the EU either as a result of the rejection of the EU austerity measures as being too painful for its citizens or of an unwillingness to fund other countries as also being too painful for their nation. The final comment I make here, regardless of the stress tests, is that if a large European bank gets into trouble, the fallout would be much worse than if the same event took place in America. This is because of the interrelated holdings of sovereign debt and bank debt held from one institution to the next and the reverberations that would result from a failure or even a near failure. This is a risk that must be calculated that is not currently found in the American financial system. This risk is not made up in current spreads, meaning there is not enough yield premium in the bond markets at present for certain sovereign and bank credits, and it remains a far safer value to remain in U.S. credits rather than their European counterparts.

BBB-rated BABS

I—like all of you, I am sure—occasionally listen to the television equity evangelists. Sometimes it is painful for me to hear these people drone on about stocks as if they were the only alternative for investments. Recently, I have heard a number of these folks advising the public to buy dividend stocks and be safe with a 4 percent return, and, frankly, it makes me shudder. In the first place, equities are at the bottom of the capital structure and the most likely to get in trouble if there is any market downdraft. Senior to equities, of course, are preferred stocks and then subordinated debt and finally senior debt, which must get paid or the company goes into bankruptcy. I make the obvious point that if the senior debt is not paid, then the entire management probably loses their jobs. In the case of a dividend or a preferred dividend, it is the whim of the board whether to pay it or not.

In the case of BBB credits in normal corporate bonds, there is some fall-off from A-rated to the next rung down. In the case of Build America Bonds (BABs) or taxable municipal credits, there is just a giant abyss that can now be exploited. Some of the BBB BABs now yield over 8 percent, and while the maturity is long dated, they are certainly of a shorter duration than equities, which are perpetual. In the case of municipal credits, which have a far lower default rate than corporate credits and bonds with partial federal government backing as well, I would make the suggestion that many people and institutions, especially those searching for total return, would be far, far better off owning 8+ percent BABs than owning equities in most cases and even similarly rated corporate names. For those of you who have never given due consideration to the BABs market I would offer my viewpoint that today is a good day to begin!

The EU Ambassador Now Speaks for Britain

August 13, 2010

Yesterday, the new ambassador from the EU claimed that he now spoke for Great Britain. He said that he was the first point of contact for Europe—all of Europe. Now this person from Portugal may well be a fine fellow but that he now spoke for the country of Great Britain has given me a great deal of consternation. Winston Churchill must be somewhere in a state of absolute apoplexy. It has been some years since someone rose from their grave, but I would bet a fiver than Sir Winston is damn well trying. World War II was fought so that Germany and France could manipulate a European Union, and now some chap from the Pyrenees takes precedence over the Queen of England and the British Parliament? The world has come to this?

From Stettin in the Baltic to Trieste in the Adriatic, an iron curtain has descended across the Continent.
—Winston Churchill

Frankly, I find this just appalling. If John Bull, Big Ben, or Blimey were in my presence, I would rap any of them across their knuckles and tell them that they have surely lost their minds and maybe their country. Even the Bard must be outraged as he attempts to wake from his slumber. What may have been is apparently now gone and the world is poorer by its disappearance!

There be many Caesars ere such another Julius. Britain is a world by itself, and we will nothing pay for wearing our own noses.
—William Shakespeare, *Cymbeline*

I recall, without the aid of Google, that Adolf Hitler once said that he would accomplish something that Napoleon had not—to land on the shores of Britain. Although he failed, it appears that the unassuming Frau Merkel has succeeded. The British have finally succumbed to appeasement, which is a case where the crocodile eats you later rather than earlier, but eaten you are nonetheless.

I am flying home this morning, and Angela and Tara will take care of business. One can only hope that the British come to their senses before they are offering sauerbraten in Piccadilly Circus and the English are being held subject to Germanic law. I feel like Europe has entered the Fifth Reich—and all without one shot being fired!

The economic division in Europe is sharpening. Germany reports great numbers this morning for their GDP, and France has a decent GDP announcement, while Greece, Spain, and Ireland, in particular, continue to struggle. In Greece, the unemployment rate has now hit 12 percent, while their GDP declined at a 6 percent rate. The pressure continues unabated in the EU, as there is now a clear distinction between the "haves and have-nots."

Part II

Learning to Dance Until It Moves

Chapter 6

CPI Linked Securities

nflation and deflation are the yin and yang of the investment world. They are like some laws of physics that cannot be turned on or off and continually impact how everything moves, spins, and turns. In a very real sense, they are primal forces that exist just by the mere fact that a financial system is in place, like gravity exists with the creation of the first piece of matter. While both frighten investors if they move much off the midline, deflation is the far more frightening devil, as central banks do not know how to deal with it and have much less expe-

By a continuing process of inflation, government can confiscate, secretly and unobserved, an important part of the wealth of their citizens.

—John Maynard Keynes

Inflation is as violent as a mugger, as frightening as an armed robber and as deadly as a hit man.

—Ronald Regan

rience with how to manage deflationary environments. In either case, however, it is not just their existence but their magnitude or the amount of inflation or deflation that exists that can severely move markets in one direction or another.

The major factor to assess along with these two armed bandits is growth. The determinant is whether the growth in the economy is less or more than the amount of inflation or deflation. If costs and prices of goods and services are less than some accurate measure of the increase or decrease in the economy, then you have either inflation or deflation, but again, it is the amount of either that is what moves the markets and increases or decreases the value of bonds, equities, and anything else you can imagine.

Inflation is taxation without legislation.
                    —Milton Friedman

During most of the last century ex the Great Depression and a few other minor glitches, we have had inflation in America and most of the world. Inflation is actually a good thing in small amounts and becomes toxic only when there is too much of it. This could be compared to a glass or two of red wine, which the doctors tell us is good for us as compared to a few bottles of the stuff that might send any of us reeling down the street so that some is good, but over-indulgence not so much.

The primary measuring stick for inflation in America is the Consumer Price Index (CPI). To be quite honest, it is a convoluted index that is poorly constructed, full of ambiguities, and about as complex as some equation devised by Einstein.

The truth is that the American government has purposefully designed it this way so inflation is dampened. There are some reasons, none good, that this was done, but the purpose was to keep the government, pension funds, and many other institutions from having to pay too much money. This is because many people's retirements are tied to the CPI as a measure of inflation so that their yearly pensions are based on the increase or decrease in this index. There are also all kinds of private contracts and surcharges that have clauses calling for increases or decreases in pricing, depending on the monthly change in CPI. Many professional investors, including myself, have argued for years about the viability of the CPI, but in the end there it is and that is what we are forced to use.

All markets, it seems to me, are the subjects of two masters: greed and fear.

Everything else we discuss and get lost in analyzing are subsets of these two taskmasters. Many things change depending on which one is driving the cart at any point in time, and fortunes get made and lost based on not only which one is at the helm but how much they are applying the whip. Consequently, it is in a time where fear is in the driver's seat and where inflation is the cause of concern that institutions and individuals alike clamor for something—anything—that will offset the losses in fixed income securities that occur when inflation is ravaging the countryside.

Now the U.S. government recognized this demand, and there is a very liquid market in bonds backed by the "full faith and credit" of the United States, which are commonly known as TIPS, or Treasury Inflation Protected Securities. Here is another case of a poor construction, where most of the advantage goes to the issuer, our government, but it is again what there is so that if you want to be in this sector and get the safety of the credit, then this is what you buy. The space is dominated by about six large institutions that run special funds of different types that utilize these securities. I deal with and know a number of the people that are the big dogs of the TIPS world, and it is a game where inflationary expectations are paired off against Treasuries and where offsets, hedges, and the use of leverage are applied on a continuing basis. This arena is a very specialized place, and the yields are generally right up against the normal fixed coupon treasuries, which do not adjust for inflation, but there is one component that is left out of the equation, and that is credit, which allows for much higher yields and also is reflective of more risk.

The market for bonds tied to inflation, known as "linkers" on the continent, that are tied to corporate credits, which increase both the risk factor and the yield factor, are known as CIPS, or Corporate Inflation Protected Securities.

This market is much less liquid than the government market and less liquid than normal corporate bonds with fixed coupons, but a decent market does exist in these securities. These securities were first introduced around 1996–1997, but many of them were of poor construction where they were issued at large premiums and where the underwriters pretty much gouged the buyers based on giving them some methodology for dealing with inflation beyond the government construct.

There were a number of issuances in the early days, and then the market went mostly dormant as the inflation fears ebbed. It was in 2003 that I rediscovered these bonds, and then I proceeded to help create a market for these bonds, working closely with several of the lead banks and major dealers.

In the beginning, the going was tough. I believed in these bonds, and the timing was right, but for Mark Grant from some regional dealer to tell some King of the Road securities firm how he wanted them done, how he wanted the structure designed, that he wanted no derivatives in the indenture at all, and a number of other details that compose the present-day structure of CIPS was not an easy task. More than once during the process I felt like giving up, and more than once I almost threw in the towel. However, I am a tenacious fellow and very focused when challenged, and I knew enough that just because some New York yahoo tells me that it cannot be done, while I may have a moment or two of despair, I will charge at it again—and I did.

I recall with great clarity that one of my firm's traders was at my house after I was rebuffed by one investment bank on the structure of the CIPS composition.

He looked at me and said, "Well, at least you tried." My response was my somewhat famous line that I used to tell all of my young salespeople and traders when I ran capital markets at various investment banks: "When you meet an obstacle; you can go around it, go under it, go over it, go through it, or in the last instance when nothing else works—dance until it moves."

I danced, and in the fall of 2003 in association with Merrill Lynch, I did my first CIPS deal, which was for the Student Loan Marketing Association (SLMA). The deal size was $225 million, and I placed $193 million of the bonds. I thought my friends at Merrill were going to come unglued, and, as my assistant Angela (also known as the Wizard's apprentice) can tell you, I actually went outside and danced in the streets. In the world of lead banks where the syndicate department is a major part of the firm, they have "lead tables." These are published monthly by various sources and report on which bank has done what as the lead manager or a comanager. These tables are important because it is what each investment bank touts around to show the issuers so they can get more business. For a regional investment bank these "lead tables" have no real meaning, however, so if you looked at the prospectuses at the time, we were not listed on the cover because it made no difference to us. In truth, however, I helped structure and distribute many of the deals, and I look back on that time of my professional life with great satisfaction.

CIPS are not foolproof, and the credit of the issuer is always a determinative factor, but the ones I did were always the senior debt of the issuer, had no derivative in the indenture, and paid income monthly based on the change in the CPI, and many remain outstanding to this day. When inflation becomes a concern, these securities do well and will get issued again, I am sure; in the meantime, they provide reasonable protection for that time when inflation once again rears its ugly head and the prices of fixed coupon securities decline in price.

Structured Products

January 27, 2006

thought it would be a good exercise to take a look at structured products this morning. I have a definite view on what makes sense or not. Let me begin by saying that I make no reference to any lead bank or anyone's sacred product. I don't need someone huffing and puffing down my neck on a pleasant morning in January. I am entitled to my opinion, and you are entitled to yours, and that is just that. Since this is my commentary and not yours, you will just have to respect that herein contains what I honestly think.

I am engaged in doing the first callable CIPS bond that I am aware has come to market. This is interesting for a number of reasons. First, since the bond floats with the CPI, it seems reasonable to conclude that if the bonds were called, they would be called in an environment of higher inflation and likely of higher yields. This would indicate that you would get your principal returned in market conditions where you may wish to put the money into nominals at higher yields than were obtainable when you first bought the CIPS. The typical value of a call is lessened, in my view, when the call is on a bond that already floats with inflation. The call, in fact, becomes a put, in some ways, as inflation would force the call and give you back your money at a time when you may want it back.

The other part of the structure that I find appealing on this deal is the floor. It is very nice to have a floor and not have a cap. All CIPS deals, as far as I know, have had zero floors, which is better than TIPS, which could theoretically go negative. Here we find a 2.50 percent floor and no cap at all. Let inflation run to 20 percent and you get the spread or the bonds are called. Finally, I find an AAA bond at the offered spread something for serious consideration. I think that +225−230 is an attractive level for a bond of this credit quality, and I invite you to give some thought to the current offering:

Issuer:	Toyota Motor Credit
Lead manager:	Deutsche Bank
Ratings:	AAA/AAA
CPI spread:	+225–230; price to be set
Price:	$100
Maturity:	10 years
Structure:	10 year/noncall 1 year
Floor:	2.50%
Cap:	None
Size:	TBD
Denoms:	10m × 1m

There have been a number of different deals done recently that are linked to commodities. These require a practiced eye, in my view. Some of these structures could provide protection against inflation and also give you some upside when considering appreciating commodity prices. The key here, I think, is what is in the basket. If the basket is designed for Little Red Riding Hood to deliver to the Big Bad Wolf, then I think I would pass on the structure. I would look for deals without caps, and I would pay special attention to the composition of the choices of Commodities. I would want a broad-based basket and not one composed of just metals or any other specific product group. There is probably not great liquidity in these products, but they could have a place in a diversified portfolio.

Another area that is being pushed by the Street is bonds tied to currencies. I think this is a trickier product. It may be useful if you have international exposure or have a very strong view on the dollar, such as Warren Buffett's recent foray. What you are really betting on here, of course, is either the appreciation or depreciation of the dollar. It does not seem quite patriotic to vote against your own currency, but that, in fact, is really the best in most circumstances. When I think of this kind of bet, I always think of George Soros and what he might be doing. Since I have no idea what he may be doing, I am fearful that I could be on the other side of a bet with him. I am not comfortable with that thought! Here, you really have to look carefully at what currencies are in the basket. Most of us—not all of us, I am sure—have no reasonable idea whether the Malaysian ringitt or the Thai baht is reasonably priced versus the dollar. I find this product intellectually interesting, and I might show it out if I liked the basket, but I find it a more difficult call than the commodities product.

Another product that gets floated out is collateralized debt obligations (CDOs) that contain bonds of various credit qualities and/or origins. I suppose these provide some diversity, but these are not my favorite vehicles for diversification. It is tough enough to monitor the bonds that you own, much less some vast amount of credits from this country and/ or that country and bonds from other parts of the world.

Let us think this through. It is highly probable that you own some structured products in your portfolio. TIPS, in fact, as well as CIPS, are structured products. Bonds with calls, puts, and so on are also structured products. There is no reason to stick your nose up in the air and say you buy only nominals when, in fact, there is some kind of structure attached to many of the bonds that you probably own. The question then becomes what provides value for your holdings and what will give you a return that is commensurate with your risk. Some of you are focused on liquidity, and many of these products do not give you the same fluidity as some large nominal issue, but then this must be weighed against the potential return. When interest rates are low and the curve is flat, it may well be the time to add some additional products to the mix. You have to pay attention to what edge you can obtain when managing money. The preservation of capital is always key, but making money is Grant's Rule 2.

Expect to see a lot more products adjusted for inflation in 2006. I think there will be a number of mortgage products, asset-backed products, and even munis that will get adjusted. There are good reasons for this, in my opinion. I never argue that anyone should bet on inflation, try to outguess inflation, or trade based on the inflation numbers. I just say, and I absolutely believe, there is bound to be inflation in some amount or another and part of your portfolio better be tied to inflation no matter what it may be doing at the moment. As an example, the current coupon on the SLMA CIPS of 2/1/14 is a 6.40 percent. This is something to consider when you are looking at a 10-year Treasury yielding a 4.51. SLMA is hardly a credit that trades at +189 over the curve.

The Time Is Right

July 29, 2008

I have met John Thain of Merrill Lynch twice in my life. First was at the syndicate desk of Goldman Sachs many moons past, and again recently on the executive floor of their world headquarters. He did not strike me then nor did he strike me recently as a man who goes back on his word. He has the reputation of a straight shooter, so one must ask what has caused his turnabout on the question of funding for the investment bank that he oversees. It is often much too easy to point fingers and to proclaim wrongdoing when that course may not be in keeping with reality. There is no way around the broader truth that the recent actions of Mr. Thain caused more uncertainty than was previously present, but then the financial realities of Merrill's balance sheet may have forced him into a corner. I would suspect that Mr. Thain did what he felt must be done and was not very happy about having to do it. That is an educated guess on my part, but I will stand on that belief.

The more relevant question now, when peering through the mist, is: Are the write-offs for Merrill Lynch now over or at least largely completed? A careful reading of the recent series of transactions brings me to a conclusion that there were a number of fairly complex deals that had been engineered and then released to the public all at one time. I point specifically to the funding issues, the new arrangement with the Singapore Wealth Fund, the issuance of new stock to outstanding holders, the capital raise, and the selling of their CDO debt at a substantial loss for which Merrill provided the funding in what I suspect is a far-reaching attempt by management at Merrill to clean up their balance sheet. I will say this, having been on the board of directors of four investment banks myself: You can do this once, just once, before the board makes other plans for your future.

I think the recently announced actions of Merrill Lynch bring the firm to a crossroads. The paths have converged in the woods, and each step is now critical to the firm's well-being. Choose wisely!

The Merrill Fallout

As part of Merrill's recent announcements was the sale of $30.6 billion worth of CDOs to a Texas-based firm. These assets were sold for $6.7 billion, which is a 78 percent loss. Now Merrill had apparently marked down many of these securities in prior quarters, but there is no way to know what other firms have done with their positions. The majority of these securitizations include mortgage bonds of various classes, which will now get marked down by the pricing services and must be reflected on the books of other investment banks, commercial banks, insurance companies, and money managers. This distressed sale of assets may well cause problems for other financial institutions as the marks-to-market are now set and not just a theoretical value divined by some accountant. I look for further losses in other financial credits as a result of the actions taken yesterday by Merrill.

Inflation

The last CPI number showed the highest rate of inflation since 1991 and is indicative to me of far worse numbers to come. The recent drop in the price of oil is just 14 percent off of its recent all-time high. Many people seem to be breathing a sigh of relief with, in my opinion, the recent and momentary lower cost for oil, but allow me to present a broader landscape. Prices that manufacturers paid for basic materials rose 70 percent in the three months ending in June. That figure is just heart stopping, and there is virtually no company on the planet that has large enough margins to absorb that kind of increase without passing a substantial amount of it along to the consumer. During the same time period, according to the Bureau of Labor Statistics, prices for intermediate goods made from basic materials rose about 27 percent, while finished products rose 14 percent in what I perceive as a rock-solid indicative sign of inflation to come during the rest of 2008. The codirector of the Center for Economic Policy and Research stated recently, "While these increases have not for the most part been passed on at the retail level, it is inevitable that they will be at some point." I continue to think that to own securities linked to inflation may well be one of the best bets during this difficult year.

FNMA and Freddie Mac

I have a novel solution for the problems confronting these two agencies. Let me first state that part of both of their charters is to provide affordable housing to the people in America. Once President Bush has signed the pending legislation and it has become law, it allows the U.S. government to inject what cash is needed into these two government-sponsored enterprises to sustain their existence. There is a precedent for the course I am about to suggest, which is the Government National Mortgage Association (GNMA). This agency is part of the government and has a 100 percent full faith and credit guarantee by the United States. I believe that it is a basic part of the American experience for citizens to be able to buy and afford housing in our country. Given the recent problems with these two agencies and the increasing cost of their borrowing to provide mortgages for housing, it certainly appears that the mortgage rates they provide will have to increase due to their own cost of capital. So my solution is this: Have the government tender for these two companies. Let's fess up to a failed experiment and absorb these two housing agencies back into the fold of the central government and keep their financing costs at the lowest possible level. The solution may be somewhat controversial and complicated at inception, but it solves the basic problems confronting the Federal National Mortgage Association (FNMA) and Freddie Mac in one fell swoop. It is the right time to shoulder the burden and get on with the business of sustaining these two agencies without the task of running the gauntlet of facing 1,000 cuts of the knife while everyone speculates about the exact nature of the federal guarantee. The time has come to make the guarantee explicit and unquestionable.

The Value of CIPS

August 15, 2008

I f I have been a proponent of anything over the past several years, it has been to bonds tied to inflation. As most of you know, I am not a fan of TIPS because I think it is a flawed structure that is great for the U.S. government and a poor construct for investors. The credit discussion is applicable in CIPS, but there is absolutely no doubt in my mind that a bond that pays monthly and readjusts to CPI monthly is a far superior option to the set coupon and adjustment for CPI at maturity that represents the fundamentals of TIPS. One of the lesser discussed components of the TIPS market is that breakevens are set by market forces and that the market is mostly controlled by about six large institutional investors that use derivatives and other complex strategies to increase their yield. All of this is fine, but it does not change the fundamental structural value that CIPS have over TIPS. As a matter of fact, the only two negatives that can be attributed to CIPS, and they were real ones, was that the marks-to-market from the pricing services were just plain lousy for a while, which is no longer true, and the spreads were too tight to TIPS in the initial going, which is now no longer the case. Additionally, I would make the argument that when bonds linked to inflation are trading at wider yields than corresponding fixed coupons, it is the time to be loading up on inflation protection, which is currently the case for most issuances now.

Now some of the large financial institutions make the argument that they can replicate CIPS at a cheaper level than a new issue. This is not a given. There are some key factors that must be contemplated when addressing this issue. A CIPS bond is priced with three inherent components: the funding level of the issuer, the cost of the swap from the London Interbank Offered Rate (LIBOR) to inflation, and the markup in the deal. Clearly, some deals are priced with more of a retail markup, but this is certainly not true in all cases. When corporations need to fund, as many do now, the yield on a CIPS bond is better than the offsetting nominal, as yields are tied to the CPI Index and not to benchmark Treasuries. Now here are the additional points to consider when one makes the argument that CIPS can be constructed more cheaply than in a new deal: The CIPS bond is generally the exact same senior obligation as a nominal bond with no swap or derivative as part of the indenture. The issuer may engage in a derivative transaction swapping their LIBOR funding level for Inflation, but this is not part of the risk of the CIPS holder, and it is a separate transaction outside of the debt issuance generally between the issuer and some investment bank. That swap carries two risks: the value of the derivative itself, which will vacillate with market conditions, and the counterparty risk that is associated with the swap. In this day and age, these are not small issues, and a value must be attributed to each of them or, in reverse, the CIPS owner has neither of these risks and holds plain vanilla senior debt that ranks equally with the fixed coupon obligations of the issuer and adjust for inflation like a LIBOR floater adjusts off some short funding rate. I would make the argument that in current conditions, given the value that I attribute to the risk component of holding a derivative and the counterparty risk associated with the derivative, you cannot, in terms of real value and risk, create a synthetic CIPS as cheaply as you can buy a new issue. A synthetic CIPS and an actual CIPS are, in fact, not an apple-to-apple comparison because of the greater risk distinctions that I have stipulated.

CPI was reported at 5.6 percent yesterday and marked the largest increase in inflation since 1991. Some people think this rise in CPI will be a momentary spike, but I am not one of them. The construct of the CPI is convoluted and complicated, and some thought needs to be put into understanding how it actually works, which is to hold the CPI down so as not to have to pay out large amounts of money to Social Security and pension recipients, but having said that, the replacement component and other factors that make up the CPI construct will cause the CPI number to be much higher and for a longer period of time than the conventional wisdom would dictate. The same factors that do not allow CPI to increase easily will be the same factors that do not allow it to decrease easily. Moreover, since CPI uses rental values instead of housing values, please note that the costs of renting have been increasing while housing has obviously been declining. What this means is that the idiocy of using rental costs as a replacement for housing costs is now about to bite the government in the backside, as this component is a significant part of the CPI.

Wages are not keeping up with inflation either, and this will be addressed over time by employers. This number is now a negative 3.1 percent and this is what gets talked about in the press, but this is not the whole story. Social Security recipients and other pensioners who have incomes tied to the CPI are now set to get the largest increase in their monthly checks since 1982. The money is a large enough amount that it should prove to be stimulative to the economy and is a real factor to be considered when looking at GDP in future quarters.

General Comment

I have been on Wall Street for a very long time now—34 years. I can tell you, all of you, that we will muddle through the current mess. The financial system has been strained, as it has been strained before, but it has not broken. With each passing day and the accumulation of facts and time, it is more and more apparent to me that we will make it out of here alive. America has run most of the way through the gauntlet, and Europe is about to head down the same path, yet the system will survive and return to more normal times. The fear and depression that currently exists in the psychology of the professional and retail investor alike will dissipate as survival become apparent, and the markets will react accordingly. Inflation is a fact of life, and by many measures a mandated path, as no central bank wants to go through the dangers of a deflating economy. Protect your core assets, preserve your capital, take a few shots at making money, and pay special attention to the potential ravages caused by higher-than-expected inflation rates.

Luck is what happens when preparation meets opportunity.

—Seneca

Here are a few bonds tied to inflation that I think have value:

10y PACLIF 7.14% INFLATION NOTE @ 96.75%

Issuer: Pacific Life (Aa3/AA) 144a
Maturity: 6/2/18 (10 years)
Price: 96.75% ★★ NO CAP & NO CALL ★★
Cusip: 6944P0AJ4
Coupon: YoY CPI + 2.12% → Current Coupon 7.72%
{3136F9RQ8 Corp DES <GO>} FNMA 06/10/20 CPI YO+1.25
  6.85% now 20000 97.50

Prudential (A3/A+) 8/10/2018 @ 99.50
  {74432RAN3 Corp DES <GO>}
  −6.75% for 1 month; -Then CPI YOY + 2.75%
  ★★ Sep. cpn = 6.75%; Oct. cpn = 7.772% Nov. cpn 8.35%

Cusip: 48123LJY1 (on Bloomberg soon)
  Issuer: JPMorgan Chase & Co.
  Type: Registered Note
  Index: US CPI Urban Consumers, Non-Seasonally Adjusted
  Settlement: 28Aug08
  Maturity: 28Aug13
  Pricing date: 25Aug13
  Coupon: YoY Inflation multiplied by [130% − 135% (7.28% − 7.56%);
    to be set at pricing date] paid Monthly, Actual/365. Subject to
    minimum coupon of 0.00%
  Price: $100.0

5y Citi 150% Inflation
  Issuer: Citigroup Funding Inc (AA−/Aa3)
  Settle: August 25, 2008
  Price: $100.00 ★★ NO CAP & NO CALL ★★
  Coupon: 150% × YoY CPI (5.60 CPI × 1.50% = 8.40%)
  Pay: Monthly, Act/365
  YoY CPI: YoY CPI observed on a 3-mo lag {cpurnsa index hp <go>}

The Mouse Trap Is Baited

April 13, 2010

With the recent French admission of sorts that they could have the money within a week and other comments by the Germans and Irish, we all know with certainty that the money for any Greek bailout is not presently available. You may argue all that you wish and say that it is a certainty if you like, but no one can make a factual claim that the money is anywhere to be presently utilized. My feelings about all of this are abundantly clear and certainly not what the European Union wants to hear, and that is that they are leveraging a hoax, or a ruse if you like, so that bond investors pick up the tab for Greece and not them. We will see who gets duped and how this all plays out, and perhaps it will work; the Brooklyn Bridge has been sold several times, but perhaps not in anything but the shortest of runs. We will all see.

In baiting a mousetrap with cheese, always leave room for the mouse.
—Greek proverb

It is a funny thing about making claims in the financial world, especially when you control some of the purse strings either directly or indirectly, which is the Provence of nations, you can cause some manipulation in the beginning, but then the edge runs out and the walk across the abyss begins. We will all stand back and watch what floats or does not, and since the underpinnings are the financial condition of Greece, then nothing has changed except increased costs for borrowing and an economic platform that is further rattled by that actuality. I, for one, am content to sip my Grand Marnier and not be a participant in this circus, but I, like you, will continue to be amused by the antics of the proffered play as the actors have such inventive lines.

As I grow older, I pay less attention to what men say. I just watch what they do.
—Andrew Carnegie

More Mundane Matters:

Launched:	10y Inflation Linked Bond
Issuer:	Major U.S. Bank
CUSIP:	Will be on Bloomberg today
Coupon:	y1: 6.00% fixed, monthly pay
y2–10: CPI YoY + 2.50%,	monthly pay
Cap:	8.00%, floored at 0%
Reset:	Monthly {CPI YoY Index GP <GO>}
Settle:	04/28/10
Maturity:	04/28/20
Price:	$100
Denoms:	1m × 1m
Close:	4/22

Here is a new issue, name on request, that addresses the possibility of upcoming inflation. There continues to be a deep division about inflation, but here is one manner to account for it if you are in the inflationary camp. With the floor set at zero and the cap of 8 percent, it is my view that the band is more than reasonable to account for any scenario that is likely in the intermediate term. One other salient factor here is the spread at +250 bps over inflation, it is considerably higher than the spread of comparable bonds to LIBOR in the same name and also a much better spread than over Treasuries for a fixed coupon. Certainly, no panacea, but these types of bonds are a good tool in your arsenal to confront a stabilizing to improved economy and my view of higher yields soon all across the curve.

The Deflation Trade

August 18, 2010

I have spoken about this concept before. I think that later today you will see a real offering—finally. While many of you do not pay much attention to structured trades, I think this one has merit. It will certainly not be as liquid as Treasuries, but then that is not why this idea should be considered. The basic concept is a coupon minus CPI, which is the deflation component of the trade. The ceiling here is zero, as defined as the coupon if CPI matched or was higher than the coupon then your monthly income would not go negative. The upside potential has no cap on it, as in if we do go into deflation (coupon minus CPI) where the CPI goes negative, then you get full value of the decline. There will also be no call in this structure, and there is no derivative at all in the indenture—straight vanilla senior debt of the issuer. I am going to name these bonds DIPS (Deflation Investment Protected Securities). The trade has value for two reasons: First is the directional focus, which considers your opinion on deflation/inflation, but the second strategy is even more compelling. This is the hedge concept where you have a hedge against a deflationary environment for your portfolios. You might take some time to consider this idea when it comes out today!

Year-Over-Year CPI Numbers (2009-2010)

7/10	1.2%
6/10	1.1%
5/10	2.0%
4/10	2.2%

(Continued)

Year-Over-Year CPI
Numbers (2009-2010)
(Continued)

3/10	2.3%
2/10	2.1%
1/10	2.6%
12/09	2.7%
11/09	1.8%
10/09	−0.2%
9/09	−1.3%
8/09	−1.5%
7/09	−2.1%
6/09	−1.4%
5/09	−1.3%
4/09	−0.7%
3/09	−0.4%
2/09	0.2%
1/09	0.00%

As an example, then: If the coupon was 7.25 percent and the CPI was the highest it has been during the past 18 months, or 2.7 percent, then you would receive 7.25 percent minus 2.70 percent = 4.55 percent. Then if the maturity was 10 years, the correlation would be 4.55 percent minus the 10-year (2.63 percent) for a spread of +192 bps to the 10-year Treasury. One other interesting comparison is to the flip side of this trade, TIPS or bonds tied to inflation, and the data can be pulled up on Bloomberg Function TII <Govt> <Go>. Please note the yield of the 10-year TIPS: 0.92 percent. This, to my knowledge, will be the first trade of its kind as I present a structure to you that reflects my view of our upcoming bond markets. Past this, regardless of your viewpoint, is the fact that there is no other security that I am aware of that protects you against deflation. For inflation there are TIPS, CIPS, and some other

Continued reaction to last week's Federal Reserve Committee statements about the threat of deflation has triggered a rally in the bond market, driving long-term yields to the lowest level since 1958.

—Frank Nothaft

inflation–linked securities, but for deflation there is nothing. Do not hesitate to contact me if you wish to discuss this concept further.

In the example that I have presented, let us suppose that the CPI fell to −2.70 percent which is the antithesis of the high note of the past year and a half; then your return would be 9.95 percent for that month in a time when it would be exceedingly likely that yields would be almost nil. Consequently, here is a trade that provides return when almost no return will be found in anything else. Further, for those of you that hold TIPS, it is an offset to your positions and one that is certainly more attractive in its yield and spread than what can be found in the Treasury inflation market presently. For those more adventurous souls there is also both a carry trade here and an arbitrage play in owning the deflation-linked trade against owning the inflation trade; the current advantage, in my view, is to deflation.

> *Often the difference between a successful person and a failure is not one has better abilities or ideas, but the courage that one has to bet on one's ideas, to take a calculated risk—and to act.*
>
> —Andre Malraux

Chapter 7

The Wisdom of Buying Senior Debt to Preferred Stock

A s I write the introduction to this chapter, I am fascinated by the way it has all played out. It is a long process as I review what I have actually written. The process, though, has been enlightening as I go back and think about what I have said before—something I never do in the normal course of things. Often, I am surprised by what I said or amused with my own comments, which I guess is a good thing, as the writing of something while you are in the middle of it is decidedly different than looking at it with hindsight when you know the outcome.

I tend to be my own harshest critic, but I got a few things right and for that I am thankful.

I would say that prior to the financial catastrophe some two years ago now, very little thought was given to the capital structure. The prevailing notion was that bonds paid a coupon and that preferred stock paid a dividend and that one was no better or worse than the other. It seems silly now, but back then I would say that this was the conventional wisdom.

See how much we have learned in the past several years—perhaps it takes a crisis to bring all of us back to our senses.

The capital structure, with lots of subsets and derivations, looks like this:

1. Senior debt
2. Subordinated debt
3. Preferred stock
4. Equities

During the financial crisis, the American government was taking positions in the preferred stock of various financial institutions. At the time, there were a number of large money managers that were making public comments that they were going to follow in the government's footsteps and also buy the same class of securities that the country was buying. I recall looking at it all and sending a message to a number of these people who were my clients and telling them that they were taking the second-best course. Emails came flying back asking me what was the best course. Something similar to the childhood game of "OK Mr. Smarty Pants; put up or shut up"—and I put up. I told them to buy the senior debt of these same corporations and be senior to the government for the first time in memory. The response was almost instantaneous, "Offerings . . . offerings."

In fact, with our 20/20 hindsight now, the call was correct. Many major banks slashed their equity dividends and cut or delayed their preferred dividends, but there is not one large bank—not one—that has not paid its senior debt in full and on time. As a matter of fact, while equities still languish to this day and the prices of many bank stocks are nowhere near where they were when the crisis began, the senior debt tightened and tightened to Treasuries, and yields went down dramatically while prices increased so that the play was a huge benefit for many investors who followed this course. When you can buy a position that is in front of the country's position, buy it—always.

There is also a distinction here that has become evident but should be emphasized. A bank or any other corporation can cut, suspend, or eliminate its equity dividend or its preferred dividend with some Thursday lunchtime board meeting over cold ham sandwiches. It is just a simple vote, and then the public relations team churns out the "move to save money" jargon, and things proceed ahead. This is nothing more than a majority vote of the board at almost every company in America, and having served on a number of boards myself, I know quite well how it goes. The public, until maybe recently, never really understood the difference between the various classes of securities, and many were seriously hurt by their lack of knowledge. Even now, I am not positive that a lot of investors get the joke, and this is exemplified by Ms. Muffy, who is a commentator on one of the national TV business channels. IBM recently came out with a bond that paid 1 percent, while their equity has a dividend that pays 2 percent. She spoke for a three-minute sound bite about why anyone in their right mind would buy the bond instead of the stock. This is why her name is Muffy, I suppose—not her real name, of course, but she was bringing all of the wisdom of a Muffy from a cheerleading clinic to her audience.

You buy bonds to preserve your capital. You buy every other class of securities for appreciation; that is my viewpoint. Even in the case of preferreds, the call is either that the company's financials will improve and therefore the value of the preferred will improve in price or that interest rates are going down so the value of the preferred will improve in price. This is called "appreciation," and that is why you buy them. In the case of senior debt, either it gets paid or the company goes into bankruptcy and their management gets plastered on the wall of shame and is most likely terminated. Senior debt is a class in and of itself, and to not take stock of the distinction is foolhardiness squared.

In times of financial calamity, there is one singular attribute that stands out from every other one, and that is to keep your principal intact. The time that it takes to make your money back can be years, and the cost to your income, cash flow, and living money can put you in all kinds of places that you do not wish to enter. This principle has been a guiding light of mine for my decades on Wall Street. The further down in the capital structure you are in your investments, the more risk you are undertaking. The difference between an equity and a preferred stock is miles and miles from the security of senior debt, and yet the public is often bamboozled by the press and by mutual funds that proscribe nirvana only in terms of these lesser classes of securities. This is wrongheaded thinking and a dangerous course of action that often results in sizeable losses for the uninitiated and for those guided by the less-than-responsible retail brokers who are often as ignorant as their charges. Not all, mind you, but many, and it is a travesty that results time and again in unnecessary jeopardy for their clients.

All of this is especially pronounced in our current economic environment.

Interest rates are just off absolute zero while the Dow Jones Average hit its high of 14,164.53 on October 9, 2007, which is still down almost 24 percent as I write this piece. In the meantime, short yields are so paltry that the length of time to make back your losses is exacerbated. As an example, if you own a 5-year bond with a 1 percent yield, then when the bond matures, you have made a cumulative 5 percent while in a somewhat higher interest rate environment, with a 2 percent yield on the same bond and the same maturity; you would make 10 percent on your money. The differential is 50 percent and is quite pronounced when regarding it from this angle.

The one other factor that bears mentioning when comparing senior debt to preferred stock is volatility. Preferreds went down way more and took longer to regain their footing than senior debt during our recent crisis. Even if the coupon was paying, the mark-to-market or price of the security in almost all of these securities was hammered. Had anyone needed to sell because of their financial position, then it was quite painful for many people and institutions alike to take the hit. Senior debt performed much better and did not suffer nearly the losses of almost all preferred stocks; safety is forever and always a criterion of serious investing.

Ahoy—Your Key to the Treasure!

November 17, 2008

Robert Louis Stevenson, *Treasure Island,* the stuff of our boyhood dreams. Pirates in search of golden doubloons, and the Wizard has found the map. Arrgh! Perhaps it is more accurate to say that I have observed the map, and any rummy bloke with some sight, eye patch or not, can read the rather clear signs that the government is laying out for us so you too can get your fair share of the treasure.

> **George Merry:** *Long John, don't you go crossing no spirit!*
> **Long John Silver:** *Spirit, eh? Maybe. But man, beast, or spirit. . . I don't care if it's Beelzebub himself. I'M GONNA GET THAT LOOT!*
> —Robert Louis Stevenson,
> *Treasure Island*

Now you may think that I have been too long on the stern of my boat in the sun, but an American I be and not a mad dog or an Englishman. You just have to listen carefully to them that guards the Treasury and you will find your way to the "X" that marks the spot. Here is the deal: The boys in this administration or the next administration are not going to allow the companies that are receiving taxpayer money to go broke. They will move heaven and earth, call in favors, push buttons, demand, plead, scold, or anything else you might imagine so that they do not have to go back to Congress and tell them that they invested the public's money in this corporation or that corporation and that the money is now gone. Not going to happen! So all you have to do now is connect the dots and you will know where the treasure is buried.

The Treasury in all of its bureaucratic wisdom has decided to take equity stakes or own preferred stock in various banks, finance companies, and insurance companies, and we have the opportunity to own debt that is senior to the government's position, often now with yields that are just off the charts, knowing that the government has set a floor for these institutions. This is the stuff of dreams, legends, and stories that will be told around the fireplaces of some club long after the present financial crisis has cleared itself up and dissipated.

So let me advise you what to do specifically—let me lay the bosun's chart out on the table and point out quite clearly where the loot is buried. Aye, you rathscallion, here be the way to the treasure. When the government takes an equity or preferred position in some company then rush about as quickly as your wooden leg allows and buy the senior debt of that company. Some names such as the national banks have already tightened back insofar as there is no value to be gained, as the treasure has now been plucked before you arrived, but those names are hardly the end of the list. Here are names that I believe will benefit from the actions of the Treasury; if you wish to join the band of merry men, then you will set your course.

Bank Names
- NCC Bank
- M&I Bank
- Sovereign Bank
- Fifth Third Bank
- Huntington National Bank
- M&T Bank
- KeyCorp
- Zions Bank
- Comerica Bank
- Suntrust
- BB&T Bank
- First Horizon Bank
- First Tenn National Bank
- Capital One

Financial Credits and Insurance Company Credits
- American Express
- AEGON
- Hartford
- Genworth
- Lincoln National

- AIG
- CIT
- Metlife
- Prudential
- Principal
- Nationwide
- SLM

Now avast matey and swashbuckler alike; heed the words of ye olde practicer of the lost arts.

Here be the way to the treasure!

I love those moments. I like to wave at them as they pass by.
—Captain Jack Sparrow

The Gift

November 18, 2008

I have had several long talks recently with some very smart people in our business, both in the United States and in Europe. The topic has been my view on asset allocation with a focus on senior debt of companies where the government has invested funds. After these discussions, it has dawned on me that perhaps I am not communicating well. It is either that or it is that people are so stuck in a quagmire, they can't see the forest for the trees. To me, it is just plain obvious that the market doesn't get it or there would not be the kinds of yields presently available to purchase. In these situations, one should always ask himself to review his conclusions, as I have taken a decidedly different tack in my thinking than the consensus view. So I sat down this morning on the back of my boat, where I am presently situated in South Beach, and reviewed my thinking, and I cannot find fault with my rationale.

First and foremost, we are in an economic crisis that shows no sign of abating anytime soon. Without a lot of hyperbole, it is my opinion that to be in the stock market makes no sense presently, and to purchase equities for dividends is just the stuff of idiocy, as earnings are down and will probably get worse and dividends at a whole host of companies will get cut to preserve capital. If I were forced into a corner, I would guess 6,500 for the Dow and hope that I was correct. When I look at mortgages and know that under this administration and even more so under the next administration, monthly payments for many individuals will be lowered or defrayed or the final maturity extended, or some combination of those three, then why would I want to buy any securitization of mortgages, which may well be affected by the preservation of the homeowner? Let me be clear: The interest of homeowners is an inverse interest to the owner of securitizations. The government is going to help the homeowners, and the investors be damned. Asset-backed securities have no appeal for me now, as the value of any asset is going to decline in a recession, and the valuation of these pools is anyone's guess presently.

When I consider agency debt, I conclude that there is not enough yield to make them interesting, and no one knows what the guarantee really means anymore. I do not like to purchase securities that I do not understand, and I have no idea any longer what *explicit* or *implicit* means. When the stuff gets blown into the fan, which is where I fear we are heading, I am not at all certain just who will guarantee what. Perhaps at a spread of +300 to 400 bps, I may find them interesting once again, but not at present levels. To this equation you have to add a supply issue with the new Federal Deposit Insurance Corporation (FDIC)–backed debt coming at some point, which will certainly widen the agency market. Treasuries may have some value for the guarantee and liquidity, but at the present levels of yield it is pretty tough to get excited about them, knowing that as soon as the economic crisis abates, their yields will be rising like a balloon off of the Arizona desert. Consequently, while 12- to 18-month maturities may not whack you too hard from here, I would certainly not want to own longer-dated maturities at this point in time.

The Gift

Now in senior corporate debt, the government has given you a gift. It is sitting there on the table in front of you, red ribbon, nicely wrapped, just waiting to be opened, and yet many of you are staring at the table and haven't yet noticed that the present is sitting there. Now very carefully readjust your eyes, blink a few times, and smile at the manna from heaven. Several times yesterday, as I explained this to a few money managers, I felt like I was turning on the light, and you could almost hear the light bulb pop as it dawned on my friends that they were missing the obvious.

The government—unknowingly, unwittingly, dumb, blind, or without thinking it through—has allowed for you to invest along with them in a number of corporations and has given you the opportunity to own senior debt while they buy equity or preferred stock or take warrants. Think about this: They put up the money and you get to own a capital position that is senior to theirs. If this is not a gift, then I am Rudolph Valentino, which is clearly not the case. My friends, this is Christmas, your birthday, and your anniversary all rolled up in a giant holiday celebration, and most of you are missing the party!

I am sending you the invitation; you have the damned thing in your hands, so open the letter. Who, in their wildest dreams, would have thought for one moment that the U.S. government would inject capital into a whole slug of companies and allow you to be their partner and let you own senior securities to their investment and get yields that dwarf Warren Buffett's returns when putting up capital. I am telling you that not to take advantage of what you are being given is just a travesty of poor thinking. I provided several lists in my commentary yesterday of what to consider; go back and look at them. These companies, my friends, are now truly government-sponsored enterprises, and not to recognize their value is just plain wrongheaded thinking. The government's money trumps ratings and financials and is a clear statement that the company will survive.

Smell the roses, wake up to the glorious dawning of a new day, enjoy the gift you are being given because at some point the rest of the world will wake up from their slumber and recognize just what is sitting on the table. I would liken this opportunity to debtor-in-possession financing, where returns are 9 percent to more than 40 percent annually, and yet the obvious is being ignored by many of you. Take off your blinders and come to the party!

Take the obvious, add a cupful of brains, a generous pinch of imagination, a bucketful of courage and daring, stir well and bring to a boil.

—Bernard Baruch

The Most Unique of Opportunities

November 19, 2008

Several weeks ago, I wrote about the trouble ahead for the mortgage-backed securities sector. I had a number of people write to me and ask me what I was talking about or make an argument that I was incorrect in my thinking. Sometimes I just think it is that no one wants to confront reality when it is unpleasant. Yesterday, the mortgage area got whacked as the light dawned and people got a glimpse of the carnage ahead.

> *The unintended consequences of a series of government actions are putting further pressure on the valuation of mortgage assets.*
>
> The *Financial Times* this morning

Now last week one major index representing mortgages, the ABX Index, fell 17 percent. In my opinion, the outlook for mortgage-backed securitizations is not good and is going to get worse. The two major housing agencies have already put in place antiforeclosure initiatives that may well benefit the homeowner but will quite negatively impact valuations for mortgage-backed securities and cause any model now in existence to price the existing pools—worthless. If you are beginning to suspect that I might be right, I invite you to include in your consideration the next administration and the policies they have proclaimed. Mortgage payments for people in financial difficulty are going to get extended, defrayed, deferred, or perhaps get eliminated under the new regulations, and if you think this is as bad as it will get, then I implore you to reexamine your thinking. I would not want to bet that the government is going to provide money to holders of the existing securitizations to make up the difference between the loss in income from the diminished pools and the income that was supposed to be available. If nothing else, think major extension or perhaps worse as the income for the securitizations diminishes as the homeowner is helped in a variety of ways that we don't even know about yet. This is one asset class that is in decline, and the situation will only get worse—perhaps much worse. In fact, I think it is quite likely that the era when mortgage-backed securities traded on their average life may well be a methodology of the past, as no one will be able to calculate an average life accurately and that at some point in time mortgages securitizations may well be calculated and traded to their actual maturity.

Unintended Consequences

The Treasury is careening from one wall of financial initiatives to the next, and the consequences of this, while quite negative for mortgage-backed assets, are extremely positive for the senior debt owners of credits where the government has injected capital and taken positions "junior" to senior debt by owning preferred stock and warrants. I know I am redundant here, but I find it just incredible that it is possible to have a superior call on assets to the taxpayers, after federal money has been put up to help these companies, and get the yields that are currently available in the marketplace because investors as a class are focused on financial impairment when the public monies will at least partially cure those issues and senior debt in these same companies is allowed to trump the public's money. As far as I am concerned there is nowhere else to invest now, nowhere more compelling than stepping in and buying the senior debt of companies that have been helped or are about to be helped by the government. Perhaps it is just the incredibility that one could be senior to the taxpayers that has almost everyone frozen in a vacuum, but I would like to suggest that you should thaw out and take advantage of this unbelievable opportunity before the world wakes up and the window shuts. When the taxpayer's money is up, then heaven and hell will be moved before that money will be lost, and you, as a debt owner, must get paid before the taxpayer under the present convoluted scheme. But a gift is a gift, and I'll take it!

Sometimes we stare so long at a door that is closing that we see too late the one that is open.

—Alexander Graham Bell

Following is an updated list of companies to consider. I hope you come to fully appreciate the singular opportunity that is presently available.

Bank Names
- NCC Bank
- M&I Bank
- Sovereign Bank
- Fifth Third Bank
- Huntington National Bank
- M&T BANK
- Key Corp
- Zions Bank
- Comerica Bank
- Suntrust
- BB&T Bank
- First Horizon Bank
- First Tenn National Bank
- Capital One

Financial Credits and Insurance Company Credits
- American Express
- AEGON
- Hartford
- Genworth
- Lincoln National
- AIG
- CIT
- Metlife
- Prudential Insurance
- Principal Insurance
- Nationwide Insurance
- Protective Life
- SLM

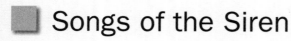

Songs of the Siren

November 20, 2008

I feel that it is useful, from time to time, to reiterate Grant's Rules. They have been around for more than five years now and written about with great irregularity during this time period, but there was some method in my madness when I first conjured them up. They seem simple enough at first glance and of no great importance, and yet they have been the cornerstone of my musings since first inscribed. I recall the time when they first appeared and the anguish that was placed into their rather simplistic formation as I tried to lay out the "watchword of my faith" when it comes to investing.

Grant's Rules
- Rules 1–10: Preserve Your Capital
- Rule 11: Make Money
- Rule 12: When a Company Is under Federal Investigation for Fraud or Improper Accounting—Sell
- Rule 13: When a Company Gets a "Going Concern" Letter from Its Auditors—Sell

My career has now spanned more than three decades, and I have survived a number of downturns and financial debacles. I would like to think that I get the joke, and that is that capital must be preserved at any and all costs. The stuff is just too hard to come by, and it allows you to have a stake in the game when things turn, but, more importantly, it allows you to survive when the streets are awash in blood. Today, my friends, without any doubt, it is a matter of financial survival.

In looking out over the broad landscape of the world at present, I can only conclude that financially we are in real trouble and that surviving this will be a matter of historical experience and prudent thinking. The U.S. banking system is not what it was in the 1930s, and the complexity of financial instruments was not a glint in anyone's eye during the Depression. The role of the Federal Reserve Bank was substantially different in those times, and we are about to see if the regulations put into place as a result of the financial collapse of the 1930s do, in fact, work.

One principle of mine that is certainly playing itself out is to be out of equities and into debt during a severe downturn. It is just foolish to think that earnings or dividends are going to remain intact when America and the rest of the world are in a financial shambles. It is the stuff of nonsense to think that real estate, commodities, and other hard assets will hold their past value when we are in a global recession. So, at present, I suggest being out of equities, commodities, and real estate and any securitization tied to any of them unless backed by some governmental entity for both principal and interest; yet, even there, one must be mindful of certain caveats. For instance, I would be shedding agency debt like an old pair of shoes as the new FDIC guaranteed debt is now days away from appearing, and I think this will widen out agency spreads, if one even understands the guarantee of their credits anymore, like a bull running through a cornfield. A few months out, agency debt could well be wider by 100 to 200 basis points as people flock to the FDIC debt, which will have better yields than Treasuries and put tremendous pressure on agencies by both their guarantee and their spreads. I do not want to be in euro debt anymore either, as I think the continent does not have anywhere near the regulations necessary to sustain a sound financial system during this kind of economic malaise. The European Central Bank (ECB), by design, just does not have the tools or the firepower available to them to provide adequate stability, and we are just now beginning to see the cracks in their system as national interests begin to trump the interests of the region. I have been and remain very bearish on the euro as a result of the structure and limited powers, if nothing else, of the ECB—just not enough juice to fill the glass.

In general, I want to be in relatively short senior corporate debt now to capture yield at the historically high spreads now available and to have the first call on assets if surviving becomes an issue or to be in short Treasuries for liquidity. I continue to just find it fascinating that we can buy debt now that is senior to the government's position in some companies, and I will make the startling comment that I think this debt is now safer—much safer—than owning other credits such as Citicorp.

To be specific, I would rather own AIG Holdco debt with yields of 10 to 14 percent as both a matter of yield and safety with $152 billion of taxpayer money injected than to buy Citi debt at present spreads. Yesterday, Citi's stock fell 23 percent in just one day and is now down 33 percent for the week as their management and balance sheet come into question. Another company where I do not believe spreads or ratings will hold is General Electric (GE). Now many people think of GE as a manufacturing company, but their financials do not support this view as GE Credit produces a large share of their former revenues and profits, which I do not think will remain consistent during this economic crisis.

It is natural for man to indulge in the illusions of hope. We are apt to shut our eyes against a painful truth, and listen to the song of that siren till she transforms us into beasts. . . . For my part, whatever anguish of spirit it may cost, I am willing to know the whole truth, to know the worst, and to provide for it.
—Patrick Henry, 1736–1799

My thinking is the following: The money of the taxpayer trumps the ratings agencies, trumps the financials, trumps almost any and every monetary concern. If you can own debt senior to the taxpayers', which is now currently possible, then this is the place to be both in terms of safety and yield, as the market just has not figured this out yet given current spreads in some credits.

With Apologies to My Mother

November 28, 2008

After writing a humorous piece yesterday, "The Special Thanksgiving Day Report," I am in trouble. My mother is now convinced that all of you now think that she lives in a double-wide trailer far out in the boondocks and she isn't happy with me that I may have left all of you this supposed impression. Now we all have mothers, and this just won't do. All Thanksgiving Day I was assaulted with furtive glances, the ones I am sure we are all aware of that only a mother can give you, and a multitude of comments that expressed her displeasure. So, for the record, she lives in a lovely house in a gated community where there are lots of very nice and educated people. I hope this gets me off the hook. I am sure each one of you understands the problem, and I appreciate your understanding of this public acknowledgment. Whew!

Hold Positions Senior to the U.S. Government

This strategy has been the watchword of my current thinking. While there is some risk associated with this play, I think it is now and will be in the future the most rewarding of investments. The government has now invested a substantial amount of money in several companies, including AIG and Citigroup. This morning, I will use Citigroup as the example for my reasoning. The details of the Citigroup bailout are quite specific and upfront which is differentiated from many of the Treasury's plans of late. The projection is that Citi has $309 billion in troubled assets and that Citi will absorb the first $29 billion in losses and then the government will absorb 90 percent of any losses above that number up to the ceiling of $309 billion. In exchange for this "insurance policy," the government receives preferred stock with a nice rate of return. All well and good, but the real kicker, to investors, is that you can buy the "first call on assets" debt that is senior to the government's position. While a number of venerated investors have spoken publicly about being partners with the government, here is an opportunity to have a better position than the government; this is almost without historical precedence in American financial history.

I would take a long and hard consideration here of your portfolios. You can go out in the secondary market and buy the debt of Citi, AIG, and several other companies that ranks higher than the government's position at yields that are at historically wide spread to Treasuries with the solace that the government will lose its money, all of their invested taxpayer's money, before you will lose yours. Now you may not be a great fan of Citi or AIG's credit, but that is no longer the whole story and you must shift around your thinking here. Looked at in another manner, the government has not only given Citi or AIG an insurance policy, but, if you own the senior debt, they have given you one, and that is just an incredibly valuable option to be handed for free. Now Citi's fixed and floating senior and subordinated debt, both ranking higher than the government's preferred stock, yields about +350 to 750 over corresponding Treasuries. In the case of the AIG holding company debt, the yields are 12 to 14 percent through five years or so. This is just a gift, my friends, and you should, in my humble opinion, be taking advantage of it.

Other Opportunities

Take a look at the Royal Bank of Scotland (RBS), which recently purchased ABN Amro Bank. Here is a venerable and established institution on the continent with a sizeable presence in the United States that is now 57.9 percent owned by the British government. Think of that carefully because the British government owns an equity position while you can buy their senior debt. This is just another wonderful opportunity to own debt that is senior to the governmental position and at quite attractive yields—just one more gift for the holidays!

The recent announcement by the Treasury outlining their program to buy troubled assets provides another interesting play: to buy the debt of CIT. The government has announced a plan to buy up to $200 billion of consumer and small business loans, and this is just a boon for CIT. The company has also applied for bank status, following in the footsteps of Goldman Sachs, Morgan Stanley, and others, and I expect the application to be granted; then they will be eligible for Troubled Asset Relief Program (TARP) funding.

American Express applied and was granted bank holding company status last Monday. Here is one more case where you can buy debt and be senior to the government's position. At spreads of 600 to 675 through the intermediate term, here is another credit to carefully consider. With up to $3.6 billion now of taxpayer money invested in this enterprise, others may apply for their credit cards, but I suggest buying their senior debt.

While the call may be somewhat early, I would consider the debt of some of the major old-line insurance companies. A number of them are rushing around to buy small banks to get at their fair share of the TARP money, and I imagine some, if not all, will be successful with this enterprise. Check out current yields and spreads—something to consider.

Deflation but Then Inflation

The press is running about, normal stuff, hawking the deflation story. Don't be a buyer! The deflationary cycle is likely to be short lived due to the money that the Treasury is pumping into the system. Most economists agree that inflation arises when the central banks increase the money supply in excess of the rate of gross domestic product (GDP) growth, and this has been going on for several years now. U.S. money growth is now approaching 14 percent, which is substantially higher than the reported GDP growth of 3 to 4 percent and even higher than the expected GDP numbers that are likely to show up soon. Under the present administration—and, my guess, even more so under the forthcoming administration—we will print even more money and continue to monetize the debt. The current economic crisis may well morph into an inflationary recession, which can be defined as the declination in purchasing power combined with high unemployment and rising prices. Eventually, this may be the door that is the way out of the recession, but it will be a painful process, as assets, real estate, and other commodities increase in value, but the path is strewn with financial rocks and its fair share of boulders. This road will not be limited to the United States but will be global in nature. Aside from U.S. M3 growth, now running at 16 percent, India is at 20 percent, China is at 16 percent, Russia is at 31 percent, and Brazil

Inflation is a far more devastating tax than anything that has been enacted by our legislature.

—Warren Buffett

is at 32 percent. The Consumer Price Index (CPI) numbers are really head fakes, in my judgment, given the realignment of the formula in 1980. Using the original formula of a fixed basket of goods and services, economist John Williams has recreated the original CPI and he estimates a current inflation number of 13 percent.

Unintended Consequences

December 10, 2008

Perhaps some of the most key distinctions that need to be made now are the unintended consequences of the American government's economic intervention and how they will affect you. I fear that these are not of a small nature and careful planning must now be made to avoid possible calamities resulting from various federal programs that have been tried or are likely to be implemented, and then, on the flip side, to try and take advantage of any openings that inter-

The trouble with our times is that the future is not what it used to be.
—Paul Valery, French poet, essayist, and critic, 1871–1945

vention may present to you. While I have been around long enough to see the 137th edition of serious commentators and economists alike identifying the present as a time that is totally new and different, both the present financial crisis and the marked change in attitude of the incoming administration present such distinct breaks with the past that one can truly say now that we are entering a new era. What we know for sure is that the new world will be constructed with governmental interjection into the private sector, an American and world economy reflective of the band Dire Straits and national programs constructed for the protection of the individual with a social bent toward the redeployment of wealth.

Yesterday, I was trying to explain the unintended consequence of the government's putting money into corporations at the preferred level, with warrants in some cases, to the head of a global money manager of some repute. You can now buy senior debt of these same corporations, which is ahead of the government's call on assets and at some very attractive returns. My analogy for the situation involved an 800-pound (363-kilogram) gorilla. The gorilla is going to eat—make no mistake about that and do not bet otherwise—and yet, unintentionally, he has proclaimed to the denizens of the jungle that you have the right to eat first. Now there is no animal in the jungle as big as this fellow, and when he eats, you will already have been fed. Here is a situation unknown in the past and not to take advantage of it is just plain idiocy!

Another unintended consequence of the government's actions is, I fear, quite negative for the mortgage markets. All you have to do is pay attention to what the president-elect has said and you can prudently imagine what is coming. A whole host of individual mortgages are going to get rewritten in some manner to protect homeowners. The unintended consequence here is going to be that the collateral for a vast array of securitizations is going to lose value. However things work out— defrayed, deferred, delayed, extended, or any other approach on the horizon—the value of these mortgage pools is going to be worth far less than it is at present and is thought to be given current valuations. Let me also make the point that the homeowner will have far more weight with the political set than any investor. There are many mortgage geeks currently spending vast amounts of time, energy, and money trying to buy undervalued assets in mortgages now, but I believe many of them have left out a critical point of consideration. The salient fact forthcoming is that the underlying collateral of today may well be worth far less than at present, due, to some extent, to the valuation of real estate but, to a larger extent, due to the government's encompassing desire to protect the homeowner from losing his house. In brief, the homeowner wins and the investor loses; I believe the dawning realization here will cause massive losses and markdowns in mortgage securities.

A third unintended consequence is now taking place in the U.S. Treasury market. Yields of zero or close to zero all along the curve are now making it very cheap for the government to finance all of their new social programs, while the same fear factor that is driving these low yields has caused every form of private debt to widen out to levels never seen before in the history of the country. Never before, including the Depression, have corporate bond yields, as one example, been this wide to corresponding Treasuries. Never before, in my view, has corporate debt trumped the equities markets in such a fashion. To not reduce or even eliminate equity asset allocations now is just to take the ostrich position with your head stuck in the sand, and to invest for dividends, many of which will diminish or be eliminated in this economic downturn, is a fool's game directed at the individual investor who has little or no access to the institutional world of fixed income.

Finally, there is the unintended consequence for deflation and inflation. No one can see the timeline accurately, though I suspect we are
18 months to 2 years out. Either these massive social programs work,
which is my bet, or we are all going to hell in Obama's handbasket and it
won't make any difference. So assuming that we live to fight another day,
it is deflation now across the board with incredibly high nongovernmental yields due to fear, then a substantial tightening for nongovernmental
securities in the deflationary environment as the fear factor recedes, and
then a huge dose of inflation, which will be a godsend to increase the
values of real estate and grow the economy as the unintended consequences of the government's social programs and the record growth in
money supply.

That is the Wizard's assessment of the playing field.

Gentlemen, start your engines!

Seize the Opportunity (Carpe Vicis)

May 15, 2009

S ince last fall I have had a singular strategy. This has been to own debt that is senior to the government of the United States after they take positions in certain companies, which have all been financials credits to date. You may say what you like or compare it to other solutions to win the Great Game or even label it "luck," but the strategy has worked. Every single company in this category has paid and is paying its debts. There has been no exception to date.

> Opportunities multiply as they are seized.
>
> —Sun Tzu

What can be said with great certainty is that a company with financial difficulty, after it receives billions in federal aid, is a company that has just been recapitalized courtesy of Uncle Sam and at no cost to investors. What else can be stated is that the American politicians will move both heaven and hell, and to whatever part of the galactic construct that is necessary, to make sure the taxpayers get repaid, which means that the debtholders get their money prior to the American public. The government's position in preferred stock is still junior to subordinated and senior debt, and while we fretted about what the current administration may or may not do as they entered the field and participated in the game, there has been no attempt made to abridge the capital structure. When we look back, some time from now with the past's perfect hindsight, I think we will recognize this moment in time as one of the great opportunities of the century when an individual investor or a private institution could own debt that was senior to the government and with no cost or penalty.

The next question is not "Can we succeed in spite of our awareness of the present conditions?" nor "Would it be better to go back to sleep?" but "Can we achieve greater success by this awareness?"

In fact, our cognizance of what the government has done has opened up a whole new world of opportunities, and those who have seized the opportunities have prospered. Today, Friday, May 15, 2009, we have been given even greater opportunities, and I am bristling with excitement to seize them when the market opens some hours from now. This morning, the Wizard's eyes are bright and shinning and his face is radiant because he knows that Epona, the Greek goddess of prosperity, has smiled upon him once more.

Once more unto the breach, dear friends, once more;

Or close the wall up with our English dead.

In peace there's nothing so becomes a man As modest stillness and humility;

But when the blast of war blows in our ears,

Then imitate the action of the tiger. . . .

—The Immortal Bard, *Henry V*

In terms of yield, one of the enticing sectors of the fixed income markets is the debt issued by the insurance companies. I have dabbled some, but always with the awareness that I did not know where all the mines were buried in their financial statements. I have stayed more with the guaranteed investment contracts (GICs) than suggested their senior unsecured debt for this reason. Who knew what gems of disaster might be hidden in some portfolio they owned in order to increase their bottom line or cover their liabilities? Today, however, some of the leading American insurance companies have been recapitalized courtesy of the red, white, and blue and our TARP program. Here is the list:

- Hartford Insurance
- Prudential Financial
- Allstate Insurance
- Principal Financial
- Ameriprise Financial
- Lincoln National Corp.

After the late-day announcement yesterday, as examples, including the trading on the New York Stock Exchange and after hours, Hartford's

Always in motion is the future.

—Yoda, *The Empire Strikes Back*

stock rallied 26.8 percent while Lincoln National's stock rose 18.2 percent. For those of us in fixed income, this is the morning to be the tiger and grasp your prey before the hyenas and vultures line up to beat you to the kill.

The Process of Elimination

December 14, 2008

The trick of the conjurer that delights so many of us is of great interest only when we do not know how it is done. Once revealed, we feel silly because we should have known how it works. Sometimes, it is just the simplicity of magician's art that overwhelms our ability to understand the methodology of the sorcerer's craft. Sometimes, in the world of investments, we face exactly the same situation; it seems unclear how to preserve capital and make money when America and the rest of the world is in a recession or worse. People scamper for safety and

> *It doesn't matter what one reveals or what one keeps to oneself. Everything we do, everything we are, rests on our personal power. If we don't have enough personal power the most magnificent piece of wisdom can be revealed to us and it won't make a damn bit of difference.*
>
> —Don Juan (Carlos Castaneda)

return to the old playbook when the rules for "normalcy" no longer apply, and then they throw up their hands when they lose even more money and wail in aguish.

There is no reason for this; put simply and without rancor or egotistical ravings, there is just no cause for despair. What now is a time for is to think and consider clearly the investment landscape and then follow a rational and sane path while avoiding old tricks that just no longer work in this environment. In a serious economic downturn, you do not buy equities; you do not buy them for growth, you do not buy them for dividends; you do not buy them. When the tide goes out, nothing is spared, and that is just the way of it; to hold some other opinion, in my view, is nothing but short-term gambling, which is not the task we are paid to do. In times of financial peril, you do not buy high-yield bonds unless you are a masochist and enjoy tremendous amounts of pain. This is true especially, markedly, in this environment, where you are not only subject to the ravages of an economy that is collapsing but a banking and financial system that is so frightened of its own shadow that it wants to fund nothing and certainly not any credit with substantial risk. In our current malaise, you do not buy real estate because this asset class has no bottom currently. In commercial real estate, tenets are folding like card table chairs, and in residential real estate, homeowners are under more economic pressure than at any time since the Civil War and the value of land is a quantitative unknown. Moreover, to bet one way or another about what the new administration may or may not do is akin to playing black-jack with your two cards face down and the dealer asking you if you want a hit when house rules do not allow you to look at the cards. A dumb game, my friends; let's not play that one.

> *Yesterday's home runs don't win today's games.*
>
> —Babe Ruth

To those who advocate buying assets or commodities, I say, "Don't be foolish." Assets or asset-backed securities and commodities will fall to levels that are affordable during a recession or depression or whatever word you like to categorize this moment in time. Our current travesty is akin to watching the tide go out; virtually every rational person is in agreement on this point, and no one has the tide tables. No one knows how far the tide will fall or how long it will be out or when it will return. No sane person should play games with money that they do not understand. Here, we clearly have one that is in determinative of its rules much less any potential outcome. Now some people will get lucky here and some people will lose their money, power, and position, but there is no rhyme or reason to engage in this flight of sardonic fantasy.

> *When one tries to rise above Nature one is liable to fall below it.*
>
> —Sir Arthur Conan Doyle,
> *The Adventures of Sherlock Holmes*

Therefore, I have gone through the major possibilities and eliminated what does not make sense and what are we left with—Treasuries, agencies, and corporate debt—and here we turn up the magnification of the looking glass. My own Rules 1–10, Preserve Your Capital, do not require you to not make money as part of the axiom. The further we head toward zero yields, the less attractive Treasuries become because liquidity, while important, is not a replacement for a reasonable return on your money. One cannot live on a zero return without diminishing his capital, and this is an unnecessary and greatly unpleasant position to find oneself in and not required at this moment. Agencies now have a guarantee that has been greatly diminished by the bankruptcy of the Federal National Mortgage Association (FNMA) and Freddie Mac and verbiage utilizing *implicit* and *explicit* are so convoluted that the meanings of these words are rather like ancient Latin; one supposes the meaning, but no one is quite sure. It is also the case that agency debt is in a widening process as the new FDIC debt is rapidly diminishing their space. So we continue the process of elimination, and we are left with corporate debt.

Now listen up. Pay attention here because I am about to reveal the conjurer's trick. Corporate debt is no longer a single entity. The government, through its inept wanderings, has changed the playing field. Corporate debt now comes in two distinct classes, with the first being the usual debt that you can analyze in the normal, traditional manner. The second class of debt is where the government has taken a position junior to both senior and subordinated debt by putting money in select credits and taking a position of preferred stock and warrants. The government, in fact, has chosen for whatever mystifying reasons to take a position that is lesser than the debt that you can buy in the secondary market. You may term this *stupid* or *a gift* or just revel in wonderment, but that is what has taken place. The facts are staring many of you in the face, and yet you choose to ignore the obvious. It is just beyond my humble powers of comprehension as to why more of you are so resistive to the obvious. Reality is staring you squarely in the face, and yet you want to buy IBM or AT&T or Duke Power—wake up!

The one thing that the American public will not put up with, will throw out a politician for of any party, stripe, or creed is losing the money of the taxpayers. The one absolute truth about politicians is that they want to be reelected, and you can put your money on that bet and always win. Consequently, those corporations where the government has made an investment and where you can own a position more secure than the taxpayers is just a wonderful investment and at present historically high spreads to Treasuries; it is a Christmas present

In solving a problem of this sort, the grand thing is to be able to reason backward. That is a very useful accomplishment, and a very easy one, but people do not practice it much. In the everyday affairs of life it is more useful to reason forward, and so the other comes to be neglected. There are fifty who can reason synthetically for one who can reason analytically.

—Sherlock Holmes

all boxed and tied up with a red ribbon, big bow and all. Now I can't make any of you take the gift, but I have led you to the pile of them underneath the tree; choosing one or several of them is up to you. You can pick AIG or the national banks or the major regional banks or CIT or American Express or a number of other names, but these babies are lying like diamonds glittering in the sun just waiting to be scooped up. One day soon, your competitors will figure this out in a broad way and they will all be gone. Stop and smell the roses and the coffee and pick up your fair share of the bounty before the opportunity expires!

Chapter 8

AIG Debt

The story of American International Group (AIG) is a Dickensonian two-tailed narrative. Tail, in this case, does not mean someone's backside or the external appendage of some animal, but it represents a Wall Street term called a *tail event,* which is something that could happen but is unlikely to happen. Because professional managers of money are always looking forward, and considering what might take place or what could go wrong, we utilize this term as reflective of a possibility—but a distant one.

In the case of AIG, however, the tail did come around to wag the dog.

AIG may be the least understood chapter of the American financial crisis, and not just by the general public but by those in Congress who should understand why this company had to be saved. The two factors that came into play were (1) counterparty risk and (2) the derivative contracts themselves that they had in place with other companies, investment banks, and nations. *Counterparty risk* is a term where one corporation has an obligation to another corporation that is contractual in nature. This is something measured and adjusted on a daily basis by large financial institutions to assess the risks that they have with other dealers, lead banks, insurance companies, and so forth. It is a critical measure of exposure so that your company would not go down if someone else did. During normal times, this measure of risk is mostly glossed over, but in turbulent times, everyone is paying attention, close attention, rapt attention!

Right up until the time of crisis, everyone thought of AIG as a stalwart of the insurance world—well diversified, global in scope, previously manned by the conservative Hank Greenberg, and represented by some of the smarter guys in the investment community. They were the darling of each and every investment bank and a sizeable part of the cash register that rang in the financial towers of New York and London. This was the thought right up until the end, when the company notified the Federal Reserve Bank of its problems and then the tires skidded and then blew out on the road. When there is so much at risk that the entire global financial system could potentially go down, it is called *systemic risk*; this was the risk represented at the time by AIG. The Fed and the country just could not let them collapse because, if they had, many other major corporations and even some countries might have followed in their footsteps.

"Strong stuff," you think, and you are 100 percent correct, as many large financial institutions were scared—and rightly so.

I recall all of this vividly as the hand holding that I was doing at the time with some of my clients had eclipsed the holding stage and headed right into hand wringing as we discussed what might be done to reduce potential damage.

During those several weeks, at the apex of the crisis, it was virtually a 24-hour death watch, as no one knew what was going to happen or how they would be affected, though we all knew there was no upside to where anyone stood.

It was going to be bad, really bad, very bad, or corpses were going to lay in waste on the Street, and we all waited to watch an outcome that was far out of our control.

AIG had lots of forward trades on, with settlements weeks, if not longer, well out on the time horizon, and these were checked first. Next, they had written many complex derivative trades on everything, from the noninversion of the yield curve to mortgage transactions that were guaranteed to contracts of assurance against losses if some company went bankrupt; they were responsible for thousands of credit default swap (CDS) transactions, and the entire list is long and the amount of money involved was huge. Aside from these one-off structures, they had the normal reinsurance agreements with most of the large insurance companies in the world, which could have suffered dramatically if they were gone because there was no one else to step in and fill their shoes at the time. In other words, a mess so large and so intertwined that the entire financial system of the world could have collapsed if they were not propped up, hence the "systemic risk."

Now there are other parts of the story where we do not know all of the facts, and it is likely that we will not ever learn all of them. Because AIG had such a giant presence in Asia, there has been rumor and speculation that the governments of Japan and China raised the flag of serious consequence if something was not done. Given the number of U.S. Treasuries owned by these two nations, their cry of anguish could not be ignored, and this is thought by many to have played into the equation. I would not doubt this personally, and the rapidity of the response by the Fed leads one to this conclusion. It was apparent that Congress was going along at the time as I would guess that the boys in our central bank were issuing tales of horror behind closed doors if something was not done.

Now, in late September 2010, the government has announced that it is going to swap its preferred stock position in AIG and convert it to common shares and then sell it in the open marketplace. This is a very positive indication for AIG in my view and a definite nod that things are improving. Sometime in the beginning of November AIG should receive about $15.5 billion from Met Life for the subsidiary they have bought, and AIG also plans a public offering in Asia for one of their units. AIG's $21 billion credit line with the government may get paid off sooner than expected. Now I have seen calls to buy the equity of AIG and "partner up with the government," but I believe this is the second-best choice.

The debt structure for AIG breaks up into the AIG/Sun America guaranteed investment contracts (GICs) and then AIG/Holdco and both of these have appreciated significantly in price and the value is already gone from them for the most part. Then there is AIG/International Lease Finance Corporation (ILFC), which recently did a public bond issuance, and finally AIG/American General. It is these last two credits where I think value still resides. It is my opinion that AIG will do anything and everything to make sure all of these bonds gets paid, and the government must obviously believe that this will happen as well or they wouldn't be discussing conversion. What risk that was inherent in all of these bonds is significantly less than in times past, and I think that they are all "money good."

Our Undiscernible Future

October 31, 2008

We do not know where we are going these days, and that makes the predicting of the future more difficult than usual. One generally has the light cast off by the lamp of the past to provide some direction, but I fear this moment in time does not allow the glow of that light to be reflective on the bricks that lie to the fore. It is not just that but the unquantifiable amount of variables that now present themselves that causes this Wizard's bumbling when trying to anticipate the shards thrown by the future back at us unenviable mortals mired in the present.

First, let me tell you that I do not know where the upcoming election will take the United States economically. I have a sense now that we do not know what we are doing under the present administration, and I am more fearful regarding future choices when I try to visualize next Wednesday or next January when we turn out for the changing of the guard. In our present circumstances, it is like a rather drunken sailor who has plenty of liquor but is not drinking well, and the quantity and quality of the rum one might expect over the next few months is woefully difficult to assess. I find this a frustrating moment, though not without precedent, but I do wonder more than usual about the consequences of the direction that we all may get pushed.

It seems apparent to me now that the entire globe is now in financial decline and that while some have come up with reasonably good ideas, there is no sort of a plan anywhere that one can grasp and imagine the future with any sort of clarity. One certainly does not exist in America, and if they have one locked up in Denmark, then no one is sharing it with the rest of us. If one must choose one of the Ancients now, then it would be our old nemesis fear that is leading our collective charge into the battleground of the future, and he is the leading general now with good reason as companies as well as countries stand at the brink of financial implosion.

One area that I continue to like is the senior debt of some of our largest insurance companies. You may ask why, and with good reason, when I make this observation; it comes down to a distinction between the banking and insurance companies and a manufacturing company such as General Motors. If GM were to go bankrupt—a 70/30 chance now, in my opinion—it has little or no effect on the car sitting in your driveway. The car will still run, you can still get it serviced, it still has some value, and it will still perform the task of transportation, which is why you bought it. This is not the case in the financial services business, and this is why governments—ours or anyone else's—will not allow the larger of these institutions to fall into decay. We have watched this with America's larger banks, and we are now beginning the process of watching it with some of the insurance companies. Consequently, as the process unfolds and insurance company debt trades like bonds about to default, there is an opportunity to buy these credits at levels not seen in decades. I cannot say with certainty which specific companies will be impacted and by how much, but I can predict with a great deal of certainty that the group will be here tomorrow, the day after tomorrow, and so forth into the next decade. I advise staying relatively short in maturity, and I advise making clear distinctions between one company and the other, but in the end some homework and some diligence will prove out current purchases in this sector as we round the corner at some point in the future.

My fears of country defaults increase almost daily as I turn my attention to the travails in Europe and especially eastern Europe. Their currencies are getting shredded against the dollar in the Baltic/Balkan regions, and they just do not have the capital or industry to be able to stand this kind of strain for a long period of time. Please observe that these countries are not a note in a bottle that will not affect other countries and international banks around them if one or more defaults. My single greatest concern now is that an implosion in one of these countries or in a country formerly part of the Soviet bloc will set off a string of events that will make the AIG upheaval look like the proverbial tempest in a teacup and send the euro not only back to parity with the dollar but force it to a substantial discount.

Less likely but still in the realm of possibility are defaults by some larger countries. Argentina is one example as they recently paid 15 percent for a loan from Venezuela or Russia, where cash reserves are dwindling at a remarkable rate. If the world's stalled economies keep pushing oil lower for a sustained period of time, then very serious financial deterioration may well take place in a number of countries where oil is the prime provider of revenues. The Wizard advises sticking close to home when the weather may well get nasty!

His God Was Compound Interest

November 14, 2008

I am a great fan of Dickens. I always have the picture of W. C. Fields carved in my mind when I remember his portrayal in *David Copperfield*, giving his sage wisdom on income exceeding expenditures—good advice then, good advice now. We are currently sunk in a topsy-turvy world where many things don't make sense and everyone is frightened of everyone else, of their financial future, and of losing more money. Now this is all rational thinking and there is a certain sense of prudence to be found in these fears, but this kind of thinking does not accomplish much. Fear is really like a kind of silent killer, as it stymies your ability to wrestle with the problems at hand and it destroys any ability you might have to improve your situation. Fear also has a tendency to force you back to principles that you have relied on in the past, which is not bad in itself but not very useful if the past has radically changed direction so that it has altered the course of the future; and that, my friends, is where I think that we rest now in our present circumstances.

> *The father of this pleasant grandfather, of the neighbourhood of Mount Pleasant, was a horny-skinned, two-legged, money-getting species of spider who spun webs to catch unwary flies and retired into holes until they were entrapped. The name of this old pagan's god was Compound Interest.*
>
> —Charles Dickens, *Bleak House*

The times are not normal at present, and while we may all agree with that premise, I fear that many of you have retired into your spider's den and have no interest in coming out any time soon. Now look, all of you brilliant soothsayers of the past several years who looked and acted like geniuses and have now been humbled, it is time to return to the game, and while the persistent licking of your wounds might salve your

As I said just now, the world has gone past me. I don't blame it; but I no longer understand it. Tradesmen are not the same as they used to be, apprentices are not the same, business is not the same, business commodities are not the same. Seven-eighths of my stock is old-fashioned. I am an old-fashioned man in an old-fashioned shop, in a street that is not the same as I remember it. I have fallen behind the time, and am too old to catch it again.

— Charles Dickens, *Dombey and Son*

vexations, and while the eating of a slice or two of humble pie may cure your momentary hunger, we have work to do; the alteration of circumstances does not change the task to which you have been entrusted.

The quotation from *Dombey and son* by Charles Dickens is not you, and don't let it become you. I swear, listening to some of you that are much younger than I, I recently get the impression that you have retired from business life and you have morphed into old men. This has to stop!

AIG

Let us consider this unfortunate credit this morning. Here is a case of a company with some great insurance businesses, some great assets, and a fine reputation in their corner of the world that did a really crummy job in investing its own resources. The government has opined and announced it "too big to fail," and they have bought in at the equity and preferred stock level; yet there is senior debt available, which has a call on assets that is more secure than the government's position. How often do you see that? Almost never, and yet the market is valuing the senior debt at just stupid levels, in my view, given the federal bailout. What is the risk here — that the company will fail? Not a chance, in my opinion. The road could turn this way or that way, but the taxpayer's money is up and the mess at AIG will get straightened out. There is no way that I would want to own their stock, but the senior debt is just a gift at the present yields available in the corporate market. There is senior debt around now in 4-year and 7-year maturities of American General, a wholly owned sub of AIG, which is yielding more than 20 percent. If the consensus view on AIG is such that it allows these yields, then so be it for the green eye-shades in the counting houses, but I take the view that you should reap the rewards of their poor thinking. Give this some consideration!

A Few Other Names

Allow me to step up the backdrop for my next few comments here. The present administration and certainly the next one are advocates for the consumer, the individual, and the common man, whoever and wherever he may be. The major banks and the regional banks are not going to be allowed to fail, and while owning their stock may be a travesty, the ownership of their debt is exactly where to invest. A good example of just this thinking was the recent purchase of National City Corporation (NCC) by PNC; bad news for the equity holders and a giant move to the upside for the bondholders. Think M&I, Key Bank, Fifth Third, Sovereign (being bought out by Santander), Manufacturers and Traders, BB&T, Capital One, Suntrust, and others. You should consider American Express; this company is not going anywhere and will receive what help is necessary to insure that. Take advantage of the fear and the forced selling and the current mentality of the general market that ascribes a fundamental misunderstanding to current valuations while the government steps in to buy positions in these companies that will be junior to the debt you own.

Unintended Consequences and Opportunities

November 22, 2008

Since I can see who reads *Out of the Box* each day, I will report to you that when I write something on the weekend there are many more people than you might suspect who read my commentary. I guess this is because so many of us get online with some frequency to peek in to see if there is anything that we might have missed. An innate curiosity seems to be part of our crowd, and the weekend is also a time when one has a few moments to reflect in peace as we are all not besieged with meetings, phone calls, and every other such thing that demands our time during our normal workdays.

I have decided to take a shot at a subject this morning, which is really quite difficult for many people, as we are all resistant to change—the asset allocation model of the human being or "reinvention" and "repositioning." The ability to perform these two functions well is, in my opinion, every bit as important as the reallocation of money that gets performed in your asset models. The necessity to change your thinking is driven by the capriciousness of market conditions and the economy, and I think it is an innate part of being a successful money manager. Consequently, when market conditions change, as they have done recently in the most radical of ways, you have to be able to adjust your thinking to the new circumstances; let us call this a necessary "reinvention" because if you cannot do this or you will not do this, then you will get left behind. You can trust me on this one, given the number of bodies that I have seen lost on the way when people were not able to make the attitudinal

> *Whosoever desires constant success must change his conduct with the times.*
> —Niccolo Machiavelli

shift that is mandated as the financial markets adjust around you. Let me make a further point here that it makes absolutely no difference whether you like it or not, so get on with it.

Now next week, we are likely to see the emergence of a new asset class, which will be around for three years: Federal Deposit Insurance Corporation (FDIC)-insured debt. This insertion into America's capital structure will be placed just behind our "full faith and credit" debt and will most probably cause some marked changes in the current securities that are presently available. It will most certainly drive up yields in agencies, as this new debt has a better guarantee and will be perceived as "safer," and they may also impact Treasuries as the guarantee is so close to Treasuries that many people will want the additional yield at a time when Treasuries have almost no yield as investors continue to clamor for liquidity and safe harbor. Agencies will widen 100 to 200 bps from present levels as a result of this new debt, and I would be swapping agency paper for this new debt as each opportunity emerges, or totally come out of agencies now and go into Treasuries and then back into FDIC debt as it become available.

AIG Debt

Here is one space that is a good example of the argument I have been making recently about senior corporate debt. To be honest with you, while I can be nice and say that the ability to buy senior AIG debt, which holds a superior position to the government's injection of $152 billion of taxpayer money, was an unintended consequence of Paulson's capricious decision making, it is frankly just a travesty for the American public that you can buy securities senior to the government's position, but there you are—the debt is readily available. AIG debt breaks down into three distinct classes: the holding company debt currently yielding 12 to 14 percent, the AIG/ILFC debt currently yielding 14 to 20 percent, and AIG/American General debt, with yields in the 40 percent area. Now think about this: You can buy a senior call on assets to the American government's call on assets at yields like that. In my humble opinion, the consensus opinion obviated by the yields available is just plain dumb and a great opportunity to back up the cart and load up. You may well ask—and you should ask—why this is possible, and the answers are twofold: fear and the fact that this type of opportunity has not been available ever before that I am aware of, and the investing public just does not know what to make of this situation. All one can say here is that one should be thankful for the poor decision making of the Treasury and enjoy the opportunity.

Look, my friends, times of severe economic crisis always present unique investment opportunities, and you have to "reinvent" your thinking and "reposition" the structure that you have previously created to win the game. Here, we arrive at the second absolutely necessary shift that must be taken because of the financial crisis. The structure that you have created, that you live by and with, to invest money, must now be altered to adjust to the current radical shift in circumstances. This is not an easy thing, and it requires some work as the structure in which you live controls not only your thinking but puts walls around your ability to make the important changes that are now mandated by the economic malaise of the present. Let me attempt to explain this in a simple manner: The size and shape of a container determines and defines the volume of a gas that resides in the container, as a gas will always expand to fit the container. There is no other construct available in this universe for a gas or for asset models. In times of acute strain and crisis, you must change the size and shape of the container.

In the time of economic crisis, when critical extensions of governmental power are likely to occur . . . there is little opportunity for a meaningful vote on whether or not, as a matter of principle, the powers of the state should be extended. Instead, there is likely to be an insistent demand for emergency action of some sort and relatively little consideration of what the permanent effect will be.

—Economist Calvin Hoover,
Economy, Liberty and the State, 1959

The new FDIC debt offerings, the investment of the public's money at an equity level in a number of corporations, the unknown definition of any agency's guarantee, the bankrupting of two agencies of the federal government—all have changed the financial landscape in functionally radical ways, and these considerations must now change both your thinking and the structure that defines how you make your decisions when investing money.

The Church Separates from the State

December 26, 2008

Y ou have never heard me, not once in all of these years, suggest considering General Motors or GMAC as an investment. Frankly, GM is one of the worst-run companies in America and a corporation that rests on its laurels, but the laurels, in my view, are all that is left. Yet now we are presented with a different set of circumstances that separates the finance company from the parent, and the separation is quite significant. I must admit that this is an uphill climb for my thinking, and I have been mulling it all morning. On Christmas Eve, GMAC was granted the right to become a bank holding company. Under the government's plan, GM will now own less than 10 percent of GMAC, and Cerberus can own only 14.9 percent of the voting shares or 33 percent of the total equity. GMAC's sub, GMAC Bank, will also now become a commercial bank, regulated by the Fed, and it starts its new life with assets of $33 billion and deposits of $17 billion. GMAC, with total consolidated assets of $211.3 billion, will be the parent of the bank, and this seems to answer the question of continuing support, for the warranties of General Motors vehicles as the warranty, if borne by GMAC, will have government sponsorship. Yet, flipped on its side, it also appears that the government is now positioning General Motors to be placed in some kind of prepackaged bankruptcy, as it has answered the "warranty issue" without directly making any statement. This is a "watch what I do and not pay attention to what I say" situation. In fact, last month, GMAC did not write a single lease for GM, and they financed just 6 percent of GM's retail sales.

I would say now that for those of you willing to take some speculative risk, GMAC is now an interesting play, while GM appears to have a very short time span left as an independent corporation outside of Chapter 11. I continue to think that the holding of debt that is superior to the government's position, read here the major national and regional banks, CIT, American Express, and others may prove to be some of the best investments made in your career, and GMAC has just wandered into the camp by federal fiat. I would also guess that the GMAC of today and the one we may find in three years will have a very different makeup, client base, and corporate purpose than at present, as the government is highly unlikely to let either GM or Cerberus mandate the terms and conditions of managing the company. Not for the faint of heart, but I like the risk/reward ratio now.

AIG

One of the great plays of this cycle keeps getting better! AIG breaks down into three plays, really: AIG, the holding company, with yields of 12 to 14 percent; AIG/ILFC, with yields running around 17 to 20 percent; and AIG/American General Finance, where yields can be found in the 33 to 40 percent range. Rather than hand wringing and gnashing of teeth, I think the opportunity here is just remarkable because of what the government has done. Not only have they taken a junior stake to either the subordinated or senior debt, but they keep improving the balance sheet for AIG. Think of this: The Feds have helped to the tune of $150 billion to shore up AIG's financials, and you can own their debt

I can no other answer make, but, thanks, and thanks.
—William Shakespeare, *Twelfth Night*

at the yield levels indicated and have a better call on assets than the government. On Wednesday, a fund established by the Federal Reserve Bank of New York, Maiden Lane III, acquired an additional $16 billion worth of AIG's bonds and said they tore up the AIG guarantee. This was just the latest round of purchases, which now total $62.1 billion. Think of this for a moment; not only has the U.S. government injected cash, but they are now canceling their debt on a systematic basis, which shores up AIG's balance sheet and makes the outstanding debt much less risky by any perspective you would like to imagine. I just shake my head when I think of all of this, but I say "thank you" and mean it!

The Wizard's Apprentice

July 29, 2009

Please join me this morning in welcoming Tara Schuerman as my newest apprentice. She will be working for junior wizard Ms. O'ffill and will concentrate on back office and clearing issues. Tara joins us after stints at Wells Fargo and Bear Stearns. Tara has been schooled in eye of Newt and Rockne, potions and notions, stirring the pot, sleight of hand, and other tricks of the trade. Both ladies will be joining me for dinner this evening, where Ms. Schuerman will undergo the welcoming Wizarding ritual of the Grand Marnier reduction après dinner. Bear in mind that if you are not exceptionally nice to her, you may end up as a quite ugly warted toad. Thank you!

Never forget that three lefts make a right. The road to Mastery is paved with twists. Since Hogwarts is no longer available; I shall have to teach her myself.
—The Wizard

A Specific Moment in Time

Quite some time ago, I warned all of you about the bond insurers. I can tell you that I received a huge amount of flak for making that call, especially from many people associated with municipal bonds. Some people in my own firm even called for the offing of my head, but I remained resolute in my opinion and the most senior members of my firm were gracious enough to be supportive of my judgment. We all know what has taken place since then, and just yesterday Standard & Poor's (S&P) slashed the rating of Ambac 11 notches to "CC." Vindication may well be left to the Almighty, but I am not far behind this morning. Trying to protect your clients is not an easy business, and writing a commentary each day, trust me here, is like exposing your neck to the executioner's

The mob is man voluntarily descending to the nature of the beast. Its fit hour of activity is night. Its actions are insane like its whole constitution. It persecutes a principle; it would whip a right; it would tar and feather justice, by inflicting fire and outrage upon the houses and persons of those who have these. It resembles the prank of boys, who run with fire-engines to put out the ruddy aurora streaming to the stars.

—Ralph Waldo Emerson

blade, but experience and common sense most often prevail, and the tough issues must be looked at dead in the eye; the truth must be told as well as one can discern it, and while no one may congratulate me for the call all these months later; I surely stand on solid ground this morning.

Build America Bonds (BABs)

This program will be ending soon if not resurrected. Let me encourage you to consider buying some of these securities now before the program ends. These bonds will become gems that sparkle in your portfolios in the not-too-distant future. I believe that the compression in virtually all of these credits will be quite dramatic because there will be nothing like them after the program shuts down and as people want the additional security that they provide. Choose what credits you like, pick the maturities that suit your strategy, but don't be left one day wishing that you owned some. Take some time this morning to look at the spreads available here and compare them to other corporate credits. This entire sector is cheap by almost any standard you can define. If liquidity is on your mind, then look at some of the larger state credits, but my best observation is that one day soon, beyond the financials and the government's involvement, there will also be a scarcity value associated with these bonds.

Finding Value

I learned during my long stretch on Wall Street that each and every time the country enters a period of financial difficulty, the insurance companies are decried in the press. There has not been a single exception to this in my 35 years of watching the markets—not one. Miraculously, incredibly, and invariably, almost all of the larger well-known names return to financial health. I am being sarcastic here, for those of you who are still sleeping last night off, but it truly boggles my mind that many people never get this play right. The great compression that has taken place in bonds will be one boon to these companies, as will the beginnings of stabilization in real estate and the bounce that has taken place in the stock market. Now there is still quite a lot of upside potential in many of these credits, and I would turn my attention to the insurance sector as one of the more positive bets to make. If you can find cheap GICs, all the better; but even the senior debt will do here, as the bonds in the insurance sector have lagged the general move upward in prices.

A baby has brains, but it doesn't know much. Experience is the only thing that brings knowledge, and the longer you are on earth the more experience you are sure to get.

—L. Frank Baum,
The Wonderful Wizard of Oz

The Implications of AIG

August 9, 2009

The AIG Effect

There is no question that the recent financial results announced by AIG startled a lot of people. A profit—well, well, where did that come from? Yet, in retrospect, it should not have been a surprise. We have now reached the other side of worrying about what is in the portfolio of an insurance company to finally enjoying the gains that accompany the tremendous compression that has taken place in bonds of all sorts, durations and ratings. A careful reading of AIG's latest pronouncement shows large portfolio gains, and there are several spillover effects from all of this.

First, the stock of AIG has just been on a tear and short sellers' squeeze or actual recognition of substantial improvement in the company or rumors of a sale of ILFC; pick what you like, but the results are pronounced. Then there is the question of their debt. For those of you who have not trafficked in the name, this company has bonds that trade in distinctly different categories and at markedly different yields. There is AIG Life and then AIG/ILFC and then AIG/Holdco, and finally AIG/ American General Insurance, the Life bonds being the most expensive and the Am Gen bonds trading with the most yield. This is all based on the thought that the company may be split up or pieces sold off, and who knows who would be guaranteeing and paying the debt. What is particularly interesting is that the bonds have rallied some but nowhere near what the equity has done, and there is now a large disconnect between the two. I can tell you this: One of the major lead banks now thinks that the bonds may have a 10-point run in front of them in the short term as people come to accept that AIG is not a dead horse and can produce profits all on their own. In my opinion, there is a great opportunity here if you can stomach some risk, as I think there is way more opportunity here than meets the eye.

The Spillover

While AIG has more derivatives and complex products in its portfolio than most of the other major insurance companies, results should be indicative for the class. It is my view that there will be other "positive" surprises and good results forthcoming across the board in the insurance company sector as the compression in bonds rolls out and significantly improves earnings for virtually every insurance company. Given current spreads, it will be AIG, LNC, GNW, AFLAC, PRU, HIG, and others who will most likely move up rather significantly in price. There is still plenty of opportunity present here, though I suspect those of you who dawdle will be left behind.

Looking further afield, this same compression will also roll into "positive" surprises for the major banks. Their portfolios will be affected in just the same fashion, and the turn that has come in bonds may well be the catalyst for some surprising upside earnings in this sector. Considering current spreads here, I would be considering Citigroup, Bank of America, J. P. Morgan, and even Morgan Stanley, with Citi, the laggard of the group, getting the biggest pop in the short term. Just as inflation is a friend to real estate and other hard assets, compression is the friend of virtually any company in any part of the financial sector.

If all of this holds and earnings do improve, then we should also look to a move up for the equity markets in general for the balance of the year. An increase in earnings may well also mark an increase in lending with more cash available, and all of this, in total, may then indicate to the Fed that things have actually improved, which will end the low rate environment as the Fed allows interest rates to rise as we enter phase two of the recovery, which will be higher interest rates and higher yields in Treasuries. It will only be compression that may offset the decline in prices of matched securities in other markets. All of this is good in my view; we are at the cusp of the beginning of the healing process as the American economy first and then the rest of the world begin the long ascent back to normality. As a general comment, this is the time to be a borrower and lock up the low rates presently available, for they may not be available again for a number of years.

As I like to look at reality and avoid hyperbole, I think we are also getting this signal from the market itself. There is a huge yield disparity between fixed coupons and London Interbank Offered Rate (LIBOR) floaters now, of any category, which is indicating, in my opinion, that higher rates are coming and hence the move into floaters.

The Biggest Bang for Your Buck

Play the laggards! You may not want to hold them until death do us part, but they should be a good bet for the balance of the year. The names would be Citigroup, senior or sub debt and even the equity; Bank of America; Genworth; LNC; Hartford; Pru; AIG; or other bank and insurance companies where spreads have not compressed as much as the industry leaders. That additional risk will be more than offset by the bounce you will get as earnings improve! Further afield try Halifax Bank of Scotland (HBOS), Royal Bank of Scotland (RBS), Hong Kong and Shanghai Banking Corporation (HSBC, a credit way undervalued, in my view) and even some of the bonds of the large foreign insurers if you can find them. We are entering stage two of the recovery; don't get left behind!

Citigroup, AIG, and Peg Legs

August 28, 2009

I do not often suggest the consideration of an equity. The stock market isn't really my gig, and I am generally loath to enter areas where my primary base of knowledge is out of bounds. My observation about Citi (C) was really connected to my consideration of them as a bond market credit but I felt that, at under $4, something should be said about their stock. This was all 10 days ago, and we all know that at over $5 their equity becomes marginable and that many trust departments, insurance companies, and the like can buy their stock, while they are prohibited from doing so under $5. Citi's stock price closed at $5.05 yesterday and is approximately $5.30 in preopening activity this morning. All of this has prompted me, once again, to look at their financials and consider future results. However I slice and dice the numbers, run the normal ratios, or ponder the real appreciation that must be going on in their portfolios as a matter of compression, the results come out on the positive side of the balance sheet. I make no prediction about the upside potential, nor will I join the crowd in making some major splash announcement calling for the overall market to close at a specific number by year end. The Wizard's crystal ball remains focused on fixed income, but the direction for both, I would say, is up.

Then as I turn around and look at their debt and the available spreads, I also see further compression ahead. Citi, afterall, is the laggard of the major banks, and spreads of +400 for their subordinated debt can be found with some patience. There will come a point—this fall, in my opinion—where people will suddenly recognize that Citi is not only going to survive but that it may actually prosper. In my view, the risk–reward ratio lies sturdily in the reward camp at these spreads, and I would be considering this credit.

Major Upside Surprises

Here is a call I will make: There will be a substantial improvement in earnings for many financial credits in the quarters to come. The bulk of this will come from two quarters: portfolio compression and a marked improvement in marks-to-market and the benefits accrued from a yield curve that will only get steeper as the Fed holds short interest rates in check. The most leveraged of plays—you may read AIG here, which was brought to its knees during the downward cycle—will show earnings growth past all expectations as we have reached the nadir and reversed. The equity folks seemed to have grasped this with AIG's stock at $9.48 on July 9 and a closing price yesterday of $47.84. We old fogies in fixed income have given their bonds a nod, but only that, as yields have come in somewhat, but still, returns of over 10 percent in most cases and as high as 18 percent for short maturities in some of their subs. This, my friends, is a classic disconnect, and I feel personally that the stock market folks are beating us to the punch.

Now with all of the issues and problems the AIG/Matched Funding bonds are still rated A3/A− while AIG/SunAmerica is A1/A+, AIG/Holdco is A3/A−, and the AIG/ILFC bonds are also investment grade. Given current spreads, one may only assume that the consensus of our crowd is not getting this joke, but I assure you, as I have seen so often before, the light will dawn. This situation will be the classic rubber band story—pulled to the last limits on the downside, but cracking back with vengeance as the economy and bond market, cash and derivatives, improves. Just as Prudential and Hartford and the rest of them have returned to more normal spreads, here is the absolute laggard, and its time is coming. You want upside potential—here it is, though I would be staying shorter than 9/1/13, the date the large government loan is due, as a matter of my conservative nature. It is not too late to join this game yet, but soon the value represented in these credits will be more recognizable and the gates will begin to shut.

Now since I am sitting on my boat at some small island in the Bahamas, I shall rephrase all of this for you so you can join this adventure:

Here be the treasure you seadogs. If ye can't see the X clearly on the map then the Captain suggests that you open your eyes before yer lids ferment in tar. Now there's a good lad and up the rigging to see what lies on the horizon. Tis sure as Long John's peg leg that nothing can be gained by standing on the stern and peering forward. So up with you and on to the bowsprit and no quarter given or taken as we plunge ahead!

One Place to Go and
One Place to Avoid

September 22, 2009

O ur world is strewn with opportunity. Each day as we arise and
look at the financial world, there are just a myriad of new
and exciting contingencies that stare us directly in the face. Yes,
true, some days more than others, but a little patience and some vigilance
thrown in with some considered thinking and a diligent approach—all
kinds of doors to examine and perhaps open. Along with the possibility
of entering new spaces, we may also find information that will cause
us to close or avoid certain doors that have become just too risky to
enter. That is the other side of the paradigm—not the negative side,
just the other side, where we may have gained some wisdom from past
experiences. It is first the observation and then the thinking that leads
to extrapolation, and it is here where the opportunity abounds. One
must always ask, "What does it mean?" and then be prepared to follow your thoughts down the path of relevance to the financial markets
and your positions. It is here where the minds of the best and brightest
dwell, and it is here where we must all aspire to gain admittance.

So as we begin today, I visualize one large opportunity and one large
space to avoid as I consider recent events. The pending black hole is one
that I have discussed before many times, and it seems to be getting darker
and larger—securitizations tied to commercial real estate. Moody's Real
Commercial Property Price Index dropped like a rock last month, down
5.1 percent. This was after what appeared to be some stabilization in
June with a drop of just 1 percent. This index is down 39 percent from
its October 2007 high as troubled assets, defined as in default or close to
them, doubled to 23 percent from March to July. These figures come
from Real Capital Analytics, which is a firm that compiles this kind

of data. These numbers are record-breaking figures on the downside as commercial property sales close in on what looks like an 18-year low. Office sale prices are down more than 20 percent in many major cities, while apartment prices, down 24 percent nationally, are much worse in some place such as Florida, where they are down 44 percent.

At some point, at some time, there will be an end to this, but not any time soon in my opinion. The end may well be tied to the beginning of some real and not imagined inflation, as that road, however painful, is the only road that will end this mess. However, as I have stated before as tied to the bond markets, that discussion, while intellectually interesting perhaps, is one that is premature and not necessary to have quite yet. I do make the point this morning that for those of you who own securities tied to commercial real estate, the pain has some way to go. If one could take some profits in bonds of a different sort and balance them out against an exit strategy in some of the commercial securitizations, that seems like a good option to me. When I first stated my opinion about these securitizations more than a year ago, I received any number of polite but firm emails suggesting that I had perhaps erred in judgment and was being overly negative. I continue to stand upon terra firma; I will make the point today that the situation, in my view, will continue to worsen. I do not think the bottom is yet in sight.

The Positive—AIG

I have been a consistent advocate of buying AIG bonds for quite some time now. If you have read my commentary with any kind of regularity, you know that I have been firm in my conviction here. Yesterday, we got several quite pleasant surprises in regards to AIG. Forget Moody's and S&P and all the other ratings agencies because yesterday the U.S. Government Accountability Office (GAO) publicly opined on AIG, which is a rare event for any corporation. The government office said they were showing signs of stabilizing. The GAO, in its report, stated that AIG's property/casualty, life, and retirement services units all had capital above the minimum requirements. For the second quarter, AIG had a pretax operating profit of $1.3 billion, and given recent market conditions, I would suggest that quarter three could be even better. Yesterday was also marked with Congressman Towns, Chairman of the House Oversight Committee, instructing his staff to examine ways the government could cut its stake in AIG, cut the interest rates that AIG is paying to the government for their loan, and extending the term of the loan. AIG's stock was up 21 percent on all of this news, and this only crystallizes my view that the bonds are a good bet. For safety, buy the GICs and then the Holdco, with ILFC being somewhat more risky and the American General bonds being the riskiest but with the most yield. Yields are in dramatically from six months ago, but it is my view that there is much further to go in these credits!

Hold On, I'm Coming
March 10, 2010

AIG

There was a certain amount of pleasure yesterday when one of the major dealers asked me if I could cough up some short AIG paper at a yield of 2.86 percent. This was the bid, and as I stared at it on the screen, I just smiled. I have been suggesting this credit for you to consider for over a year now; it is there in black and white for those of you who want to go back and check, and I have been heavily involved in this name. I recall buying AIG for clients with yields of 30 percent and 40 percent, and now the bid was under 3 percent. Now let me tell you, with its recent sales of assets and the remaining book of business, the credit is now has a debt-to-asset ratio of something between 130 and 150 percent. The safest bet with the least yield is now AIG/Holco, though I suggest AIG/ILFC and AIG/Am Gen if you want to capture some further compression. In my mind, it is no longer even a question of parental guarantees for the subs; the entire company is now past the hump, and they even own 20 percent of Met Life now after the sale of their sub to them, and life, once again, is good! You may have thought there was just too much risk in this name before, but now you should reconsider your position.

Citigroup

The water pours down the tributary, and the rumor mill grinds it out once again. If nothing else, the stock of Citi indicated something was happening yesterday, as it was up almost 9 percent on the day. The rumors center around the government's selling its stake and that there are several single buyers that want to purchase the entire piece, which would give them virtual control of the enterprise. Names rolling around are HSBC, Barclays, and even Goldman Sachs to capture the retail base. Then there are the recent articles in the press suggesting that all of those old bad assets may have some value after all. The rocket scientists must just have returned from vacation, as the compression in the fixed income markets leads one rather quickly to this obvious conclusion that I have been speaking about for months. Of course, I did not figure it out myself, as it was the Wizard who had marked it on his chalkboard of financial acumen. There is only one problem with the old fellow's markings, and you can trust me here, his hand writing is just abysmal and it can take hours to figure out what he wrote down. Fortunately, I have the Sages to help me here, but it usually just bores them to help and they return to rolling belly up in the afternoon sun. No requests for suntan block, oddly enough.

Other Bank Credits

I would surmise that many of you are underweight financial credits. The value of that strategy has now ended. If the assets of Citigroup have now increased in value, then this has not happened in a vacuum. It certainly is not that their assets are now worth more while Bank of America or J. P. Morgan or many of the larger regional banks do not also have improved assets. What does remain, though, with the exception of JPM, whose debt is probably fully valued, is one last further bout of compression as people begin to recognize that what went down has started to come up and the light dawns once again and ends the murky night. I note also the recent call by the Fed for banks not to buy back their shares or increase dividends—more assets then to back their debt and a real plus for those of us in fixed income. Take some profits now in the industrials that are trading at Treasuries +50 and redeploy it before the Fed begins to move and absolute value is lost in the changing of the guard. Yesterday's winning play most often becomes tomorrow's losing scheme, and I think it is time to make some changes here.

Fixed-to-Float Bonds

When the turn comes, there will not be enough of these securities on the planet to satiate demand! Make your move first, find names you like, and buy them in what size you can. If all you buy now are vanilla floaters, you will suffer until the turn comes with yields at present levels, but if you can get a nice fixed coupon for a year or so that then rolls over to a LIBOR floater, happiness will be the hallmark of that play. Not that you want to be happy, of course; everyone knows that bond buyers grin only when the office door is closed and after they turn out the lights so no one can see them. It is just the way of things, as we are more used to wailing and wringing our hands and casting aspersions in the wind, but that time is past for the moment, so you will just have to suffer.

Chapter 9

Fixed-to-Float Bonds

F ixed-to-float is not the Goodyear blimp tethered to the ground
and then suddenly unhooked and released into the atmosphere. If
this is your starting point, then you have miles to go before you
sleep. This reference is to a certain kind of bonds that are designed to
take advantage of a change in interest rates.

The vast majority of bonds have a fixed coupon and a fixed maturity
date so that the coupon is paid twice a year and continues to do so until
the bond matures, and then you get the last interest payment and also the
return of your principal. This is a "plain vanilla" bond, and this is what
they are known as on Wall Street. The problem with these bonds is
that when interest rates begin to rise, the "mark-to-market" or value
of these securities declines in a generally inverse ratio with the rise in
interest rates or yield; as yields go up, the price of the outstanding bonds
goes down.

For the vast majority of individuals, this is not a huge problem. People
generally do not buy bonds to trade them and do so only if there are
large profits or if they are forced to sell them to raise cash. However, in
my world, the arena of very large institutional accounts, this is not the
case. Here, the current valuations of bonds are looked at on a daily basis
and decisions are made whether to buy, hold, or sell certain securities

based on a wide variety of factors, and one of these is their current price. My world is a landscape where the normal trade, the everyday garden variety, is $5 million, and many trades take place on a daily basis that are multiples of this amount. To put this in perspective, I would guess that the smallest of the institutional accounts that I do business with has a billion dollars under management and that a few are over a trillion dollars, so that while the bonds are the same for individuals and institutions, what is done with them is a wholly different affair.

Now the Great Game cannot be played without a viewpoint, and if yours is that interest rates are about to head higher for any reason, what is it that you do?

It is here, at this juxtaposition, that money managers begin to consider bonds with different structures to protect their portfolios and to take advantage of rising rates. The point of departure is that no bond, none, does well in all interest rate environments, so different structures must be considered at different times. The common notion that asset allocation is strictly a question of how much to put into bonds or equities or real estate or commodities and so on is a simplistic notion that does not even come close to the choices that are available and made daily by those engaged in managing money.

Fixed-to-float securities are bonds that pay a defined coupon for a given period of time, and then they float or change what they pay based on some other criteria, which is very specifically stated in the indenture. Generally, but not always, when the bonds morph to floating rate securities, it is at a given spread over the London Interbank Offered Rate (LIBOR) so that as short-term rates rise, the bonds pay at a spread to this short-term rate, which is reset daily in London. This structure tries to accomplish two goals: It keeps the bonds from severe declines in price, and the coupon payments rise right along with short-term rates so that cash flows can also increase. Having said all of this, though, even in this well-defined space, it gets vastly more complex. There are hybrids and trust preferred securities (TruPS) and perpetuals that all come into play here besides much shorter bonds that are designed specifically for the issues I have just discussed.

A man may build a complicated piece of mechanism, or pilot a steamboat, but not more than five out of ten know how the apple got into the dumpling.
—Edward Boyden

Now I live in a unique place in the universe. It is a very small niche that I have created after many years of being on Wall Street, and it is a creation of my own design. Not only do a get to write my commentary and advise a lot of really smart people about financial matters, which they sometimes pay attention to and sometimes not, but then I get to interact with many of the lead banks and create what I think is valuable in the present circumstances. To be honest with you, it often amazes me that anyone is interested in my opinion and then that the Masters of the Universe at the major dealers will pay attention to what I want and create it for me. Yet both of these are what goes on and have for years, so I have come to the realization that I must know something of interest or think in a certain way that has some value. I am not offering an overdose of humility here but a smile at myself as I work hard daily to continually sort out the complexities of the financial marketplace.

In the area of structured finance, which is where new products get created, I know almost everyone and have for many years; I also run this part of my firm.

It is a simple phone call after all of this time; here is my idea and let's do it. Even better than this, sometimes, because most of these people also get my commentary, is when they call me and say that I had a good idea and what about making something to take advantage of it. Then a discussion ensues, conference calls take place, black boxes get run, and numbers are spewed across computer screens until finally a new bond structure is created or a variation of one already in existence, and the whole process is quite exciting. Now many of my friends here are quantitative types that live in the world of permutations and mathematical formulas that often leads them down paths where few people can understand what they are doing. Often during this process, I have to drag them back to reality and explain one more time that yes, they may be right, but that this will be impossible to sell because no one will be able to understand it. I always remember that the other side of the page of "sell" is "buy," and if no one is buying, the idea is moot.

I also act as a filter for my clients. Unlike the world of individual brokerage, where an account only deals with one person, in the institutional arena they deal with 5 or 10 or more investment banks on a daily basis. Where I differentiate myself is that I will not show out any offering or propose any idea that I do not believe in, which is a very different paradigm than at most dealers. Most account coverage is driven by the traders and the investment bankers of some firm,

Sometimes the questions are complicated and the answers are simple.
— Dr. Seuss

but in my case I make the decision of what to propose and to whom. In today's world, where interest rates will absolutely rise at some point, the only question being when, I think everyone is well advised to own some fixed-to-float securities, and then it is only a question of the appropriate structure and of the credit of the issuer.

The Camp Followers

November 13, 2009

Yields

With the last of the Treasury auctions for 2009 behind us, there are two schools of thought for the balance of the year. One camp is entrenched in the view that the curve will flatten, while the other is predicting higher yields. The result is likely based on three occurrences. The first is the underlying strength of the economy that will get reported and signal a continuing improvement or stability but little growth. The second will be the equity market utilized as a forward indicator for quarters one and two of 2010. Finally, everyone will continue to watch the Fed for any signs that the raising of rates will begin in the near and not the distant future.

It may be that the element of human psychology will drive the train. Always difficult to pin down, but an economic crisis causes fear, then acceptance, and finally a positive move to the fore, as people will refuse to be held down for any longer than is necessary. It is here that causes me to place my bet on higher yields. I think the overall economy improves more than is expected, that banks and insurance companies report out numbers higher than the consensus estimates, and a nod to the Fed—never to be admitted, of course—that inflation is ultimately the only way out of the asset malaise, and it will be subtly encouraged if never revealed aloud to anyone. Consequently, my bet is on higher yields forthcoming, with the knowledge that even if I am wrong for the moment, we will surely get them in 2010, so I will not be wrong for long and that is what makes my bet the safer play.

The Municipal Bond Arena

After my commentary yesterday, I received the following from one of the senior executives at one of the large international banks. The Municipal Bond Department reports to him, and his comment was telling:

> *Loving your Muni write up this morning. . . . It's a train wreck just waiting to happen.*

Fixed-to-Float

Here is one area that I think will prove to be a winner. I am aware that the final maturity of some of these issues is problematic for some accounts, and this makes the selection process tough for some of you, but I am a big fan of this play as we face higher yields at some upcoming point. All of the variables must be examined, of course, to make a wise decision, but the examination is worth the time. The key components are the yields to maturity and to call, trying to obtain a call in 2012, and in if possible and finally assessing the floating part of the indenture, comparing it to the current floating rate notes available in the credit and making an educated guess concerning the probability of the call. The fallback position is that the bonds do not get called and that you are comfortable with the floating rate provisions for an extended period of time. Having said that, given the current spreads, likely to widen as yields rise, when the bond becomes a true floater, it will appreciate in value from its fixed-to-float mark. Consequently, regardless of the course chosen by the issuing corporation re the call, there is not only extra yield here but a good chance of appreciation regardless of how the situation plays itself out.

The Fixed-to-Float Opportunity

November 17, 2009

I am going to give you an example, and it is just that, an example and not an offering, of bonds that you should be considering at this point in the cycle. Please bear in mind that the yield to maturity is based on the present LIBOR fix and that the yield to maturity (YTM) is a variable number, depending on the stated LIBOR rate. This is critical to understand my strategy.

2MM SWISS RE (SCHREI) A3/A− 3.25 11/21/21-11 $89.00
XS0138467401 (IN $) FIXED–TO–FLOAT 3.67% YTM/9.54% YTC

Here, we have an A-rated credit with a final maturity of 2021, which is not out in the ozone. Here, we have a call or a fixed coupon becoming a floater in 2011, which is within the range of taking advantage of rates heading higher. If called, we get a very nice return, and if not called, then these bonds will float at six-month LIBOR +180 bps while we are able to buy this credit at a nice discount of $89, which will either be called at $100 or rise in appreciation, in my view, if the bonds go to a floater. Here, my friends, is one of the sweet spots in fixed income if only we could find enough bonds.

Rumors of the Wizard in New York

November 20, 2009

I don't venture out of my lair so much these days. I dislike leaving the two Sages to their own devices, and I refuse to wear either socks or ties except to please my friend who runs the investments for one of the large New York insurance companies, and then only because he takes such pleasure in seeing a piece of cloth tied around my neck in some fashion statement that reflects the sheer idiocy of the male species. In any event, I will be found freezing from December 1 through December 4 in the Big Apple. I have a significant number of meetings already booked, but I will try to make some time in my schedule if you wish to see the twinkle in my eye; let me know and I will try to arrange it.

Fixed-To-Float: Some Further Explanation

I have fielded a lot of questions recently about this structure. Obviously, what seems apparent to me has slipped by some of you, so I thought I would explain the conjuror's trick; everything is simple after all once it has been explained. To correctly analyze these securities one need merely borrow from the mortgage-backed playbook and include some assumptions. Let us take an example; this is not an offering, but it will work just fine as an indicative example.

AIG/ILFC 5.9 12/21/65 W/ a 12/10 CALL $50.00 4.47%
YTM 85.89% YTC 44965TAA5

Now all this is what pops up on Bloomberg on the yield to call (YTC) page, but it is not the whole story. The yield to maturity is calculated based on the corresponding LIBOR rate stated in the indenture, which in this case is 3-month LIBOR, which is currently 0.266 percent, and that is the number used to calculate the YTM. So head over to the Yield Analysis (YA) page and put in the dollar price and then in the second box down on the right indicated by the "benchmark," as exemplified below, change the 3-month LIBOR rate to 1.2666 percent, which assumes a 100 bps rise in 3-month LIBOR at some point in the future, and you will see that the YTM is now 6.28 percent while the YTC remains the same, or if you think LIBOR will rise to 2.266 percent (up 200 bps), then the YTM is 8.14 percent and so forth. I would argue that with LIBOR barely above zero, there is only one direction to go at present.

BENCHMARK C :	0.2666% + Spread
Assumed Coupon =	1.8166% APPLIED FROM
First Floater Fix Date:	12/21/10 TO
Maturity Date:	12/21/65

Speaking of Zero

Very short term interest rates, as reflected by Treasuries maturing in January of 2010, have actually turned negative while the current 3-month bill yields 0.13. I saw a number of articles in the press this morning citing a flight back to safety; don't believe it. This speculation does not contain one grain of truth. What is, in fact, happening is this: All of the major banks now must close their books on 12/31/09, as mandated by the government, and each of them wants to show the most pristine of balance sheets and hence the squeeze. This situation has pulled down yields in all short maturities, with even the 2-year trading at its low yield for the past year. This is just window dressing, and buying securities attached to these rates must be taken into consideration as the probability of a bounceback after year-end is quite high.

2010—The Specifics

December 31, 2009

It is going to be a tough year; make no mistake about it. Do not fool yourself into thinking that either good absolute or relative returns will be easy to accomplish as compared to your brethren. Enjoy today in all its fullness, as it will be the last day to rest on your laurels or other parts of your anatomy for some time to come.

This suspense is terrible. I hope it will last.

—Oscar Wilde

A tide of rising rates spares no man or portfolio, and I suspect the winners of 2010 will have to have some quite specific strategies that are employed and fastidiously utilized as we roll through the coming 12 months. Fixed coupons in all but some unique cases will be losers, and LIBOR floaters will preserve capital but provide inadequate returns. Fixed-to-float bonds where the call is inside of 2012 and the floating spread is higher than corresponding spreads should hold up well, but many of these represent maturities too long for some portfolios. Bonds tied to inflation may well prove valuable, though probably not until the second half of the year. Staying quite short is another avenue while waiting for yields to rise, but here the bet is simply a call on interest rates.

Nothing wilts faster than laurels that have been rested upon.

—Percy Bysshe Shelley

The funny part about Wall Street, of course, is the line that we draw in the sand on this day every year. Today, performance ends; today, holdings to be regarded by clients are cast in stone, and the first trading day of the new year is the point of the new embarkation. Today we are here, and tomorrow we are there, and the timeline shift is of substantive magnitude.

As I have stated before, I think 2010 plays out in three steps:

1. Rising yields as driven by the cowboys and worries about the Fed's moves to come
2. The Fed's raising short rates and everyone concerned about just how far it will go and for how long
3. Worries about inflation, the cost of commodities, both energy and basic goods, as the country does the one thing that it must do, which is to reinflate

The concerns surrounding all of this will be:

1. The health of many sovereign credits and their ability to repay their debt
2. High-yield credits that will no longer be able to borrow at artificially low rates, so creditworthiness will become an issue
3. Municipal credits that are in disarray, as many revenue bases will no longer support both their debt and social services
4. A worsening position for both commercial real estate and their securitizations that are saddled with rising yields and little economic growth, so that values continue to erode until the inflationary cycle begins
5. Bond portfolios that are continually dragged down by marks-to-market as yields continue to rise and spreads widen out again, with the resultant reaction of the dealers shying away from trading risk
6. New issuance by the Treasury causing supply problems that will impact any and all debt regardless of its nature as base rates rise, which will also cause a steepening yield curve with two-to-tens out to +315/325 bps

Additional plays include:

1. Buy deeply discounted bonds. They will not decline as much in value as current coupons, and instead of buying one unit, buy 1.5 units and use the leverage as an offset to higher yields, both for income and later appreciation as they roll down the curve.
2. Consider any new product that rolls across tied to 5- or 10-year constant maturity swaps (CMSs) or constant maturity Treasuries (CMTs), and while you give up liquidity, you gain in pricing.

3. Consider replacing some agency debt with agency step-up debt, but pay close attention to the structure, as some of these are not done properly.

4. Roll out of vanilla muni credits and into Build America Bonds (BABs) as a much safer way to preserve capital and avoid risk.

5. Consider the laggards in the financial sector for both equity and debt plays, as the steepness of the yield curve will benefit them and be a huge help to their balance sheets.

6. Take another look at some of the regional banks and do your homework; most will muddle through all of this, and there are some decent opportunities in the short end in some of the names. Spreads are out of line here, in my opinion.

In the final analysis, 2010 will be a treacherous year. Having said that, problems are just that and must be dealt with accordingly. I am fond of quoting the Wizard here:

When facing an obstacle you can go around it, go through it, go under it, go over it or, when nothing else works; dance till it moves.

Yesterday, everybody smoked his last cigar, took his last drink and swore his last oath. Today, we are a pious and exemplary community. Thirty days from now, we shall have cast our reformation to the winds and gone to cutting our ancient shortcomings considerably shorter than ever.

—Mark Twain

Prepare to Dance!

The two Sages and I wish you and your families all of the very best for the next year. May you find joy, retain health, achieve peace, and have the grandest of adventures that will lead you to great success in all of your endeavors.

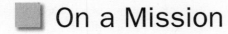# On a Mission

January 8, 2010

Making the Right Moves

Recently, I wrote about the difficulties of our present situation, and I received a call from a friend of mine and one of the senior traders at one of the major dealers, who told me that he felt like I was holding back. I had identified all of the problems, and he was on board with my assessment of the market. He had read my thoughts all the way to the end, but where was the solution? Yes, exactly, where is the solution? That is exactly what I have been mulling about for weeks, and the sad but true conclusion is that there isn't a very good one for most of you. I like the long fixed-to-float bonds well enough if the call and then flip to float is 2012 or so and in and the floating spread is more than what is available in today's market, but many of you can only own so many ozone maturities, so that is only a partial answer to my quest. I find either CMTs or CMSs attached to the 5- or 10-year a reasonable option for investing now, but those bonds are nowhere to be found. There has been a huge rush, of course, to buy LIBOR floaters, but that answer is not going to be a good one until the Fed moves off the dime, which I think is probably about 6 months out and other of my distinguished brethren think will be a year to 18 months out, so, in either scenario, it doesn't help for the present time. In fact, with all my wandering about on the economic landscape, there is no all-encompassing solution unless, and here is the conclusion, that I push on the structural whiz-bangs and get them to create the solution.

> *I am not a prophet nor of great religious conviction so I cannot move mountains but I can damn well kick up enough sand on the beach to get your attention.*
> —Mr. Trader, Senior Sage

I am dancing!

When presented with the inevitable obstacles of life you may go around them, under them, over them, through them or when nothing else works: Dance till they move.

—The Wizard

See first that the design is wise and just; that ascertained, pursue it resolutely.

—William Shakespeare

You will ask; you will pop it up under my nose, "What about liquidity?" These will not be Treasuries or agencies, and you will not get the kind of liquidity, but then a fixed coupon corporate doesn't give that to you, either. The issuers, to the extent that I am involved, will all be household–type names, and there should be a number of dealers that will bid on them at any time if that is what is needed.

What I am going to try to effectuate are a series of fixed-to-float bonds in various maturities and with various terms and utilizing various issuers that will address the structural issue of how to deal with short rates pegged by the Fed, a steepening curve, yields that will be rising across the board, and the eventual move by the Fed to start raising short rates and causing even higher yields and lower prices. It seems to me that either you join me, at least to some extent, in my dance or you are going to face portfolios that are back in price and on the slippery slope to going down more. In other words, there is just no good answer to our present dilemma, so I am going to try to create the answer.

I am in pursuit!

The Casting of Magic
January 10, 2010

January 5, 2009: the second-largest amount of new issuance for corporate bonds on record. The total was $19.5 billion, and all of it issued by financial institutions. What was particularly interesting was that General Electric (GE) sold debt at +130 bps, actually a better spread than their last issuance, which had a Federal Deposit Insurance Corporation (FDIC) guarantee. This should give you some indication of the voracious appetite that now exists for bonds after our recent brush with financial calamity. The investment attitude of a generation has been changed by our recent experience, and people and institutions alike have backed up from equities in general, have backed away from index funds, and are demanding safety of principal over opportunities for appreciation. For those of you who have not gotten this message and figured it out in your approach to your clients, you are making a mistake. It is January 11, and U.S. issuance of investment-grade corporate bonds is already $38.1 billion and $1.86 billion of high-yield debt. Last year saw a record influx of $143 billion into bond funds, and the money keeps rolling in into 2010, with new money pouring in for an unabated 53 weeks.

The Unappeal of Money Market Funds

Not everyone may understand the financial ins and outs of the Fed or the double talk of some of the governors, but what everyone does get is that money market funds yield just this side of nothing and that nothing is not an acceptable return. I think that this is one other driver of the rush into bonds with investment-grade debt now yielding 4.75 percent utilizing one Bank of America index. It isn't complicated; people don't want the capital risk of equities, they don't want the miniscule return of the shortest of funds, and they are putting their money in the segment of fixed income where some safety is attainable and where some return is perceived.

Bathing in the Light of the Lord

For those of you that have positioned yourselves as "bond experts," you now find yourself in the sweetest spot of your lives. Money is flowing into the coffers, you are loved in the press, and you have become the experts of the investment world. Life, in short, is good! I have the somewhat radical view that bonds are for income and equities are for appreciation. That idea is catching on, however, and the old notion that one should buy stock for dividends is slowly losing its value. The general public never really got it until recently; a corporation can stop paying their dividend at any time on the whim of the board of directors, but if they stopped paying their debt, then some kind of bankruptcy was the conclusion and just a major distinction between the two. In fact, for the first time in more than 50 years, American corporations announced more dividend cuts in 2009 than increases. According to recent data supplied by S&P, just 778 companies in 2009 announced either dividend increases or resumptions of their dividends, and this is the smallest number since 1955, when S&P began tracking these statistics.

Until one is committed, there is hesitancy, the chance to draw back, always ineffectiveness. Concerning all acts of initiative (and creation), there is one elementary truth the ignorance of which kills countless ideas and splendid plans. The moment one definitely commits oneself, then providence moves too. All sorts of things occur to help one that would never otherwise have occurred. A whole stream of events issues from the decision, raising in one's favor all manner of unforeseen incidents and meetings and material assistance, which no man could have dreamed would have come his way. Whatever you can do, or dream you can, begin it. Boldness has genius, power and magic in it. Begin it now.

—Johann Wolfgang Von Goethe

My Well-Known Call

It was some 18 months ago, and hindsight is 20/20, and the government was buying the preferred stock of many large financial issuers. I suggested here, in documented black and white, that the play was not to buy the preferred stock and partner up with the government, but to take the senior position to Uncle Sam and buy the senior debt of those same corporations. Lots of sleepless nights, countless moments of aggravation, and an incredible amount of strain, but in the end a 100 percent winning call and there is no rational denial. Even in the one case where the Treasury allowed CIT to head into default, we got new bonds that have appreciated since issuance and new equity in CIT that has appreciated in value. In all of the other instances, the credits paid their debt, and the compression since then is a documented fact.

My Current Call: Buy Fixed-to-Float Securities

This is a call on structure and timing when it seems just obvious to me that interest rates are going to rise and some kind of protection must be found. In a recent example—and this is not a suggestion to purchase these securities but one example of a recent deal—the Barclays 5-year pays 3.25 percent for the first year, which is +300 bps to 3-month LIBOR, and it then floats at +150 over the same LIBOR rate. Yes, there is a cap, and I don't like caps any more than the rest of you, but that is the only way to construct these things at present. If these bonds get called after one year, then you get your money back in a time when rates are rising; if they don't get called, then you own a 4-year floater that is floating at a higher rate than if Barclays did a straight LIBOR floater today. Now many of you consider this type of bond on an OAS (option-adjusted spread) basis, but that is only part of the story. If that is your sole method for determining the value of these types of bonds, then you are making a mistake. The flip side is the evaluation of your portfolios, using the exact same OAS if yields rise by 100 bps/200 bps and so forth. We do know that the average move for the last three moves by the Fed is +425 bps, and hence some extrapolation must be done when assessing the value of a fixed-to-float security. It is my hope, and I will dance as quickly as I can to accomplish it, that there are many more similar issuances in a whole host of names so that there is an opportunity to own this type of security. There is just not a better option that I can think of to deal with our present environment. This is the Wizard's conjuring at its best; if it doesn't exist, then cast the magic spell and make it so.

Magic is a faculty of wonderful virtue, full of most high mysteries, containing the most profound contemplation of most secret things, together with the nature, power, quality, substance and virtues thereof, as also the knowledge of whole Nature, and it doth instruct us concerning the differing and agreement of things amongst themselves, whence it produceth its wonderful effects, by uniting the virtues of things through the application of them one to the other.

—Heinrich Cornelius Agrippa, three books of occult philosophy or magic

The Most Undervalued Bonds

February 1, 2010

There is a segment of capital markets where the bonds are not well understood because if they were, they would be trading at much higher prices. I have discussed them before and suggested them before, but today I am going to provide a much more thorough analysis because I have concluded that I have not communicated well in getting my point across. Too many of you have called me or emailed me, and it is quite obvious that I have not conveyed the punchline in a well-understood manner. These bonds are fixed-to-float bonds, and they are the one segment of the marketplace, possibly because of their long-dated maturities, that have not compressed to a point where value is lost. There are bonds in the short end where some value is still left that I like, such as various shades of AIG or the Student Loan Marketing Association (SLMA), but here it is a matter of credit consideration. In the case of fixed-to-float bonds, it is a case of not fully appreciating the structure and certainly of not evaluating it correctly.

I am going to use some real-time examples of these securities to make my point today. These are real bonds that I have seen in the market in the past few days, and I use them for example only; they are not offerings. Let's first consider the makeup of these bonds. They have been issued in size by many banks, as they count as Tier I capital and hence their long maturities, but there are also shorter-dated bonds that float by, if you will, from time to time. This structure has also been issued by many insurance companies and even some utilities. The basic components for consideration are the length they remain fixed before they either get called or float, the floating provision meaning the spread as compared with shorter vanilla floaters in the same name, and finally some assumption that you must make about when and by how much the Fed may raise LIBOR rates. The analytics on Bloomberg are fine, as far as they go, but they do not tell the whole story, and that is why, I think, that these bonds are not fully valued.

What is being missed by almost everyone is the real meaning of when these bonds flip, and this is where the joke has been missed. It states clearly in the indentures of these bonds when they may get called, and people look at the call provision, as they should, and think that it is a maybe–maybe proposition, just as they should, and they lose the appreciation of what is really there at that point. If they get called, in many cases, great; a home run with high returns, but people do not fully appreciate the value of the flip if they do not get called, and this is where the value is incorrectly perceived. The analytics on the Bloomberg YTC page calculate a yield to maturity based on the current rate of LIBOR (0.25 bps for 3-month LIBOR now), and that is what you see as the underlying component for the yield at maturity, but that number, as we all know, is fluid, and everyone—virtually without exception, yours truly included—thinks the Fed is going to raise rates at some point; it is just a question of when. Then we look at the YTC and do not take the final and critical step of realizing that the call yield is also the flip yield so that the bond retains the call yield to the flip date, and then one owns a long-dated LIBOR floater from that date forward if the bonds are not called. It is really similar to a caterpillar that morphs into a butterfly, and you have two distinctly different securities as part of one bond issuance.

Major Intl. Ins. Co. 6.854 5/49-16 CALL $86.50 YTM 4.59% YTC 9.77% BAA1/A−

In my first example, you own this credit with a 6.854 coupon that will pay you 9.77 percent till the flip date. If they are called, that is the end of the story and you owned these insurance company bonds for six years, yielding 9.77 percent. Now if you bought a straight fixed bond in this name, it might be at +250 to the 5-year, for a yield of 5.82 percent. Let's look at the cash flow differential on 10 million bonds: $977 million a year versus $582 million a year, for a $395 million difference. Then let's consider, being the pragmatists that we are, that the bonds do not get called but they flip or morph into a long-dated floating rate bond. These particular bonds float over 6-month LIBOR at 217.8 bps. Six-month LIBOR is currently 0.38 bps, so the yield would be 2.558 percent. Yet here is the second place where the point is missed. We know that for the last three Fed moves the average change has been +425 bps in LIBOR, but today, to make my point clear, I will cut that in half and base my numbers on the assumption that the Fed moves just half of that, or 212.5 bps, which would give you a YTM of 4.30 percent, with the additional feature in the structure that they float continuously over LIBOR at a rate that this company would certainly not have to pay if they issued a plain vanilla floater given the yields in floating rate bonds at present.

Given market pricing, it is obviously the assumption of the marketplace that these bonds are equivalent to, say, agency callables, and, in plain fact, they are not. The fixed-to-float bonds are a horse of a different color entirely, and that is why I am making an attempt to explain the pigmentation. Agency callable bonds have a yield to call that is just what we all know it as, but the fixed-to-floaters are really a yield-to-morph or yield-to-flip, and then they are a totally different kind of security.

Large U.S. Bank 7.7 5/49–13 CALL $98.00 YTM 4.86%
YTC 8.42% BA1/A−

Here, we have a bond issued by one of the major U.S. banks with a 7.70 percent coupon trading at $98 with a yield until 5/13 of 8.42 percent; compare that to Wells Fargo & Co.'s 3-year maturities at your leisure, but it is +707 bps over the 3-year presently. If not called, then the bond flips to a LIBOR floater at +389 bps over 3-month LIBOR, which would be 4.14 percent if LIBOR remained at 0.25 percent, and utilizing my one-half of the average rise in LIBOR number, 212.5 bps, you would own a floating rate note yielding 6.265 percent that floated with 3-month LIBOR if it continued to rise, preserving your mark-to-market value.

A U.S. Utility (SUB) 6.35 10/1/66–16 $94.00
3.55%/7.51% A3/BBB+

Here is an example of a fixed-to-float issued by an American utility company. You have a locked in 7.51 percent yield to flip, which is +519 bps over the 5-year Treasury, and then if not called, it flips into a bond that floats at +206.75 bps over 3-month LIBOR, which would be 2.32 percent now or 4.19 percent, based on my conservative assumption

about the rise in LIBOR rates. You will
note that in this security, like all of my
examples, the YTM on Bloomberg is
misleading as it assumes the 7.51 percent
YTC or flip, which is locked in and then
meshes in the rest of the YTM assuming

It's not that I'm so smart, it's just that I stay with problems longer.
—Albert Einstein

the present rate of 3-month LIBOR at 0.25 percent. The yield to call is
an absolute number and is set while the YTM is a fluid number based on
the LIBOR rate at any point in time.

Play to Win
March 11, 2010

I play to win. I intensely do not like to lose, and I write my commentary in hopes of helping you win. Execution is fine, and we all pay attention to it and it is a matter of eighths. An idea, however, is a horse of a different color. A good idea, whether to buy or sell or stand pat, is worth points, and often the tally is scores of points. There is nothing of more value than I can share with you or that anyone can provide you that is more important than an opinion or a strategy that works. Even those of you in the very large institutions who have regular investment committee meetings may have missed something, or I may make a point that you did not consider, and hopefully this gives you an edge.

There is no room for second place. There is only one place in my game and that is first place.

—Football coach Vince Lombardi

Having said that, I do business with a lot of institutions all over the globe, and many of these people are not delighted that the readership of *Out of the Box* is so broad, and I understand their point. Now Bloomberg gives you the opportunity to see just who has read what and I occasionally pay attention to this. Last week, I cut off a major insurance company, even though I received emails from several people there, imploring me not to do it, and I did it because they were reading my commentary virtually every day but not doing any business with me and that is just wrong. If you do not find OOTB useful, then fine—ask to be removed from the list and that will be that. However, if you are reading it regularly and not doing business with me, then I ask you to change this; one way or another, you make the call. This is not a joke; make your choice, and we both can get on with what is important to each of us. I am up each day at 4:00 A.M., and it takes me hours to write my piece; there is no sense wasting the effort on people who do not think that my commentary has value. The service, I am sorry to tell you, is not free; just as you expect to get paid for your labors, so do I.

Fixed-To-Float Bonds

I have written about this often enough, but I still do not think many of you get the advantage of these bonds. True, they have longer maturities and it may screw up your duration picture, and that may be reason enough not to buy them, but you should carefully explore the value they represent. Not only do they give you an outsized yield, but the return is so far outside of fixed coupon bonds as to be compelling. Let us assume a YTC of 10 percent, which is certainly achievable in high-quality credits. You see, this is not really a YTC as we generally understand it such as with agency securities. The YTC is really a double value in these bonds because it is also the yield to flip or when the fixed coupon portion expires and the bonds become floaters. So we take the 10 percent yield to flip and let us assume, for the sake of example, a call/flip in five years. Here, you get a yield of 10 percent per year for five years or a 50 percent return during that time period. Then let us assume that the bonds are not called and continue on as floaters and let's assume that you lose 10 percent on the mark-to-market when the bonds flip to floaters. So for that five-year period, you made 50 percent minus 10 percent, which equates to a 40 percent return for those five years, giving you an all-in 8 percent annual return until the flip. In the fixed coupon securities of these securities, you cannot get within points of that kind of return now, and therein lies their value. Now if the bonds actually get called, home run; but even if they don't, you are left with a long-dated floater that rolls with 3- or 6-month LIBOR. Then at the flip date, if not called, you get the option to hold them or sell them, and you have made out like a bandit, and boy will it help your cash flows. Here is an idea that you should seriously consider!

Leverage

To the extent that you can you should be leveraging your portfolios at these very low interest rates. Lend out what bonds are appropriate, and try to do it at a fixed level off of LIBOR for several years; this should be fixed and not floating. Then utilize the extra cash for a multiple of your present returns on capital. If your circumstances allow for this, do it now before rates begin to rise. The Fed and our current economic conditions are allowing for this opportunity, and you should take it!

Sovereign Debt

The crisis is not over, close to over, or anywhere near to over. In my view, none of this debt should be bought unless all of the financials are clear and the derivatives associated with the country and its banks are explicitly stated. The current spreads in a lot of these names are just stupid, and the sector along with the euro is a short if there is anything to be done. You would not blindly accept the assurance of some corporation as to its financials, so why would you do this with a sovereign credit? This has been a mistake that has gone on much too long in the capital markets, and it is one in the process of correcting. As to the politicians and their grandiose comments in the press, leave the fairy tales to your kids.

The Major Regional Banks

The word in the press is that Barclays is on the move. The equities of some of these credits jumped up markedly yesterday. Now I have no special information, but I have seen these cycles often enough. First, the stock moves, and then the bonds compress, and while Barclays may well be leading the charge, suddenly other acquirers appear. Many of the regional bank names have been market laggards and, with the passage of time, the ills of a year ago are getting cured. Do your homework and pick the names you like, but we are at the beginning of this cycle, and there is money to be made in this space.

Chapter 10

Grant's Gambit

While there is nothing new under the sun, I occasionally look around to see if I can find it. This is an offshoot of the wisdom of my father's mother, who was well known for saying, "The higher, the fewer, the never, the less." I am not sure if I understood it when she said it, and I am not sure if I understand it now, but it seems to prompt me to sometimes muse about different ways of doing things. These are generally times of strong French roast coffee and Honduran cigars, when the smells of the morning lift my senses out past where they usually reside. If bonds are bought for income and stocks for appreciation, my thought for many years now, is there a way to get appreciation from bonds?

This notion is out past the general concept of interest rates falling and bonds appreciating in the normal manner of things but pondering if there was an edge in fixed income that could somehow be exploited to get some additional appreciation. I played around with this for a number of months, actually, and finally concluded that it was possible in certain situations. As the idea materialized, I gave it a name: Grant's Gambit.

There are several distinct plays here, and the first involves bonds being called.

The government has decided, in its infinite wisdom, that trust preferred securities (TruPS) and hybrids and perpetual bank bonds will no

■ 255 ■

longer be counted as Tier I capital. Without boring you with all the technical specifications, this means that these bonds, once presumed not to be called, will probably be called now. There is no guarantee—and let me repeat that about six times—but the likelihood of a call by the issuing bank has now greatly increased. The reason is that if the bank can no longer use it for its capital considerations, then the decision is going to get made mostly on financial considerations. Can they refinance the bond if they call it at a cheaper cost to them?

Now to head down this course requires some knowledge. The variables are the coupon rate, the spread to the London Interbank Offered Rate (LIBOR) or whatever when the bond flips from a coupon to a floating rate bond, the yield to maturity (YTM), the yield to call (YTC), and finally a calculated opinion about whether this particular issuer will call the bonds or not. Some of these securities have yields to call of more than 20 percent and can be just great purchases if they are called while you rest in the security of senior or subordinated debt in the meantime—much less risk than equities even if not called. Here is equity-like appreciation and one sector of Grant's Gambit.

The next play has to do with compression and buying bonds at a discount. We have had a huge amount of compression in the bond markets recently as the inflows into bonds funds have been gigantic, while at the same there has been a very large amount of money that has moved out of equity funds. Compression is when a bond tightens in spread to Treasuries. U.S. Treasury bonds are the benchmark against which almost all bonds are judged. Let me give you a simple example: If a bond has a 6 percent coupon and you can buy it at $90 and it goes to $94, then you have made 6 percent in interest plus 4 percent in appreciation, for a total of a 10 percent return. This can be done in senior debt of some bonds with a "plain vanilla." This can happen either because of compression or, just the same as in equities, the credit improves and has a higher value. The most notable example now of this is the banking sector, where there are still good spreads left and where the financials are in an upward swing for many banks. After this, it is on a credit-by-credit assessment, but it is possible to get appreciation from bonds just like you do in stocks if care and knowledge are applied to what is available.

To play this game requires a different mind-set than the one used generally for buying bonds. Usually, a bond purchase involves looking at the rating, the maturity, and the yield, and bonds are bought for safety and income. It is not that these considerations disappear; it is that we have added the possibility of gain into the mix. There is a bet that is being made here, but a bet that is far less risky than equities, with the chance of almost as much appreciation, and so much so that the risk–reward equation is heavily tilted toward finding value in bonds versus the equity option. You could also use some bank exchange-traded fund (ETF) as another way to play this game and spread out your risk, though a knowledgeable adviser should be able to outperform the ETF; diversification is always your friend and perhaps not your best friend in some situations such as these. You will note that Warren Buffett is not out buying a slew of companies, but one at a time where he can correctly assess the proposition of value.

Time is always the great eraser of fear, and the farther away we get from our recent financial calamity, the less these opportunities will exist. The financial markets are nothing if not dynamic; they move in a constant spin while you are awake and while you sleep and even on the weekends with some political or economic pronouncement or another they adjust first in Australia and Japan and then in London, so by the time you wake up to start your day, things have already adjusted to the consensus perception. It does not stop—not ever.

Grant's Gambit

July 4, 2010

There have been very few new institutions added to my distribution list in the past several years. Consequently, I start today's commentary assuming that most of you are familiar with Grant's Rules. They were first penned almost 10 years ago and not one change has been made in them since then. For those of you who have adopted them into your thinking, I believe that they have served us well. "Preservation of Capital" comes first followed by "Make Money," and the recent crises in both credit and solvency have proved the value of those two statements and emphasized, in particular, the order of their importance. Today, however, I proceed past the "Rules" and examine two of Grant's axioms, which leads us to a perhaps novel investing approach.

The first axiom is that bonds should be bought for yield and equities should be bought for appreciation. I am not a believer in buying stocks for dividends, and while I recognize the dividend as part of the total return of an equity, I also recognize that dividends can get torn asunder in times of economic hardship—a lesson learned by many in our recent downturn. A corporation will go to the ends of the earth to preserve its debt payments because if they are not paid, then the company does not survive, while the ending or reduction of a dividend is a boardroom matter that can be changed in the blink of an eye while the corporation has its public relations team put out incredulous proclamations about how the cut is being done to protect shareholders' interests. "Bah humbug," says the Wizard.

The second axiom, and I make a distinct judgment here, is that while many think that a corporation is run in the interests of the shareholder, reality demonstrates, time after time, that the interests of the debtholders come first because those interests preserve a company's existence and the jobs of its management and always trump shareholders' interests.

You may not like this; you may think it is wrong, and it makes no difference, as this is the way corporations work. Consequently, as investors, the recognition of this leads one to buy debt for yield and buy stocks for appreciation, and this notional twist on "return" has been clearly documented over the past decade as bond returns have beaten equity returns as compared to U.S. Treasuries and certainly as compared to the results from A-rated equities as compared to their debt.

Now let us proceed down the path a little further and take a look at a rather novel idea that I have developed. I am sure that other people have thought of this, and I am not claiming fathering some grand invention that will change the Great Game, but it is an idea that I, personally, have not read about somewhere else and I have been mulling around in my mind for some time and have alluded to it once before in a prior commentary. I think the idea is particularly timely, as money flows into bonds and out of equities as people and institutions alike just do not want the risk associated with the stock markets after the tremendous losses incurred by many during the American financial crisis. The concept is centered on how to achieve the equity-like returns of the good old days and yet remain in the relative safety of the debt markets and on top of the capital structure. Interestingly enough, one of the reasons that this is possible has to do with the construction of the investment markets, which separates equity investors from bond investors. The mindsets of the two are most often delineated by their different tasks, which, to a great extent, is what has created the opportunity.

Let us consider an insurance company as the purest example of the general investment approach. They have a team of bond guys worried about credit, yield, duration, and the like that are looking to provide a return over and above the costs of the company. Then there is a second group that generally has less money available to them that buy stocks, and they are supposed to provide higher returns than the bond group and to make money on the margin. These folks have no concern about duration, look at price-to-earnings (P/E) multiples and all kinds of technical analysis, with only a nod to credit considerations and the dividend is generally considered only as a part of the notion of "total return," which is most often set in the receipt of "appreciation." The first group generally buys to hold, while the second group will sell something in a heartbeat. Very different viewpoints, very different methodologies of investing, and, in fact, a classic representation of the "separation of Church and State." It is therefore the historical construct of how money is invested that has limited the possibilities and now allows the innovative among you to profit from what is presently available and that is the utilization of a different mind-set.

Opportunity Knocks—Open the Door

I had the pleasure to have onboard Friday evening in Baltimore one of the legends of the equity world who is every bit as nice as he is bright. Part of our discussion centered on equities as commodities and the correlation that now exists in the marketplace. He made the point—and I think he is right—that the transparency and the computerization and the "fast trading" that now exists in stocks has transformed the equity markets forever. New strategies here have just overwhelmed the old-line "buy for the long term" strategies that have been the focus of attention for the past 100 years, and the new methodologies to play this segment of the Great Game have radically changed the dynamics of the playing field. We also discussed the bond markets and his frustrations with the lack of transparency and the ability of the lead banks to trade against their clients' interests and the pronounced differences between the two markets. I told him that, while recognizing the differences, they could also be used to his advantage, and this was a topic of lively interaction over an H. Upmann cigar and a few Grand Marniers that Nicki, the attentive stewardess on my boat, kept providing at regular intervals.

> We are all faced with a series of great opportunities brilliantly disguised as impossible situations.
>
> —Charles Swindoll

Having set the stage, we now arrive at Grant's Gambit, which is playing the debt markets to achieve the returns hoped for in equities.

Before I provide the specifics of my idea, let me place this squarely on the table; we are not buying bonds to hold them, but rather to gain some yield over time and either take advantage of compression or the advantage of prices, in general, rising and yields going lower. We are looking for appreciation, and then we are going to sell the bonds we have bought. To do this properly, you either need to set up a third team that has this directive or set up a separate portfolio so that you can clearly distinguish between the objectives of the bond portfolio and the objectives of these holdings. If you do not do one or the other or both of these, then you are doomed to failure by the confusion of your purpose. Please read this paragraph again, as it is critical to achieve success.

Next, if you are typically a bond investor, you will have to perform one of the Wizard's incantations to get this right!!! You will find a small mallet or a paper weight, and as you hit yourself gently on the side of your head, you will say the following out loud:

Equities are perpetual and have no duration, and I am not going to place any great emphasis on the maturity of these bonds when I buy them except to take advantage of the lowest price and where it is on the yield curve and nothing else.

You will repeat this procedure three times in hopes that some sense is knocked into you.

What we are looking for is debt that has a low price and that will appreciate over time either due to compression or prices rising in general, and since we are at a time when we are close to some kind of floor in short rates and low historical yields in longer maturities, we are generally seeking compression. But there are also fixed-to-float securities that we can buy and then plan to sell when we hit the call or the flip if they are not called and become LIBOR floaters. This strategy can be accomplished in investment-grade securities or high-yield securities or even in some of the hybrid products. None of the bonds we will be buying are new issues or anywhere close to par or floaters or premium bonds that may become higher premiums because there is too much to lose in the current marketplace. What we are looking for, in the first instance, are 10-year and much longer bonds, with a coupon beating the 10-year Treasury that will appreciate in value so that we can sell them and make 10 percent or more in an annual return on our money, which includes the coupon yield and the appreciation in price. This would be exemplified by a 4 percent coupon with a dollar price of $80 that goes to $86 at the end of one year or earlier, which is coupled with the coupon to give you a nice 10 percent return on your money and stay in debt at the top of the capital structure and preserve your capital.

Next you will repeat the Wizard's second incantation six times as you walk around in a circle.

I am buying these bonds to SELL them when I have reached my goal.

Those of you who are "equity guys" will look at this and think, "a layup," but you don't have the skill set to implement this program.

The "bond guys" will look at this and think, "How do I know when I am supposed to sell these?" and you will give yourself a defined goal to make the determination. To do this correctly, both equity and debt people will need to move their minds around so that you will effectively change your world. Grant's Gambit is a hybrid strategy of investing to both "Preserve Capital" and "Make Money." You may check with me to get real offerings to begin.

Opportunities are never lost; someone will take the one you miss.

Bearing the Scars of Battle

July 7, 2010

O n May 11, *Wishes Granted* left Fort Lauderdale and headed up the eastern shores of America. Tomorrow, we will roll into the harbor of New York City. I admit, without hesitation, that this has been a dream of mine for decades. I recall coming to New York as a young bright-eyed kid who gasped in awe that there were trading rooms that big and that the legendary Titans ruled them because, in those days of yore, cigar smoke could be seen from one end of the room to the other and the strut of the big traders was evidenced wherever you looked and cursing was no more thought about than the resident leftover sandwich from yesterday that could be found half eaten on most desks.

I can tell you with some pride that I did play Liar's Poker at Salomon Brothers and that I saw the long bond trader at Kidder throw his phone up against the wall and that the head of the syndicate department at Merrill once told me that if I ever screwed him up or sold bonds to the Street, I would be finished. I can also report that more than 30 years later, we are still the best of friends. I bear the scars of battle and look proudly at each of them. Thirty-six years after I began my trek, I look back with pride and wonder and the smile of Christopher Robin, and now it will be my boat that sails proudly past the Statue of Liberty and a dream of my lifetime will come to pass.

Wall Street and the Great Game has fascinated me for all of my life. It is an obsession of sorts for many of us and the best video game on Earth. I awake each day like many of you and am excited to see what is going on and to try to figure out how to win the day's events. There are no regrets when I look back, and I cherish the days ahead. For those of you at the beginning of your journey, I wish for you no more or less than the intoxicating joy that I have felt, the incredible highs and the moments of anguish when the mettle of your constitution is tested by

To light a candle is to cast a shadow.
—A Wizard of Earthsea

the wiles of your opponents and your backbone is steeled by your own personal determination. Always, always take the high road. Your word is everything and honor above all else when in the throes of battle that some other direction is suggested. Ours is a game of reputation and to ever stray from the concept of being a "stand-up guy" is to head toward the early end of your career.

Experience in the Great Game is a hard-won commodity. It is not the stuff of high IQs or learning to be found in a book. Experience is not resident in black boxes, nor can it be taught at any university. It is accumulated day by day and year by year in the raging winds of doing it and learning to get it right. When I suggested the consideration yesterday of Grant's Gambit, it was not offered as an interesting twist on portfolio strategy, but brought to your attention as an alternative methodology when the equity markets are not likely to perform well. Bonds that are typically bought for yield can also be bought for appreciation, and this approach to "total return" requires a very different mind-set. In a time when the cold winds of sovereign debt crisis, liquidity crisis, and solvency crisis are on the table, especially in Europe, it is to the top of the capital structure that one must ascend and new tools developed to withstand the buffeting of the economic seas. Dividends of all sorts may come and go, but debt payments are made if companies are to survive and there are no rational arguments that may be made to counteract the truth of that. Austerity measures or unleashed spending, either side of the track, do not bode well for the stock markets, and great care must now be exercised. As equity markets decline, however, bonds will compress, Treasuries will rise in price, and the "total return" to be found in the careful selection of debt instruments may be the salvation found for many portfolios if you only pay enough attention to understand the joke.

You may trust me enough to gain some experience, and I will trust you enough to share mine with you.

Sailing Past the Statue of Liberty

July 22, 2010

As *Wishes Granted* prepares to get under way this morning I want to take a moment to thank all of you who came by to see me while I was in New York. Since I generally get up at 4:00 A.M. to write my commentary and since many of you who came for dinner stayed well past the witching hour, I now need a well-deserved rest and will take it in Greenport, which is our next destination. I would guess that the level of Grand Marnier available in NYC is probably at its lowest level in decades and there are rumors that they have had to ship additional quantities from as far away as Montreal, but these rumors are unconfirmed, of course. I can also tell you, regardless of what you may have heard, that my boat was not fined for polluting the atmosphere with cigar smoke, but it is true that a certain well-known female trader was seen smoking one of the H. Upmans on the back of my boat with the public looking on. This was also the first time I had seen anyone using both hands to smoke a cigar, and it was a nod to ingenuity on her part as both myself and her colleagues grinned at her with rapt attention.

I also wish to take a moment and thank Captain Eddie, Chef Amy, and Stewardess Nicki for the great job they did while we were in New York. Late hours and then people arriving early for breakfast were the normal of our days in the city, and everyone did a great job. As we sail past Ellis Island and the Statue of Liberty in the early morning light, I am reminded of my own ancestors arriving from Austria so many years ago. I reserve a special moment to remember them and thank them for bequeathing me the opportunity to have such a great adventure in my own life.

With the 10-year Treasury at a 2.90 percent yield this morning, I think back over the many conversations that have taken place on my boat during the past two weeks about Grant's Gambit. Given the desire for safety that is now present in the bond markets and the lack of yield that can be found in almost anything, this is a new strategy that should prove to be useful. The premises are "Preservation of Capital," a 10-year yield declining further to 2.25 percent, continued large inflows into the debt markets, and a U.S. and world economy that will not be going anywhere quickly. The idea is to buy longer-dated securities at a discount and between the coupon and the appreciation to get 8 percent plus yields where the traditional methodologies will give you a return of maybe half of that. The concept here is to trade the bonds, not to hold them until maturity, and it is an equity market solution as applied to bonds.

The Deflation Trade

I am much more concerned about deflation rather than inflation at this point in our economy. There has never been a securitization tied to deflation that I am aware of, and it has been fascinating to work with several groups at the lead banks to try to develop a product that takes deflation into account and gives investors an offset to deflation without concocting something so obscure or complicated that the construction itself would scare off potential owners of this bond. Stand by; I am getting close, but in the meantime you may wish to consider the utilization of this security both as a directional trade and of using it as a hedge against your own portfolios.

My alphabet starts with this letter called yuzz. It's the letter I use to spell yuzz-a-ma-tuzz. You'll be sort of surprised what there is to be found once you go beyond "Z" and start poking around!
—Dr. Seuss

Part III

Market Issues

Chapter 11

Bear Stearns and Lehman Brothers

During my 36 years on Wall Street, I have seen most things. I have witnessed the big lie, the bigger lie, and lies so vast in scope they cannot be accurately accounted for in the English language. I have seen fortunes made and then lost as the one big bet that won inflated someone's ego past all good sense. I have witnessed the Fed move cautiously, precipitously, and then radically as each new chairman climbed out of bed in a different manner. I have been around for the bubbles and the pin pricks that burst them. I was in the game and played Liar's Poker and around when there were no computers to calculate yields, and I saw the ticker tape in action. I think I have seen just about everything except the Great Depression and, regardless of some opinions, I am not quite that old.

I have experienced elation and fear and great joy and horrible disappointment. I have been incredibly proud of some people and more disgusted than you can imagine with others. I have had the good fortune to sit at the top of several heaps and also had the experience of several heaps vanishing from underneath me.

I have come at the Great Game with focused abandon and quiet solitude and taken what I could from each. I have made more money than I ever thought possible and then spent countless hours worrying about how to keep it. I have interacted with some of the brightest minds on the planet and held my ground, and I never forget how to smile and not take myself too seriously. I have been battered and bruised and had people try to bribe me, and yet I always held to my standards and ethics, and I am perhaps proudest of that in the end. Yet having said all of that and taking some time to recall the many distinct events that charted my course, what sticks in my mind like a cauldron of red hot lava are the events surrounding the demise of Bear Stearns and Lehman Brothers.

There is no Hollywood movie, no book ever written, and no tale told around a late night campfire that can accurately reflect the terror of those experiences. I had no idea—none of us had any idea—whether the American financial system was going to survive and, make no mistake, whether the country would survive. During my long tenure on the Street, I had never seen a series of events that were that frightening as the financial system careened totally out of control and we had no idea of who was manning the helm or even if there was any helm left. What was at stake was our way of life, a return to conditions of the Great Depression or worse, and everyone of every color and stripe on Wall Street was terrified.

People at every firm were standing ready at their battle stations, checking on counterparty risk, trying to assess what other risks might be on the table, and preparing their firms for cardiac arrest. Phone calls and emails were a 24-hour thing, and I received them day and night as everyone wondered if the financial apocalypse was at hand. To quote Dickens, "It was the worst of times" and there was no "best of times" coming around the corner anytime soon.

Wild, dark times are rumbling toward us, and the prophet who wishes to write a new apocalypse will have to invent entirely new beasts, and beasts so terrible that the ancient animal symbols of St. John will seem like cooing doves and cupids in comparison.

—Heinrich Heine, 1842

And so he was right. The beasts were new and terrible and the fear palpable and the late night sweats a common occurrence that was just as likely to happen during our working hours as in bed. The castle gates were up, all able-bodied men that could be found were patrolling the walkways, door normally locked now bolted down, and the possible incursion of the Beast foremost in everyone's mind.

During this time it seemed as if every rumor were fact and every fact a rumor. No one trusted anything or anyone as we prepared for a storm that might have rivaled the one that engulfed Noah and his fabled ark. What became immediately apparent was that all of the safeguards that had been put in place since the Great Depression were not enough safeguards and that we lay exposed to financial pandemonium. We had been reckless in our preparations, foolhardy in our protective measures, and irresponsible in our collective behavior. We were in a state of siege from the various denizens that we, ourselves, had created, and the possibility was quite real that the battle would go their way. We remained alert and awake, and we shuddered in our bunkers not knowing if the next shell would fall directly on us. The cries of nearby anguish were a daily toll that we were forced to pay.

What have we learned—anything? I fear not or at least not as much as we should have from the experience. Time is a funny enterprise; it not only heals all wounds but erases much of the horror from past encounters, and as we should now be marshalling the forces that we have to not allow that experience to be a repetitive one, I think we have missed our mark once again. Attempts at corrective measures have faded into political shenanigans. The charge of the Volcker Rule was nothing more than a swordfight with windmills to disguise the president's lack of good judgment. The reports of blue-ribbon panels have been left to gather dust on the windowsills; a few good regulations have been put in place, but not enough, not nearly enough.

The viewing stands on Main Street are far from the viewing stands on Wall Street. This was one event, I assure you, where Main Street had the better and safer seats. I will be quite happy to never go through the Bear Stearns and Lehman Brothers days again, and I still remain quite sorry for the many fine people who did not cause these events but suffered tremendously from their consequences. It is not pleasant to lead your life in fear, and yet those dark days brought exactly that to mine and many other participants in the Great Game.

The entire shooting match was almost ended by foolishness, greed, and plain dumb thinking, as all control was surrendered to random events and careless rolls of the dice.

Lest we not forget again, or at the least, not during my lifetime; thank you!

The Bond Insurance Companies

December 20, 2007

Writing *Out of the Box* is often not an easy task. Sometimes there is nothing very interesting to write about, and sometimes there is too much and the compression is difficult. I have never been sure if it is easier to be serious or humorous. Fortunately, most days, I do not have to make a clear choice and I can be some combination of both. I have always maintained that Wall Street is serious stuff but that a sense of humor is a necessity in dealing with it all, which includes myself and the grand game we play. I have always been most bemused by the small-minded people who project righteous indignation about what I write and demand retribution for statements of opinion or truth. This kind of people are pitiable in their fear of the truth or an honest opinion and are, in many ways, a reversion back to a time when free thinking was banned by other countries, which is precisely the reason for the origination of the United States lest anyone forget.

I have spoken here a number of times about the bond insurers because of the wide fallout for those of us in fixed income. First there is the question of the debts of these credits, which has done nothing but widen and continue to widen, since my first comment on the companies in this sector some time ago. Now we have ACA Financial Guaranty Corporation, a smaller member of this monoline class, which was cut to "CCC" yesterday by Standard & Poor's (S&P), which is a rating close to default status and impairs the value on $61 billion worth of insured securities. To be poignant about this ratings cut, it was a 12-level cut all in a single action, which makes one wonder about where S&P was hiding during the deterioration of the ACA credit.

The ratings for the two largest monoline insurance companies, MBIA and AMBAC, were also lowered yesterday by S&P to negative outlooks. S&P also reduced the outlook on XL Capital to negative from stable and placed FGIC under review for a possible downgrade. The reality is that this whole class of insurers got "whapped" by the Peter Principle as they expanded outside of their traditional role of insuring municipal credits. The entire group, as a class, thought they were savvy enough to insure the mortgage bonds and subprime mortgage bonds and collateralized debt obligations (CDOs) and other complex structured products to garner extra fees, and the truth of it is just this: They were wrong, very wrong!

Let us take a moment to stare reality starkly in the face today. The collapse of the subprime mortgage market, alone, has so far produced about $76 billion in write-downs for commercial and investment banks. Bloomberg has estimated that industry downgrades could prompt an additional $200 billion of losses as some holders would be forced to sell securities at distressed prices. The larger picture finds that the three largest bond insurance companies, MBIA, AMBAC, and FGIC, currently insure $1,512 trillion dollars' worth of municipal and structured debt.

It is possible, if not probable, that the whole makeup of the municipal bond market will forever be impacted by the results of the bond insurance companies and their beleaguered attempts to expand outside of their traditional area of knowledgeable insurance.

The smallish ACA downgrade is already providing significant fallout as it may force Merrill, the Canadian Imperial Bank of Commerce (CIBC), Bear Stearns, and others to take significant write-downs in the next quarter. Shares of ACA Capital have now been delisted from the New York Stock Exchange (NYSE).

What is equally troubling to me is that the ACA mess may result in counterparty defaults that are now impossible to quantify as more than 30 firms had credit swap default agreements with ACA and a default could impose further sizeable losses for many of the large participants on Wall Street. I suggest caution here, Grant's Rules 1–10, "Preservation of Capital," and a sense that this is a time for extreme prudence. It is often said that money is truly made when blood is running in the streets, and I agree with this statement. But let us add Grant's corollary: Make sure it is not your blood that is running!

The Bet to Make!

March 14, 2008

D o not tell too many people but this is really a "run of the mill" market. We have them from time to time but not this pronounced for quite awhile. The markets are now getting trounced and flounced by all of the milling around. It all starts down the alley at the gin mill, where both truth and fiction become interspersed by those who have a financial interest in shucking and driving the markets, and then it proceeds to the grist mill, where everything is ground up; then to the rumor mill, where all manner of things are spewed forth; and then to the pepper mill, where the balance is scattered about as spice.

I have reached this conclusion based on the extreme volatility that is currently present in pricing any current security. It is like Bear Stearns recently: The stocks and bonds carom off the walls as rumors of its being out of cash, the original Goldman of Goldman Sachs was found refrigerated in Iceland and is coming in to help and Spitzer, now no longer governor, is coming in to run Bear, or was that Bare? Then there is Cerberus and General Motors, rumors of a split, a takeover by Three Dog Night, and a potential name change from ResCap to ResFloor to prop up the markets.

In a market where the Commodity Research Bureau (CRB) Index is hovering near its all-time highs, and commodities or basic materials are at their highest-ever cost, just ponder that for a moment. Governments across the World are admitting only to some but not too much inflation because of the formulas currently in use. We are being hoodwinked after all. We know we are being swindled by our own government and those of us in the financial markets have lost any real gauge of increased costs for goods and services. We look at the dollar at all-time lows against the euro, the 10-year Treasury at a 3.46 percent yield, the stock market sputtering along on 1.7 cylinders and you reach the conclusion that we are either at an inflection point that is the best buying opportunity of the decade or we are all about to go to hell in a handbasket.

The razor's edge cuts both ways, and here we stand on the head of Occam and wonder just which way the slice will take place. The real key, of course, is that it is not just an A or B choice and that all kinds of strategies must be empowered to win the game regardless of the inexplicable course of the universe. Only the fool will bet on only one course, and the Master of the Universe will make allowances for the greater Master to call the Fates to task. It is a game of preservation of capital and carpe diem when the opportunities can be clearly understood and the risks quantified. If you cannot quantify the risk, then do *not* buy the opportunity. That is simple, that is short, and that may well be one of the best pieces of advice that I can give any of you! I was asked recently to restate Grant's Rules, and they are as follows:

- Grant's Rules 1–10: Preserve Your Capital
- Grant's Rule 11: Make Money
- Grant's Rule 12: If a Company is Under Federal Investigation for Fraud or Accounting Issues—Sell.
- Grant's Rule 14: If a Company Gets a "Going Concern" Letter from Its Auditors—Sell.
- Grant's New Rule 15: If You Cannot Quantify the Risk, Then Do Not Buy the Opportunity.

Let us use Bear Stearns as an example this morning, but it could be any large commercial bank or investment bank—if I do not know and cannot quantify the risks at Bear, if I do not know their leverage exposure and/or their mortgage exposure and I do not have a handle on mark-to-markets for the kinds of products that they own, then I will not buy the credit as I do not know how to quantify their risk so I cannot, conversely, understand their opportunity. This concept seems so poignant to me that this is the first new rule I have added in years, and it is either some additional good sense that popped into my mind or the savagery of the current markets that have added an arrow in my accumulated experience. For the most part, at the present point, I am a buyer of safety, bonds tied to inflation, and opportunities when I perceive the risk–reward ratio vastly in my favor. I think some of the preferred stocks now are really interesting buys at current yields with an eye toward the future.

Let me leave you with this thought on the last day of the week—we are poised on a brink of some sort, and any of us with any sense find it a somewhat scary place to stand. You will hear often and daily about the world sinking into financial madness and all sorts of prognostication of gloom and doom. Smile, use the good old common sense that you inherited from your sage father and mother, and make the bet on the fact that we will be here for another day!

The Calm before the Storm

March 16, 2008

T he calm before the storm is an often interesting time of planning
and judgment. Today, Sunday, March 16, 2008, is such a day.
Living in Florida, I am no stranger to the coming of a hurricane.
You know it is coming, you have time to think about it and make decisions about what to do, and you are never quite certain if it will hit you
or not or what its impact might be on you.

Tomorrow by 9:30 EST Bear Stearns will either be sold or not, and
in that one action hangs the tale. If Bear is sold, then the Fed bailout
will seem to have worked and there will be time for other events to play
themselves out, but if the company is not sold by the opening of the bell
for the NYSE on Monday morning, then you may see the stock market
down by 500 or 1,000 points and the dollar at 165 to the euro. What
we know for sure today is that the debt of Bear was trading at around
70 cents on the dollar until the final hour of trading on Friday, and then
it dropped to 60 cents or so, while the stock of Bear, which had been
trading at $34 to $35 until the final hour, closed out the session at $30,
or down $27 on the day, or 47 percent.

What I do know today is that I am witnessing a historic moment
in the financial markets, and I am seeing my worst fear material-
izing while the lender of last resort, the Federal Reserve Bank of the
United States, has undertaken one of the tasks for which it was designed
and for which all sane participants hope never comes to pass. I am quite
aware that is strong language, but the truth must be spoken responsibly
in times of crisis and I am fearful that we have now entered a crisis.

Some history: In 1907 there was a panic on Wall Street initiated
by the Knickerbocker Trust Company of New York failing to corner United Copper Company's shares. Loans were called, margin loans
were called, and shares fell as J. P. Morgan, personally, and the secretary

of the Treasury joined forces, brought in federal money, arranged for money from a consortium of banks, and stemmed the tide. Many believe that this financial crisis caused the creation of our Fed in 1914. Then, of course, there was the Great Depression, which saw the failure of some 9,000 banks, a severe restriction of credit, failed loans, a huge diminishment in the value of hard assets, and the crash of our stock markets. Under President Franklin Roosevelt we saw a three-day bank holiday, the Glass-Steagall Act creating the Federal Deposit Insurance Corporation (FDIC) to provide a federal guarantee for money in banks, and the creation of the Federal Housing Administration (FHA) to stabilize the housing market. After incredible hardship and the passage of time, the United States finally righted itself after the Depression and went through World War II and several other wars only to arrive at 1972, when the Fed bailed out the Commonwealth Bank of Detroit, which had over $1 billion in assets. The we arrive at 1980, when First Penn, one of the oldest banking institutions in America, failed and was bailed out by the FDIC in its first large-scale operation. Then, in 1984, Continental Illinois National Bank failed after purchases of bad loans from Penn Square Bank of Oklahoma, which resulted in a $4.6 billion rescue by the Fed and the FDIC. The federal government owned 80 percent of this bank until 1994, when it was sold to Bank of America. During the late 1980s and early 1990s, we went through one of the more difficult times in our recent financial history with the crisis of the Savings and Loan Banks. From 1986 until 1989, the Federal Savings and Loan Insurance Corporation closed or provided assistance to some 296 financial institutions with assets of approximately $125 billion. All in all, some 740 institutions were closed or consolidated by various part of the federal government, with a cost that is estimated by the FDIC at $153 billion. U.S. taxpayers footed about $124 billion of that amount, though there are credible estimates utilizing more than twice that value. Then, in 1998, we had the Long Term Capital Management Crisis, which was initiated by the default on Russian bonds and promulgated the Fed to organize a $3.625 billion bailout of this hedge fund by major commercial banks and investment banks with, notably, Bear Stearns refusing to join in the group.

The Bear Stearns Bailout

This is a historic moment in the financial history of our country whether anyone recognizes the real implications of the action of the Fed yet or not. We may never know all of the actual nuances of what took place, but we now know the conclusion, and other events may be reasonably surmised. In my opinion, this event had little or nothing to do with J. P. Morgan, who was really only the messenger or the letter carrier in this affair. In point of fact, Bear Stearns was heading into financial default— later knowledge may define this more clearly—and J. P. Morgan took some of Bear's collateral to the window. The Fed voted unanimously not to hold JPM liable for the collateral, a fact that was prearranged, I am sure, and the Fed gave money to Bear Stearns, with JPM acting as the carrier once again. Why did the Fed do this, one may ask. The answer in my mind rests squarely on my largest fear, my continuing fear, which has been expressed often enough in the daily commentary that I write, *Out of the Box*. My primal fear has always been counterparty risk or, in plain speaking, major financial defaults that could take place between the major commercial and investment banks, which could trigger a real meltdown in America's and the world's financial structures—and that, my friends, no central bank on Earth can allow if at all possible. Given the complexities of many transactions, derivative transactions especially, a series of defaults on these contracts by one major financial institution could result in a domino-type effect across the landscape of counter-party obligations, and that occurrence, apparently in the Fed's view and certainly in my view, must be avoided at all costs; hence, the bailout of Bear Stearns.

Where are we now on Sunday afternoon? We are all sitting at our various posts and listening to the Weather Channel reporting on the coming hurricane. That is pretty accurate, I would have to say, given the number of phone calls that I have received from clients and the Street alike—an unprecedented number of phone calls for any weekend in all my years on the Street. There is now speculation about Lehman. One responsible party says that Bear clears for Lehman. I am not positive as to the accuracy of the statement, though I have heard it several times now and have some concern, given that their stock dropped 15 percent on Friday afternoon, that they are also in trouble, though there is just no way to know. There are comments about UBS and a major downsizing, and that they are shopping their entire retail division and getting out of derivatives in the United States. There is continuing speculation about Merrill and Citigroup and Morgan Stanley, and the worst of this is that no one really knows and that this kind of speculative environment is what can cause panics. CNBC is now reporting "deal or die" talks with

JPM and J. C. Flowers for Bear, though it is hard to really know much. The TV station reports that Dimon does not like Bear at all but is interested in the prime brokerage accounts, the clearing business, and some other specific components. all at around $15.00/share and that Flowers has real interest but in only certain parts of the firm.

Let me tell you this: If by 9:30 on Monday morning Bear Stearns has not been sold, then the credit crisis could turn into a solvency crisis and both the bond and stock markets could take some massive hits. Mark-to-market prices could turn into mark-to-fire prices, and the pricing services will adjust the marks accordingly, causing a furthering in the downward spiral of valuation for commercial and investment banks. I know of several institutions that are working over the weekend trying to quantify their counterparty risks with all of the major banks in hopes of understanding their positions and averting potential problems. We can also find some solace in the cut by the Fed of three fourths or one point that should come on Tuesday, and this should help with refinancing for some of the mortgage holders that are currently in trouble and may also help with some pricing in the credit markets.

It all comes down to this: It is my own personal viewpoint, no one else's, that we are down to it with Bear Stearns either being sold by the opening of the stock market this Monday or not. This is one of those moments in time, like an event at the Olympics—done or not, the record broken or not, the turn decided by this one defining event in time!

A Requiem for Bear Stearns

March 16, 2008

I am from the old school. I make no pretense about this, nor do I move from this position regardless of protestations. I do not hit people who are down, nor do I deride those who have failed. Today, I mourn the loss of Bear Stearns and an 85-year-old investment bank that is now lost to Wall Street with all of its history, traditions, and many years of proud existence. I offer condolences to the leaders I have known there; a nod of respect to Sy Lewis, who is no longer with us; admiration for Ace Greenberg and the fine leadership that he provided for many years; and an unfortunate farewell to Jimmy Cayne and his colleagues.

Most of all, I am saddened this morning by the loss of jobs and the change of circumstances for the many friends and brethren in arms that I have at Bear Stearns. I wish them all a grand new adventure in new circumstances. Bear Stearns now joins the ranks of the likes of White, Weld; Kidder Peabody; E. F. Hutton; and Drexel Burnham as firms that have faded into history. There may be others who wish to take the low road this morning, but I am not one of them, as I see no rejoicing in the loss of Bear Stearns or of any major commercial or investment bank.

I must say and I will say that I am not a great believer in what is being presented in the general press this morning concerning the acquisition of Bear Stearns by J. P. Morgan. I suspect there is more here of what some would like us to believe than is actually reflective of the facts. That is a deduction on my part based on the circumstances and the terms of the buyout and not based on any particular information. If pressed, I would guess that JPM was cajoled into service by the Federal Reserve Bank and by the Treasury as a perhaps unwilling savior of the financial system. What America's Fed cannot afford, nor what any central bank can afford at present, is the unwinding of the financial system based on the unraveling of counterparty obligations and defaults in derivatives contracts. One must be mindful of a stock that was $60 not so long ago and had a reported book value of $80 that is finally bought out at $2 after trading at $30 at the close of business last Friday, which seems to be a nod to some kind of value, but not much of one. One can suspect huge liabilities or poorly marked assets or little value for their prime brokerage or clearing business, but in the end, the buyer seems unwilling. Then there is the guarantee by the Fed of up to $30 billion in hard-to-mark assets, but that still does not give you any real guarantee to what might be unknown debts or obligations of Bear Stearns. In other words, the game could be afoot but not concluded, as who knows what might take place prior to the shareholders' meeting, but one may only rationally suspect a flurry of lawsuits at this price to ensue.

With such a shock to the body financial, one must ask what is next. There is nothing pleasant or heartwarming in this question, but it must be asked nonetheless. Could it be possible that Lehman, another shop deeply imbued with bond positions and trading, could somehow have similar exposure and follow Bear Stearns down the path? Who has the greatest exposure to the bond insurance companies if AMBAC or MBIA and others lose their AAA ratings? How accurate are the financials of Merrill or Morgan Stanley or UBS or Citi or any other lead commercial or investment bank that comes to mind. It is not too much of a leap of faith to suspect that the Fed must be aware of some grim realities that may be hidden from the general public if they are opening up borrowing at the window of last resort to all primary dealers for the first time in history. This knife slices both ways, and it frankly raises more questions in my mind than it answers potential problems on the immediate timeline of financial stability; but then just what can be done to avert a financial crisis, one must honestly ask.

Neither you nor I have any control over the government of the United States nor over the Treasury nor the Fed in these hectic days. We are mostly powerless and must sway in the breeze fanned by the boys who control the wind. This is mostly true but not totally true, which is a subject of strategic importance this morning. Each of you has a particular position at your institution that allows for rational thinking and prudent calls to action, and it may well be that call that is critical to your place of work. First and foremost, you must look at your own counterparty risks. Who do you have outstanding contracts with and what liabilities does that entail, and who are you trading with and for how much, and what clearing obligations do you have, and where are your assets held and all manner of questions to assess your own risks. These are the types of questions that must be asked and quantified and answered. On the credit side, what obligations do you own and how much exposure do you have to the financial credits? What if the Federal National Mortgage Association (FNMA) or Freddie were to blow up, and what mortgage obligations and municipals are insured? What does it mean if the insurance blows up? If you own equities, then you have to take a hard look at credits and be mindful of potential risks versus rewards in a much more stringent manner this morning. One area to be particularly mindful of now is the repo market. Here is an area where disaster could loom; if you are involved in this market, then I ask you to be more than vigilant as to collateral, term, counterparty, and extensions of credit. Please also check your money market funds, look at their top 10 holdings, and give due consideration to switching to funds that own only government instruments.

Grant's Rules 1–10 should be at the forefront of thought this morning and this week, as "Preservation of Capital" is now more important than any other consideration. You may wish to consider again the Cedar Concept, which invests money in a whole slew of certificates of deposit (CDs) that are backed by the FDIC as an option to commercial paper and various other short-term assets. You must be mindful of liquidity issues in your portfolio, as certain issues may not be able to be sold—getting bids on anything will probably be quite difficult this week. For those of you who are football fans, let the resounding roar of "Defense, Defense" do the wave across your mind-set now as you consider strategic options that may well be the underpinnings of your firm's survival. Too strong, you think; then please take a moment to remember the S&L crisis and the financial malaise of 1987.

My final thoughts of the morning are these: We are in a financial crisis, and it will not be ended with the Fed lowering rates this week. The economy is deleveraging, and we are caught in a downward spiral that will end only with increased liquidity and new capital entering the system. This will take place only when people understand the playing field, and I do not believe we are anywhere close to that reality. Cash is now prince, princess, and king.

Long live the king!

The Crisis Passes—
The Issues Remain

April 20, 2009

> Time heals all wounds.
>
> —Proverbs

Here, in one of the oldest sayings known to man, lies great wisdom that is applicable not only to love and death but also to financial catastrophes. I would make the observation that while the economic landscape may not have changed much, we are no longer in a crisis mode. Since we are all human beings, not little green aliens playing the Great Game, the psychology of the players is probably as important as the actual events. In fact, the general populace of investors seems to have settled into "acceptance" and no longer resides in panic and the "woe is me" mode. This is rather telling as an indicator for making investments, and unless we find further calamities in the immediate future, it may well be that we have settled down into a consensus viewpoint of stagnation where little is expected and little is actualized.

All mankind is divided into three classes: those that are immovable, those that are movable, and those that move.
—Benjamin Franklin

Historically, one can now say truthfully that the "hands-off" approach of the 1930s was found to be lacking as we tried the "activist" approach. Looking back, I find the bankruptcy of Lehman and the conservatorship of FNMA and Freddie Mac to be the worst mistakes to date, yet it is tough to castigate sins upon the decision makers in a time that called for critical judgments when so little historical precedent could be called upon to make rational choices. It is not that either of the last two administrations is blameless; it is just that the waters were so murky it is tough to condemn those who had to decide. What can also be said is that they moved; they did not sit quietly by and depend on the free enterprise system alone. Regardless of the political hogwash that was bandied about by our politicians for the benefit of the masses, our elected officials reacted strongly, with the insertion of public funds into the economy.

Consequently, it must be stated with appropriate recognition that when under the gun of not only economic failure but popular opinion, both presidents and that the Congress did, in fact, stand up on their hind legs and push the cart; for that, our elected officials, whom I often criticize, deserve credit.

> *There is no great trick to taking off your hat to be polite but pulling Dr. Seuss and a cat out of it is a more difficult thing to conjure.*
> —The Wizard

Courage was needed and courage was forthcoming, and the spirit of American leadership was not found in the trash heap, as some have contended, and the Wizard doffs his hat.

Theodor Geisel

Theodor Geisel is the real name of Dr. Seuss. It is possible that some of you did not know this. This is rather like the subordinated debt of some of the banks. Last Friday, the sub debt of Bank of America, just a few years out, was trading at around 10.5 percent, and the sub debt of Citigroup was trading at around 14 percent. These obligations are both senior to the position of the U.S. government, which owns preferred stock in these two companies, and this is one of the great plays now available in the bond market. Why own financial names for the dividend, with the attended risk, when you can own this paper with these kinds of yields? Something for you to consider this morning, as I do not think these kinds of spreads will be available indefinitely.

One Step Too Far

The recent announcement by the Treasury that banks will be allowed to repay bailout funds that they received from the U.S. government only if they pass a test to determine if it is in the national interest strikes me as one step too far and a dangerous step over the line. One might rationally think that it was enough to get the money back for the taxpayers, have the funds to be reutilized if necessary, collect the interest for the public, or even keep the warrants to provide additional returns allowing for substantial political chest beating, but to not allow the public's money to be repaid as a political decision, obviously exercising governmental control, just smacks of socialism and politicians trying to keep control, longer than necessary, of private institutions. The words may be frothy and the political reasoning may be based on calls for the common good, but the reality of it, no matter the flowery phrases, is the government's desire to control the financial system of the country. This strategy has social ramifications and is a plan seeped in a quagmire that this administration or any administration would do well to avoid, as the basis for election and reelection is quite often at odds with running a profitable corporate entity. If Congress wants to legislate social policy, then so be it, but to maintain control of the banking system so that it is political considerations that are the basis for the running of our country's largest banks is a mistake, in my view, of the first order.

> *By this means government may secretly and unobserved, confiscate the wealth of the people; and not one man in a million will detect the theft.*
>
> —John Maynard Keynes

Devastation on Wall Street

September 15, 2008

What do you say about yesterday? I felt like I was manning the gates while the barbarians were charging them. I was quoted in several articles by Reuters and have already been on CNBC this morning in Asia. I was pinned to my battle station from 4:00 A.M. yesterday until almost 10:00 last night with only short breaks to buy the new Apple 3G iPhone and then to have a quick dinner with friends. It was perhaps the most singular day of my professional career and also maybe the most frightening. I do not think, even though it was a Sunday, that I ever received so many business phone calls and emails in one day in my entire life. Early this morning, as I rose at 3:00 and headed to look at Bloomberg, I sat down in my chair, grabbed the arms, took three deep breaths, and braced myself. There is absolutely nothing pleasant about our current situation—nothing!

As I write this commentary, the S&P futures are down 44 points and I keep staring at the screen wishing it would go away or pop up and say "Correction" or "Bloomberg down for maintenance" or anything of that ilk, but to no avail. Lehman has filed for Chapter 11 bankruptcy, and Merrill has been purchased by Bank of America. AIG is in such a precarious financial position that they have approached the Federal Reserve Bank for help, and 10-year Treasuries are up two points as everyone flees to try to find some safety. This is the stuff of nightmares and business school case studies and scenarios that many of us could never imagine happening, and I sit here feeling a mixture of disappointment, fear, and anger that this has all taken place because I think it was preventable.

Now look—I am not here to bash anyone, nor do I take any joy in being critical of people who are trying their best, I am sure, to fulfill their obligations to their position and their country, but there is just no way around the fact that the decisions made by Secretary Paulson stand squarely in the middle of the current financial crisis. There is just no possible way to avoid what I consider to be the tremendously unfortunate positions that have been taken by the secretary of the Treasury.

I point specifically to:

- His refusing to pay the preferred shareholders of FNMA and Freddie Mac, which I believe were obligations of these two agencies just as much as the senior and subordinated debt; this has caused irreparable harm to both institutional and individual investors and severely damaged, in my view, the reputation of our country.
- What could be the virtual demise of the preferred stock market as a method to raise capital, given the way the FNMA and Freddie Mac preferred holders were treated.
- The scheme he concocted to guarantee the two government-sponsored enterprises' (GSEs) debt, which by my reading is no guarantee at all but rather an artifice that has bewildered investors globally by the actual specifics that underpin the verbiage.
- His apparent intransigence in the Lehman negotiations, which resulted in the exit of any and all potential suitors and a bankruptcy filing by this venerated and storied firm of 158 years.
- The almost certain losses that will now be incurred by the world's commercial and investment Banks as the GSE's conservatorship triggered defaults in the credit-default swap (CDS) markets that now must be settled.
- The further turmoil in the CDS markets that will result from Lehman's bankruptcy and its inability to stand up to its counterparty obligations.
- The financial fear that has been created, further exacerbating the lockup for the world's financial markets and God only knows what counterparty risks that now exist.
- The coming perhaps devastating marks-to-market that all of the lead dealers will now have to take, as Lehman will be forced to sell assets as a result of its Chapter 11 filing, which will set newer and, I am sure, lower benchmarks.
- Whatever part he has had in the decision by the Fed, and I include Bernanke in this one, this morning to now accept equities as collateral at the window to lend taxpayers' money to the primary dealers.

- The end game he created with Lehman that created collateral damage and ultimately forced Merrill Lynch to sell itself to Bank of America.
- The large losses that people holding Lehman's debt will now have to incur as a result of not providing any capital or taking on assets when Lehman could have been taken over and not gone into default.

It is not that I mind the change in the playing field; it is just human dynamics, after all, but the way this has all transpired was avoidable, in my opinion. I feel greatly saddened for my many friends at Merrill and Lehman, who will lose their jobs as a result of all of this, and the downsizing of a number of the houses that play the Great Game

I am standing at the edge of the abyss, casting whatever illumination I can find, and yet I see no end to the blackness nor anything resembling a floor of this chasm.

—The Wizard

and the shrinking of both Institutions and people that participate on Wall Street. Today is a break point with the past, and I am old enough and have been around long enough to be saddened as a result of the events that have taken place. It will be many years, if ever, before trust will be restored to the financial markets, and I feel acute disappointment in the manner in which the U.S. government has handled all of this.

Chapter 12

The American Credit Crisis

I t was, without a doubt, the most frightening time of my professional life on Wall Street. To be quite blunt about it, we did not know from day to day if the financial system of the country was going to survive or not. This is neither an exaggeration nor an understatement but the cold harsh truth of a time when everything was going straight to hell in a handbasket. Many professional money managers, including people who are quite familiar to many of you, were quaking in their boots, and I was right there shuddering along with them. I would wake up in the night with the sweats and head to the office in my home just to make sure we were all still here. Emails would be coming in all night long. and clients of mine across the globe, large institutional accounts, would be inquiring for my take on things and trying to figure out how deep our common sinkhole was so they could react accordingly. While it was an exciting time—an intellectually interesting time—there was nothing pleasant about it, and it is an experience that I hope not to go through again in my life.

Many years ago, I went diving in Tahiti, and as I rounded a coral head I came face to face with a great white shark. There was no cage

You ever see a shark's eyes. They have lifeless eyes, like a doll's eyes. Until they bite you, and the eyes roll over. Then there's the horrible scream, and the water turns red. And despite all the pounding and hollering, all the sharks come in, and rip you to pieces.

—Peter Benchley, *Jaws*

and no one else there, with me at about 105 feet down. As I looked at him dead in the eye and he appraised me, I knew this could be the end of it. As I made my way up to the decompression bar and as he followed me to the surface, I was well aware that the end of my life could be close at hand. As I decompressed to avoid getting the bends, he swam at me and I hit him in the head with a piece of plastic pipe that hung down from the 19-foot Boston whaler. That shark stopped and lay absolutely still in the water and turned very slowly toward me without one ounce of compassion in his eye; the world was defined in sharp contrast in that very terrifying moment. I am still alive to tell the tale, and those moments alone with the great white shark, along with those dark nights during the worst of the financial crisis, are no different and no less horrifying to me when I revisit the experiences in my mind.

Now you don't have life experiences such as these without learning something. If you don't, you are either a fool or worse. I have noticed that life does not suffer fools lightly, so I have tried to avoid that particular appendage being attached to my name for all of my many years on Wall Street. I have always contended that experience is the great teacher, which is why you have to a have a number of years under your belt before you are able to adequately deal with the catastrophes that invariably roll along and block your path. The people who experienced the Great Depression may have had enough knowledge to know how to play the American financial crisis or, as I call it, the Great Recession, but those people have long left the scene. So it was that I huddled with my friends and clients and had lengthy conversations at all times of the day and night. We tried to figure out what to do and how to protect the portfolios with which they were entrusted. I advised, they listened with great attention, and we all tried to figure out the counterparty risks, the fallout from the government's likely decisions, what collateral damage was strewn on the landscape, and where anyone could get hurt that we had not figured out yet. "What if" was always the question, and it was only the subject that got changed. Everyone was living through a time of great fear, and we weren't even sure of exactly what to be fearful of with each passing day.

What it felt like, as I think back, was that some unknown monster was out there waiting, lurking, and you didn't know when or what, but you knew it was out there.

You could hear its breath; you could smell the stench in the air but you couldn't see it, and you didn't know when it was going to attack. We all waited. No one wanted to go outside, and we collected all of our belongings and placed them squarely in the center of the room and sat there with the biggest guns we had to protect what we were paid to guard. It wasn't that "Capital Preservation" was the first rule; it was the only rule, and whatever exposure anyone had to anything that could impinge on that dictum was going to be shut down, cut off, and ended with all due haste, so the vault

> *I'm not afraid of storms, for I'm learning how to sail my ship.*
> —Louisa May Alcott, *Little Women*

doors were closed, the alarm set, and everything locked down. That was the way of it during those days, and since then many of us say nightly prayers to the gods of the marketplace that we will not be visited again by those horrendous circumstances.

It is not apparent in the press, nor is it written about much by anyone, but those days were game-changing events for many financial institutions. New rules were put into place at many money managers, and new regulations were imposed from the top down, and most are still in place today. It is not just the public that changed their investing habits due to the financial crisis as exemplified by the tremendous amount of money that has poured into bond funds, but insurance companies, pension funds, and lots of other managers of money have reallocated into bonds and out of equities to preserve their capital. The risk profile of investors has been changed, at least for this generation, because of the American credit crisis as the remnants of the fear that was felt by everyone will not be disappearing anytime soon.

Money is too hard to make and too easy to lose, and therein is a lesson that should not be forgotten!

Exaggerated Projections

December 27, 2007

oday, I shall endeavor to make some serious comments as I begin to peer into 2008. I think there are some "foundation" observations that may help shape the coming year. The first that I am noting is the Commodity Research Bureau (CRB) Index. It is currently at its high for the year and, more telling perhaps, just seven points off its 10-year high mark of 365.35 on May 11, 2006. This index represents a broad band of commodities and is giving us, I think, a real indication of higher base material prices that could translate into higher inflation as we head into next year. The 5-year average for the CRB is 280.83, which puts the current price at about 22 percent above the median score. While commodity prices are only part of the picture and must be balanced with the dollar/euro/yen equation, they do provide some indication that inflationary pressures are on the rise for the world's economies and that these denizens could spill over into significant pressures on yields sometime in the forthcoming 12 months. Two key components, oil and gold, do not seem to be backing down from their high levels, and the financial markets may focus in on this as the mortgage and leverage issues subside, which I believe will take place after quarter one of 2008 as the current purge of past mistakes comes to an end. I believe that we are nearing the end—I repeat, the end—of the coming clean of Wall Street. The structured investment vehicle superfund died, in my opinion, not because of the lack of financial trust, though that was certainly part of the equation, but because it wasn't needed as the major investment and commercial banks took their hits and received additional capital, as I had spoken about some time ago.

I had made the comment, which is always true, that the pain stops when new money enters the playing field, and we are seeing that now in one after another of the major financial institutions shoring up their capital base.

I lived through the savings and loan (S&L) crisis of some two decades past now, and I remember it with clarity. Ernie Fleisher, one of the linchpins of that era, was and is a family friend, and I recall in detail the travails of Franklin Savings & Loan and the inability for months to see what the truth was in that situation.

It was not just that specific situation, to be clear, but the entire S&L sector problems, and it was several quarters in duration before much clarity was available and maybe a full year before that mess was put behind the financial markets. Besides financial questions, there were legal questions and a host of scams indicating improper financial accounting that does not appear to be present in our current mess. I would make the observation that the S&L fiasco was similar to our current situation, though much more severe in both depth and breadth, and one can now see that we survived that horrible time. I can tell those of you who are newer to the financial scene that the present morass has been less awful by far than that experience.

I also believe that one real problem of our current crunch is the lack of longevity and hence memory and perhaps maturity in senior positions at many investment and commercial banks. There is no substitute for living through prior crises to put a current crisis into perspective. As a matter of fact, perspective may be the most important criterion for getting through a crisis and retaining one's skin. To be able to design and create derivative transactions is one thing, to formulate leveraged structures is another thing, but to understand the consequences to any singular firm or to the financial markets is a matter of longevity and wisdom. Risk management is crucial to any financial organization, and the lack of this management at almost every major financial institution, Goldman perhaps excepted, is telling about the idiocy that is sometimes Wall Street, where greed takes over prudence and common sense.

One of my memories about the S&L days was the constant who-can-top-who in projecting the amount of pending losses. It seemed that each passing week brought the next economist into the limelight projecting larger and larger numbers, and the truth, not known until much later, was that a lot of those projections were exaggerated by quantum leaps and bounds. I think we are undergoing the same sort of passionate hysteria today. It is my view that we are probably going to see about $150 billion in subprime/leveraged losses, which equates to 12 percent of the subprime market; subprime represents about 12 percent of the mortgage market, which gives you a quantifiable number of 1.44 percent of the general mortgage market as a loss. If you then take the mortgage market as a fragment of the general U.S. economy, you will begin to see that death and destruction is not awaiting America on the next corner, and this may well be a great time to take advantage of the current ridiculous psychology.

SLM Corporation

I do not often do this, but I would avoid the coming deal as a matter of principal. The way that debtholders have been treated by SLM during the failed buyout was a travesty, and I have made my opinion clear to SLM on more than one occasion. The management of this company deserves no support from the financial community at large, in my view, and there are better places to put one's money. Don't feed the hand that bit you!

Ratings Cuts

Get ready, it is about to happen soon, I think. Fitch has now stated that they may cut the ratings on a number of insured bonds issued by MBIA, AMBAC, FGIC, and Security Capital. If this happens, and I think it is imminent, watch for the fallout across bondland, including mortgages, asset-backeds, municipals, and pending costs of issuance. This action will cause forced sales and may impact the confidence of the retail investor. Nothing pretty will emerge from the gates when opened.

The gates that now
Stood open wide, belching outrageous
  flame
Far into
Chaos, since the fiend pass'd through.
            —John Milton, *Paradise Lost*
                        (Bk. X, l. 232)

The Cost of the Window

March 20, 2008

I f tomorrow is Good Friday, then what should today be—Interesting Thursday?

Sounds as good as anything else, so the Wizard proclaims "Interesting Thursday" today and gives you permission to think, cavort, and look forward to a long weekend. You may also be nice to your significant others and make money; you have my permission for all of that!

The investment banks are now allowed to go to the Fed window for the first time, but there are a number of issues here that have not yet been fully explored. The first and foremost is a matter of regulation. Let us not be idiots—the Fed is not going to say to these primary dealers, "Oh, take all the money you want, we will find a place for your daughter's dollhouse as collateral, and here is a hundred million or so against Billy's bike, and this mortgage on a Florida condo must be worth something." No, I am afraid that the world of the primary dealers that are investment banks will never again be the same, as the Fed will require oversight and regulation for the privilege of coming to the window. It may be that the primary dealers, besides the commercial banks, are now going to fall under the Fed's purview and that capital requirements and balance sheet ratios will get applied to the investment banks as the result of providing liquidity. This may not be a bad thing, as it would help to resolve the continuing issues of what any of the large investment banks really own at that point and what the risks might be for them. This would also be a way for the market to regain some faith, any kind of faith, in the accuracy of the numbers from the large investment banks. The outlook here is not good for the next several quarters, and I will explain why to you. The bids for securities now are points, tens of points, away from the mark-to-markets, but that will change as forced sales such as the Citadel Hedge Fund hits the markets and the pricing

■ 297 ■

services revalue the assets. That is just one example, but as sales that must be made are made at lower and lower prices and the marks are reset, then the value of the assets of all of the investment banks, commercial banks, money managers, and others will be lower, and I expect several more quarters of this carnage.

A Quick Trade

If you own some government issue due within a year and have a nice profit and are looking at a bid side yield of under 2 percent, then you might consider buying a block of FDIC-insured CDs where you can pick up 150 to 200 basis points and own the same credit, that of the U.S. government. You can choose your maturity and pick up a lot of yield—worth the look in my view.

In this time of fear, as opposed to greed, I believe the best strategy is to look for yield and forget about appreciation for the present. There will be a time, but not yet, when greed returns, but in the meantime it is yield that will give you a way out of this morass. This is not a time to sacrifice safety to achieve yield, though, and that has been my constant theme since last fall. The preservation of capital remains the watchword of the faith as we painfully get through 2008, and I do not think the pain has ended yet. It was just publicized recently that the average leverage for the large investment banks, Goldman, Lehman, Merrill, Morgan Stanley, and others, is approximately 30 to 1. This is a somewhat troubling number, but I wonder just where some of the hedge funds are leveraged. The demise of one of the larger ones of those, Citadel, was only a partial, and may mark the next leg down before this whole nightmare ends.

I would not be surprised to see another 1,000-point loss in the Dow Jones and another round of panic; though I do not vote against those who print the money, neither do I convince myself that the fix is in just because they show up.

In the long run I am a believer, but in the short run I remain as cautious as I have ever been both for the equity markets and for the bond markets. Those who survive all of this will emerge stronger and more profitable, but I can almost guarantee you that not all will make the cut!

A Financial Crisis Is a Normal Event

April 4, 2008

A financial crisis is a normal economic event.

The above statement is totally foreign to the way most of us think and have been taught about the financial system, and yet I believe that it is an accurate statement. We have any number of incidents of monetary upheavals since 1900 on which to base our judgment on my initial statement. Most have us hold the belief that each economic implosion was an irregular event, totally unpredictable and unique in its occurrence, and yet I will make the argument that this is not only untrue but a dangerous belief to hold if you are managing money. The common viewpoint holds that the nature of a financial crisis cannot be predicted, that the timing can't be predicted, and that since every event is unique, the prudent response to each financial disaster must also be unique. I do not believe that any of this is true.

I am not writing a treatise here; I shall leave that for the more academic of my friends, but I will tell you that each incident of economic calamity in the last 100 years was predicated on too much liquidity, easily obtainable credit, regulations that allowed for too much leverage, and a crisis that took place due to an event that imploded assets past the credence of the leverage.

You can examine the events of 1907, the Great Depression, the Long Term Capital Management debacle, the S&L freefall, or the current credit squeeze that was precipitated by the problems in the housing market. Each of my specified variables, is present in each and every crisis that I have mentioned or that you can name. This is a rather startling conclusion that I have arrived at after years of a belief that is 180 degrees from where I now stand. More than this—it is all predictable.

When there is too much money in the system, the result is fairly easy
to foresee, and that is greed as the mover of events, money that is too easily obtainable, lax regulations that allow for easily obtainable money, the
buildup of leverage in the investment banks, commercial banks, hedge
funds, and other financial pools of capital, and finally an event that strains
the leveraged money past its equity position. It is that simple and hence
predictable along with the appropriate responses.

It was not the Russian bonds that caused the Long Term Capital
blowup but the leverage of those bonds and other instruments they held.
It is not the decline in housing prices that is causing the current problems but the leverage allowed by the banks to buy a house, the leverage
allowed by the banks that could be borrowed against a house, the creation of financial instruments that were leveraged to provide the capital
for the houses, and finally the leveraged ownership of a vast array of
financial products that declined in value past the worth of the equity.
If you do not look at the incident but rather focus on the playing field,
then it is all quite predictable.

Change Your Viewpoint and You Change Your World
When there is:

- Too much money available
- Too little regulation of the sector or sectors where the money is
  being used
- Too easily obtainable credit
- Assets that are overly leveraged
- Securities that are overly leveraged to provide more capital and
  increase the breadth of the leverage

Then you will have a financial crisis.
Since we are all in the business of managing money, I am also happy
to inform you today that the correct responses in each and every crisis
are exactly the same.

It is unsettling, perhaps, to consider my opinion, but I believe I am
correct. In each catastrophe, liquidity disappears; greed is replaced by
fear; Treasuries have lower yields; every other security widens against
Treasuries; some part of the government pushes, pulls, or intervenes;
the stock market declines; money market assets grow exponentially

with the fear; and spreads of any type of financial credit gap out beyond other types of credits.

Correct Responses in a Financial Crisis

- Sell financial credits.
- Sell equities.
- Deleverage any leveraged positions immediately.
- Sell any illiquid positions possible.
- Buy U.S. governments.
- Raise cash and put it in government money market funds.
- Exercise patience and wait for the new levels as the crisis weakens and redeploy the cash.
- Focus on the playing field and not the incident.

The Financial Crisis

April 7, 2008

Today will end my commentary on the financial crisis as a normal part of the economic cycle. Each debacle of the last century has been different in nature but all rooted in the same exact hole in the playing field, which contains too much capital, lax regulations, an overabundance of credit, a large buildup in leverage, and finally an event—The Event—that strains the leverage past its equity position. It does not really matter that you cannot predict the event if you have a realistic view of the playing field. I call the playing field, when in this shape, the Conditions. The event is only a trigger, a singular causation that puts the dominos in motion, but that event does not require your focus if you have a clear view of the financial landscape.

The reaction to the crisis should always be the same, and it is not dependent on the trigger once the crisis has been identified as being under way. You buy Treasuries; you sell anything illiquid; you do everything you can to deleverage your positions; you sell agencies and corporates, mortgages, and everything else you can, and buy Treasuries and wait as they appreciate in value. You buy government money market funds and you reduce any exposure possible to credit and structure, and you avoid the equity markets like the plague until the dust has settled.

When new regulations have been proposed or put in place and the government has stepped in either by proxy or directly, and there have been several unpleasant consequences to the event that was the trigger, and leverage has markedly declined, then you begin the Turn. This is so critically important, in my view, that I would like to propose Grant's Corollary for Economic Crisis.

1. The Conditions
2. The Trigger

3. The Reaction
4. The Turn

I have described each part of the scenario now except the Turn. This is not particularly tricky and certainly not as complex as you may think as long as you focus on the playing field, the events that have actually happened, and not the Trigger. Here, in a bow to human frailty and everyone's lack of pertinent knowledge, I propose a measured return to normalcy and the recognition that the Turn offers you an unprecedented chance to make money. In fact, after some thought, I propose reentry using the Rule of Three or three different entry points in time, in case your view of the playing field is incorrect or in case you do not have critical knowledge that is defining the playing field in some other manner than you think is characterized at present. Entry point one is probably close to a time after government intervention, entry point two is after an event that changes the psychology of Wall Street, and entry level three occurs when the financial markets, in the broadest sense, have corrected 10 to 15 percent off their lows.

> *In this industry, there are only two ways up the ladder. Rung by rung or claw your way to the top. It's sure been tough on my nails.*
>
> —Jack Nicholson

General Motors

Here is a proper mess and a situation that is getting worse and could get much, much trickier. Last Friday, Appaloosa Management, a hedge fund, gave notice of "immediate termination" of their intention to invest $2.6 billion in Delphi, the parts maker once owned by General Motors. Delphi has been struggling to come out of bankruptcy, and this declination of Appaloosa throws the proverbial monkey wrench into the gears. Expected terms of the bankruptcy exit package, led by J. P. Morgan and Citigroup, were expected out soon, but the collapse of the equity agreement is a real blow to Delphi and to General Motors, with Delphi being their largest parts supplier. GM's shares closed down almost 5 percent on the day last Friday. In a side note, GM has had to shore up the capital in its ResCap unit, as this company continues to hemorrhage money following its $4.7 billion loss in 2007. I continue to be very leery of this credit.

Just Nowhere to Hide

July 10, 2008

have spent the last several days in New York in a series of meetings
with senior people at most of the lead banks. These get-togethers
began at breakfast and continued well into the evening, with certain
people—not to be named—who tried to poison me with red wine and
Grand Marnier that just kept appearing, magically, every time a bottle
began to dissipate. Given the state of the markets, it is somewhat surprising that any of us could afford adult libations any longer, but we somehow tightened our purse strings and dropped a few coins on the dining
tables. In tow with me were my CEO and the president of the company.
I had invited them to these few days so they could get a better picture of
what I did for a living—very hard to quantify the duties of a Wizard—
and because I thought it important that certain people should put a face
with a name. Also present was the head of taxable fixed income, who
had been designated to attend to make sure I did not misbehave or turn
some derivatives trader into a frog. I have not written *Out of the Box* for
the past several days, as each new morning brought no delight and the
aspirin I took had as much effect as a Peanut M&M, and I could not
find the "A" key on my laptop much less properly visualize the screen,
which must have been infected as it was exceedingly blurry, though my
spyware program must have worked as the screen looks perfectly fine
here in Dallas.

I thought it might be useful for some of you to have a sense of the
mood and tenor of Wall Street these days and to take a kind of macro
sampling of the general demeanor of the of the people at the primary
dealers. There will be no quotes or attributions. as today's commentary
represents my overall impressions of many subjects that were discussed
and not any particular meeting with one or the other of the lead commercial or investment banks.

Universally, I can report to you that no one thought the current financial mess was over or even close to being over. I can also share with you that virtually everyone did not trust the numbers released by their competitors, and some were not so sure of their own numbers. This is actually a puzzling situation, as several choices can be made in considering this dilemma, and no one choice may be totally accurate, depending on the institution. Allow me to explore this for a moment; one choice is that either we are being blatantly lied to or the truth is being hedged to ensure the survival of the institution. A second path to be deliberated is that the deterioration in assets is downward and unrelenting so that yesterday's numbers are no longer valid today. A third path is that some of the assets on the books are so complex and singular in nature that a real estimation of value may be valid within tens of points, though I have always believed that the correct assessment of price was what someone else would pay for the asset. It is likely that no one road is correct here, and each financial institution is unique, but what I can share with you absolutely is that no one trusts anyone else at present, and this is causing issues of its own as many of the lead banks have cut back dramatically on their counterparty obligations.

I began commenting last January that both the stock and bond markets could not withstand their current valuations given the level of real inflation. The stock market is playing itself out as predicated, and the bond markets are just beginning their adjustment. It is true that the yield for the 10-year Treasury is virtually identical to where it started the year, but that is not the whole story. Yields in the credit space have widened dramatically, and I make the argument that the curve must steepen, as short rates cannot withhold future inflation expectations. I would also make the more pronounced statement that mortgage expectations will not hold and that current mortgage assumptions are not valid, meaning that there is appreciably more extension risk in portfolios than most people now fully appreciate. I brought this up in several meetings in New York and there was not one peep of disagreement, which leads me to assume that the boys on the inside have a ringside seat at this game. For those of you involved in the mortgage portion of our business, I encourage you to consider using more realistic assumptions in your models and not to be cowed by duration models touted to you by some Wall Street salesman who is following the lead of his trader, who is trying to dump his positions. I would also advise you to keep a close eye on the pools themselves, as foreclosures were up 53 percent in June and this situation will only get worse in my view as we head down the backside of 2008.

The sad part is that America and most of the rest of the world are caught in a storm. While it may not be a "perfect storm," it is a raging affair that is battering at the hatches. The consumer and the corporation alike are now facing severely deteriorating assets, such as their home, their investments in the stock and bond markets, inventories, cost of transportation, and so on, while at the same time they are being squeezed by the real costs—forget the government hyperbole—of oil, food, basic materials, and most commodities that are taking up more and more of their available cash so that their cost of living or their profit margins are under serious pressure. In the traditional economic simulation, this kind of situation ends when new money comes into the system to take advantage of the revaluation of prices, but what if the current malaise is so severe and so much capital has deteriorated because of leverage and excess spending that new money is not willing to come forth or that fear itself has tied up liquidity to such an extent that money refuses to surface until levels are such that the current crisis worsens and evolves into places that one is loath to consider. This was a discussion with several firms, and I wish that I could report any optimistic views beyond "it is a two- to three-year workout," but I cannot make any such report.

FNMA and Freddie

It may be, as some have speculated, that the U.S. government will have to take over these government-sponsored enterprises, but I would not make a bet on that assumption. I have written for well over six months that I would do everything in my power to swap out of these names into the Federal Farm Credit Bank (FFCB) or the Government National Mortgage Association (GNMA) or some other agency or Treasuries, and now the reality is beginning to take hold. The equity prices for these firms are down 76 percent for FNMA for this year and 83 percent for Freddie and their bonds have not deteriorated to those kinds of levels yet, and *yet* is the operative word here. Spreads in these names are still relatively tight, given credit considerations, and I do not think it is too late to make the swaps now as I expect further deterioration in spreads and a widening to other agency debt.

Hedge Funds

United Capital went into liquidation yesterday after failing to meet a margin call from Deutsche Bank, and Sandelman cut off withdrawals.

I am afraid that this process will continue and accelerate for the rest of 2008, which will put further pressure on the financial system as marks-to-market will further drop prices down to new lows with the forced selling of certain assets. Each and every lead bank that I discussed this situation with in NYC was more than a little concerned about their hedge fund exposure. You may not have direct hedge fund exposure, but I can tell that their liquidations will certainly affect some of the prices of bonds you may own.

GMAC

Yesterday, General Motors Acceptance Corporation (GMAC) announced that it is buying the resort finance business from ResCap. You may wonder why Peter is robbing Paul. The answer is quite simple in my view: They are trying to keep ResCap from violating its bond covenants, though I suspect the move is too little and too late. I continue to think that the odds are good that ResCap does not survive and that GMAC and perhaps General Motors and Cerberus Capital get pulled down into the sinkhole. The cash that GM is burning is now thought to be in excess of a billion a month, and that kind of loss cannot last for long.

A Time for Contemplation

September 26, 2008

L et us all step back. This is a good morning to take a few steps to the rear and survey the financial landscape. This is a time to exercise clarity of thought and not to rush about in depression and panic. All is not as bad as it appears. In fact, I applaud democracy at work in America. I did not find, as all of you know, Secretary Paulson's feverish pitch for a vast sum of money based on a nonplan acceptable. You cannot and should not wave the flag of economic necessity without a well-reasoned schematic to deal with the problems and that, frankly, was never presented to Congress, only a promise to institute a plan at a later date. Not good enough; just not acceptable in my view.

Interestingly enough, it is the economic conservatives of the Republican party that are up in arms. I do not blame them. Many of you on foreign shores may be aghast as to the turn of events, but this is how it is supposed to work; there are times, certainly not as many as one would like, when political considerations yield to what is the best for the country. To present a nonplan devoid of specifics and have it approved would have been terrible for America, as it placed too much power in the Treasury and not enough in the elected representatives of the people, it would have allocated vast resources to a concept without definition and would have left investors of all classes in a kind of economic limbo that may well have produced worse results given the patterns of the recent past, and most certainly, in my opinion, would have increased the level of fear due to its incredible ambiguity. Now it seems we may arrive at a well-reasoned plan hammered

A leader is a dealer in hope.
—Napoleon Bonaparte

out by conservatives and liberals alike that will specify not only the methodology of the rescue but define the utilization of the funds. To think that one can achieve this overnight is folly, but to watch the process with the belief that it will get done in a measured fashion is really a cause for hope and not despair.

The major event of yesterday, the seizure of Washington Mutual by the regulators and the sale of most of its assets to J. P. Morgan, is also a sign that the financial system is functioning. It no doubt is under strain and is groaning and shrieking under the pressures of quite real complications, but it continues to function. In fact, the largest bank failure ever in America, eclipsing Continental Illinois, will cost the taxpayers very little, if any, money as JPM is backstopping most of the assets as our most white shoe of banks finally and with decisive timing becomes a retail bank that will attract a broad base of customers given its financial acumen and long-standing reputation. Here, in the stroke of a brush, J. P. Morgan will have access for the first time to the money of Main Street America, and firms such as Merrill Lynch and Morgan Stanley may well feel, in time, the shoe heels of JPM as people find safety in dealing with a financial institution of this stature. Here is a deal where JPM paid the government $1.9 billion to acquire the institution, which is a welcome sight of money "in" to the taxpayers instead of "out." As a matter of fact, I would consider, at current spreads, some of the debt instruments of JPM now, as they are likely to emerge from this as the behemoth of the financial world.

As a matter of comparison, the United States is not doing as badly as many as this crisis plays itself out. While the Dow Jones Index is down 16.91 percent year to date, we find the Dow Jones Euro Stox Index down 28.13 percent and the Hang Seng Index down 32.83 percent for the comparable time period. While spreads have widened significantly in debt, the vast majority are still paying, and while marks-to-market reflect the anguish of the financial crisis and the London Interbank Offered Rate (LIBOR) is just shy of 4 percent all across the short curve, please allow me to point out that it is not the drastic impairment

Rattle me out of bed early, set me going, give me as short a time as you like to bolt my meals in, and keep me at it. Keep me always at it, and I'll keep you always at it, you keep somebody else always at it. There you are with the Whole Duty of Man in a commercial country.

—Charles Dickens, *Little Dorrit*

that some of the talking heads would lead us to believe. We are in a difficult moment, it is true, but we are not closed for business.

A Brief Note from Me Personally to You Personally

Imagine for a moment that we are sitting on the back of my boat sharing a Grand Marnier and a cigar of some note. The sea is quiet and we hear the creaking of masts far off in the distance. The sun has fallen below the horizon and the world seems a quiet place. We smile in the joy of the moment, even as our foreheads are marked by the furrowing of our brows brought on by quiet contemplation.

I have often contended, my friend, that age and experience give each of us the opportunity to gain a little wisdom. It is not a guaranteed process, no doubt, but we do have the possibility. I have been on Wall Street for quite some time now, some 34 years, and I am gladdened to share with you that I have been here before. The value of time is that you may return to seldom seen locations and not be so fearful of the peculiarities of the locale. The anguish of the U.S. Congress coming to grips with reality is not to be marked with sadness or desperation, but with a marked sense of relief that these people are striving to impose a carefully thought out solution to the manifestations of economic problems brought on us by the convergence of a number of embers that have long seethed in the pit of the financial world and which have recently been ignited by the winds of convergence. The flag waving and wringing of hands and cries of panic and despair have caused me considerable alarm, and the initial proposed solutions seemed like a tattered sail in the storm, but rational thinking is returning to guide the ship after being waylaid by the masters proclaiming Armageddon and the opening of the gates of hell. Please allow me to share with you that I do not believe we are heading into Hell in a hand basket or any other conveyance and that prudent thinking, absent for some time from our political process, seems to be returning, even though it may be disguised in the quarrels of vehement men with differing opinions. All good, I say; the proclamations of debate are upon us and reasoned men are striving for an actual course with a chart in hand and not shrieking wildly that they have seen the Sirens of the Isles and causing confusion, fear, and panic.

Do not despair; do not lose hope, and do not abandon your common sense or your ability to reach sound judgments. Do not curtail your rational thinking when others are shouting "Fire" lest you get trampled in the headlong rush to the exits. The cry to battle requires a well-thought-out plan, a necessity somehow forgotten by some members of the current administration, but the generals have gathered to remind some of the participants how a war is to be fought. In any event, with our elections hard upon us, and to paraphrase one of my longtime heroes of American folklore, Yogi Berra, soon we will throw these bums out!

And Into the New Year

January 2, 2009

I t is the first day of the New Year, and it seems appropriate to take a very macro view of our present circumstances and to peer out into the mists of the future. I thought I would undertake this task, as I have heard nothing nor seen anything that is reflective of my viewpoint of what is to come. What I have seen is a lot of comparisons to the Depression or the "Great Depression," as those selling things are wont to call it in hopes of stirring the imagination and selling more newspapers or more ad time on some television station. I am not fond of emotionally charged words, as they tend to direct one's thinking process in directions that should not be undertaken based on the fear and provocative visual images that these kinds of words enlarge in our minds.

Neither, while I may be intellectually capable of it, am I going to lay out complicated paradigms or quote proverb and verse from noted economists that may have the right answer, or not, if only we mere mortals could figure out what the heck the guy was saying. No, none of that this morning, just an attempt on my part to lay out my vision of where we may be heading.

The simple truth that ends a financial crisis is money—more money, and when the new money shows up in adequate size and for a long enough period of time, then the crisis ends. This notion can be couched in all kinds of ways and with many axioms, but there you have it. In the 1929 crisis, the Hoover administration chose by decision or indecision to leave it to free enterprise to cure the problem; while this may work over some very protracted period of time, it was not adequate to pull America from the worst financial catastrophe in our history minus the Civil War, which many forget, or the inception of our country, which is now shrouded in the veils of history and respectful homage. It was not until Roosevelt was in charge and the public works programs got under way that the situation began to change because, as stated earlier, new money showed up. Now we are taking a different tack as the confluence of greed, chance, idiocy, and poor planning have once again laid us back at the lion's door.

The comparison between 1929 and now is valid, but the response and more importantly the "result" of the response will be radically different, and that is where I break from the generic wisdom of the moment. The present administration—and certainly the next one, if their pronouncements are to be believed—is going to and has been bringing in the "money of last resort," which is money/credit of the entire nation to bear on the problem. The federal government controls one thing that is singular to everything and everyone else: the monetary printing press. Any prudent reading of any measure that may be looked at indicates quite clearly that both tremendous monetary and fiscal stimulus programs are under way that will, in my opinion, end this crisis much sooner than the last one of this magnitude as new money is showing up. The government may bumble around, as I think it has, with the Lehman debacle roiling the financial markets, and the bankruptcy of our two housing agencies roiling public trust, but still the monetary floodgates are wide open, time passes, wounds are licked, and cash is flowing. So we will have deflation now caused by the decline in the world's economies, and then tremendous inflation that will cure the problem of severe price declines in basic commodities and real estate, but cause another set of problems for interest rates and the equities markets as the costs of goods and services will ratchet up wildly unless—and here is the one major rub—Congress is able to put such regulations in place that will not allow the repeat of the mistakes that caused the problems in which we now find ourselves embroiled. This issue may be the most serious of all because if it isn't done right, then we will go down, go up, and then find ourselves on an economic roller coaster from which there is no way to exit except by financial collapse. It is my view that we have adequate resources to weather the first round and climb out of the current morass, but that is all we have and we better do this right or the country itself will be in jeopardy.

The floodgates or regulations that should control the return to some sort of normalcy and prevent one more return to financial calamity should include controlling credit when available again, no more undocumented loans, oversight of hedge funds and their regulation by the Securities and Exchange Commission (SEC), the credit-default swap (CDS) market that is on some exchange and open to a much larger array of financial institutions and the public alike, the ability to borrow against assets such as real estate set with strict standards for down payments as exemplified by margin requirements for equities, strict definitions of who may use derivatives and in what capacity, what purpose, and in what size so that overleveraged risks are not allowed for America's financial institutions—period.

So the question remains as to how we play this as professional investors. The answer really lies in the time frame that one wishes to consider. First, I would not bet on the financial calamity scenario, as I think the odds of it are relatively low. My bet is on deflation now, inflation to come, and the lessening of fear over time. Just last Wednesday, two days ago, we began to see some changes under way as end-of-the-year plays were made in the oil market and the long bond. My first move now as we enter 2009, and one that I can tell you is going to be made by a number of large financial institutions that are my clients, is going to be the beginning of exiting the Treasury market and in size. This market, in my view, was the hero of 2008 and will be the Turkey of this year. I think the move is out of Treasuries, out of agencies, and into the FDIC-insured paper as long as the spread makes sense, and I would go no longer than maybe 18 months in maturity and only own this paper for liquidity purposes. I would be a buyer of corporate credits where the government has a junior position, and while spreads may have tightened in 50 bps in the last month, I think we have another 200 to 300 bps to go as we come off historically wide spreads that had never been seen before. I think that real estate has further to go in decline, and the same for securitizations tied to them. I find the equities market a fool's paradise now, and I would only remain with what does not make sense to exit. Preferred stocks at current yields have some enticement, but their value may be whipsawed by a better credit environment, long maturities, deflation then inflation, and increasing yields for all the capital markets.

For thogh we sleep or wake, or rome, or ryde,
Ay fleeth the tyme; it will no man abyde.

—Geoffrey Chaucer,
The Clerk's Tale, 1390

This will be a year, I think, to be quick on your feet, and transactional costs be damned, as they are a minuscule cost compared to finding yourself in the wrong place at the wrong time. Asset allocation may well be the most important decision of 2009, as I suspect a strong tide will be running both in and out before this year comes to an end 12 months from now.

The Lessons of a Financial Collapse

August 11, 2009

M ost of life should be spent looking forward. The moments for backward glances can be productive, though, as they allow us to assess the road we have traveled. Where we have been may be indicative of where we might go, and that judgment is useful, but what I find particularly helpful is not to apply the past to the future, but to gain from the understanding of where we have been, and here, there is a distinction of note. So this morning, in the early morning hours before the

> *Life is a succession of lessons which must be lived to be understood.*
> —Helen Keller

sun brightens up the waters that surround my boat, I have pondered the financial travesty from which we are emerging in hopes that I might learn something from the experience.

As I sat on the stern of my boat at Harbor Island in the Bahamas, several things came to mind: first, that it had been a long time since I hear heard roosters crowing in the day and that they were in prominence on this August morning, and second was that the ocean was as still and unperturbed as a small pond in my home state of Missouri, and that water like this, similar to the elusive green flash, was what boaters dream about when imagining upcoming adventures. A very good morning for a cigar, some strong black coffee, and pondering!

The first thing that came to my mind was that in the initial stages of a recession, a move out of riskier assets and into the top of the food chain should be the hallmark decision. This means out of equities and out of preferreds and into Treasuries until the length and depth and breadth of the decline can be understood. A recession is a dynamic process compounded by fear, though, and Treasuries were not the place to remain indefinitely. The second move was out of Treasuries and into corporate bonds, and, in our recent experience, safety was found in standing behind the government's position. To have remained in equities, even at this date in the recovery, was and is a painful experience signified by the poor choice of remaining at the bottom of the capital structure when the financial world is crumbling about you. The next lesson attaches itself to preferred stocks and whether it was FNMA or Freddie or the forced conversion by Citigroup or the number of corporations that decided not to pay their preferred dividends, this space was another disaster along with being in the stock market.

As a general observation, I would note that when serious financial problems arise, we should exit, to the extent possible, the lower rungs of the capital structure and do it with some haste and deliberation as we wait out the severity of the crisis. It is far easier to endure your marks-to-market and still collect your coupons rather than find your portfolios 60 percent down in equities as your dividends get suspended and face a similar fate if you are weighted down in preferreds as companies decide to stop payments to save cash. After our recent experience, there is a giant red line in my mind that separates equities and preferreds from bonds, and it shall remain there for the rest of my tenure on this planet.

Then there is Lehman and counterparty risk and the incredible importance of knowing clearly with whom you are doing business and the extent of your risk and commitments with other firms. This leads us to capricious decisions that will certainly accompany any severe economic downturn and the general word of caution that surrounds politicians making financial decisions and the clear warning marker that their motivations and hence their methodology for arriving at conclusions bear little or no resemblance to prudent business judgments.

There is also a lesson in velocity to be learned. The pace and severity of the downturn was truly like a razor-sharp knife slicing through butter, while our ratcheting back up is similar to a snail's slosh by comparison. A recession is absolutely like hitting a wall and going nowhere but straight down while the return to normalcy proceeds like a long trudge up steep stairs. "Preservation of Capital," Grant's Rules 1–10, has been constantly enforced and reinforced during this entire process, and it must be the theme of each and every day during financial declines. If your capital is mostly intact, you can live to fight another day, but when half or more of it has been lost, then the road back is incredibly difficult.

Next there is the issue of liquidity. The further afield you play from the mainstream of investing, the more chance of freefall. This was proven time and time again with one exotic product after another, as there just were no bids or the bid was so far away from any kind of perceived value that hitting it was like taking a knife stab to the gut—incredibly painful. Then there was the overreliance, by many, on the ratings agencies that proved out to be, once again, a disastrous mistake, though they do allow for the excuse to be made that it was them and not us, but still huge sums of money were lost because of them. It may be that the reliance on these people gives you legal liability coverage, but make no mistake about it: "It was you, babe," to paraphrase the singer Cher, that lost the money nevertheless.

When you sit at the feet of the Sage and he asks you what you have learned, you must be able to look him directly in the eye and recant. No minimization, no exaggerations, just the truth the best you can tell it. Then you must return to the present reality and try to apply that experience to the world about you, and be unflinching in that task. Then, with resolute purpose, you must bend your view of the future to the wisdom that you have hopefully acquired, and so the Wizard, himself, recants!

Chapter 13

The Bailout

I t is my opinion, which has not been well received by those in government, that the root cause of the American financial crisis was the United States Congress.

Had they set rules in place that limited leverage for the banks, then no bailout would ever have been needed—would never been necessary to have taken place. You can imagine how fond our politicians are of my viewpoint; not at all, but I think this is the truth of it.

The only reason a great many American families don't own an elephant is that they have never been offered an elephant for a dollar down and easy weekly payments.

—*Mad* magazine

Many people are confused by the financial meltdown and by the bailout that took place as a result of it, but I believe I can make it clear. If you own a house that costs $1 million and you have no mortgage and it declines in value by 15 percent, then you have an asset that is worth $850,000 and a potential loss, but you go on living in the house and life continues. If, however, you own a $1 million house and you have a 95 percent mortgage on the house, meaning that you owe $950,000, and the house declines in value the same 15 percent to $850,000 and your adjustable rate mortgage increases so that you must pay more each month and you can no longer afford the payments, while your equity in the house is now negative $100,000, then you have some real problems. This very simplistic example is exactly what happened to the American banks as they were all leveraged up to levels that were irresponsible in an attempt to make more money, which is all quite fine unless the underlying assets that support the leverage have a serious decline in value.

It was not that the banks were generally corrupt or fraudulent; it is that they were not regulated properly by the government. Then the economy hit the proverbial wall, first in subprime mortgages, and then the damage became collateral so that the value of almost every asset class you can imagine declined in value and the assets could not support the weight of the leverage. The bombs exploded, and everyone ran for the exit door all at the same time, and we all know what happens when that happens: splat!

So now we come to the bailout and what must be done to save the financial system, and *capricious* becomes the operative word. To be fair, perhaps, there was no way around it, and perhaps this is just what happens in a crisis, but I must say that I was not pleased with the results. Shuttling off Bear Stearns to J. P. Morgan and bankrupting Lehman Brothers were not the correct answers, and both of these responses caused unnecessary problems and systemic risks that were just not the right responses; the American financial system still has not recovered from these shocks.

The banking world is an intertwined affair, both domestically and internationally, and the counterparty obligations of these two institutions that were shunted off on all of the survivors took an additional heavy toll on everyone's assets. Then to force the remaining banks all to take Troubled Asset Relief Program (TARP) money, when some surely did not need it, is another example of very poor decision making. Next there was the Federal National Mortgage Association (FNMA) and Freddie Mac—problem children, no doubt—but to have Congress demand that they lend more and at lower rates and then to castrate them for doing so—*idiocy* would be my choice of words here. Finally, there was the decision to stop paying the dividends on the two housing agencies' preferred stock, just months after recent issuances, which brought into question the actual guarantee of the word of the United States government and sent a sonic shockwave throughout the world's financial markets that was

> *When did the future switch from being a promise to being a threat?*
> —Chuck Palahniuk

totally uncalled for and could have been avoided. It was, in fact, a bailout that caused everyone else to bail, and we are still throwing the water over the sides because of it.

As you read this chapter, you will note that I am angry. I was plenty angry then and I am still angry now. Many of the decisions made during the bailout were just poorly thought out, and while reasoned heads that made prudent judgments should have prevailed, what took place was a series of verdicts that had political and personal motivations at their roots. There is no way of getting around the facts, in the first instance, that Hank Paulson came from Goldman Sachs, and when he had the opportunity to destroy two of his main rivals, he did so while lofting the worldwide championship belt of the Wall Street Wrestling Federation high above his head. He contended then and he contends now that his decisions were all above board and in the best interests of the country, but I for one am not buying. Assets could have been propped up, as with AIG, or money could have been lent with preferred stock taken as with so many other institutions, or guarantees of assets could have been put in place for some time period—there were all kinds of options, but to cause massive counterparty defaults was thinking of the poorest kind.

> *If people behaved like governments, you'd call the cops.*
>
> —Kelvin Throop

To this date, we do not know all of the final effects from the bailouts and from the forced changes in the financial landscape. I have seen no signs of collusion or of fraud or of some tale where all of the banks acted in unison to try to do anything. I know that the banks were overleveraged and that this was done to try to make more money and that it could have been prevented by Congress or by the Securities and Exchange Commission, both of which did a lousy job in patrolling the banks. I have seen our politicians make every attempt to whip up the frenzy of the masses so as to redirect the responsibility. I have watched as the bailout money, the TARP funds, has been paid back and while the government has made profits on their intervention after the fact. All of this I have witnessed.

All of this being said, there would have been no need for any bailouts had the Great Game been properly managed.

> *The government's view of the economy could be summed up in a few short phrases: If it moves, tax it. If it keeps moving, regulate it. And if it stops moving, subsidize it.*
>
> —President Ronald Regan

The Death of Logic and Proportion

September 17, 2008

I returned home last night from dinner, read the press releases on AIG, and thought someone must have dropped some hallucinogenic substance in my drink. I went to sleep and thought surely I would get up in the morning only to find it was some weird, surrealistic dream. Nothing has changed in my coffee-infused morning. so I am stuck with the reality and just flat dumbstruck by the Treasury's decision and the course of events!

"I wonder!" said he, leaning back and staring at the ceiling. "Perhaps there are points which have escaped your Machiavellian intellect. Let us consider the problem in the light of pure reason."
—The eminent Sherlock Holmes

Let us consider the events of these financially historic, if not catastrophic, past few weeks and try to make some sense of them and what it will eventually mean for our futures. Let us reason calmly and try to be devoid of as much emotion as the circumstances will allow as we try to create a comprehensive picture of what has changed, where we are now, and where we are likely to find ourselves. Please allow me to apologize up front for my powers of observation in the present conditions as I have always held that to comment on the news is a rather mundane affair, but to extrapolate the repercussions from the news—there is the trick of it.

Let Us Examine the Facts

The U.S. Department of the Treasury has placed two agencies created by Congress into bankruptcy. A scheme has been developed that appears to guarantee their debt for some short period of time, does not pay the dividends to the preferred holders, nullifies for a generation any meaning of an implicit guarantee of a government-sponsored enterprise (GSE), voids the worth of a federal charter, and casts a pall over the entire U.S. housing market while sending shockwaves into each and every corner of the financial marketplaces. The credit-default swap (CDS) market, to this very moment, does not know the size and breadth of all of the outstanding contracts regarding the two housing agencies and has not yet figured out an agreeable plan to allow for settlements, and we still do not know the cost of the losses.

The American government takes collateral to help provide a buy-out for Bear Stearns, and then refuses to follow the same path for Lehman Brothers. Round two has now rung in the match, as again no one has any real handle on the number of CDS contracts outstanding or counterparty obligations that have been violated or derivative contracts that now have defaulted all because of the intransigence of the U.S. government that caused each and every potential buyer to fold. The Chapter 11 filing of Lehman has also caused one historic event: the "breaking of the buck," for the first time in American money market fund history, by the Reserve Fund. They apparently held almost $800 million in Lehman commercial paper and did not have the funds to backstop the loss. This unprecedented and tragic event was caused by the Lehman bankruptcy. This morning we find the venerated American broker-dealer part of Lehman has been bought by a British bank so that the United States has ceded one more part of its financial community to foreign ownership, and one can only be reminded of England long ago dismantling its empire.

Next, the American government takes over a private company, the world's largest insurance company, by force majeure, lends $85 billion to this private insurance company, AIG, not regulated by any federal agency; on the basis of its size, the government takes an 80 percent equity ownership, fires the CEO, and replaces the CEO with one of the government's choosing, and the American citizenry now owns not only an insurance company but probably the largest and most complicated book of derivative contracts in the world. The plain fact is that we have now nationalized a private company and I wonder if we are now following the playbook of France or Hugo Chavez?

I say to you frankly and unabashedly, I have never in my entire life seen such wrongheaded thinking by any member of any administration as we are now witnessing with the secretary of the Treasury. Are we now going to pay the preferred holders of AIG after we have left the same holders of the government housing agencies lying prostrate in the dust? Do we now rely on foreign ownership of our financial system much the same way as we rely on foreign ownership for our oil supply? Are we now going to nationalize GM or Ford or perhaps GE or IBM because under the Federal Reserve Act the government is empowered to do this if there are "unusual and exigent" circumstances, which were the passages the Treasury invoked when taking over Bear Stearns?

These are not only historic times but a time that I fear we will look back on with both shame and grief, and I am saddened by the implications of what our government has done that may well never be corrected!

On the Waterfront

September 23, 2008

T he sentiments of that classic movie ring through from 1954 till now as we all wonder if we are on our feet. We may be standing, but I would say that we are wobbling and that the Department of the Treasury has not been much help. The inconsistencies of their deci- sion making have been just appall- ing, and yet they have asked Congress for even more and unprecedented power, which I hope will not be given. Constitutionally, I am not sure they can be granted what they seem to demand from Congress, but that remains to be seen. The Treasury bankrupted two federally chartered GSEs, stopped the payment of the preferred div- idends, and then took an equity stake in AIG, a company they national- ized, and they have not asked them to cease their preferred dividends. Where is the sense in that? The Treasury backstopped Bear Stearns for J. P. Morgan but refused to help Lehman. Where is the sense in that? I am in favor of a plan to help homeowners and rescue the American financial system, but I do not think Secretary Paulson is making great decisions, and I have yet to find anyone who disagrees with my premise that his decisions have been woefully inconsistent. A number of peo- ple on Wall Street think that I should cut him some slack, but I ask each of you what good has come of bankrupting our housing agencies when additional capital could have been injected in exactly the same manner as AIG was treated or the government could have taken sen- ior debt from two companies they already oversaw, or both could have been totally nationalized but the path chosen has just wreaked havoc on the preferred holders, many of which are banking institutions that were

> **Terry:** *Get me on my feet.*
> **Father Barry:** *How're you doing?*
> **Terry:** *Am I on my feet?*
> —*On the Waterfront,*
> with Marlon Brando

allowed, if not encouraged, to own those shares as part of their capital structure, which makes no sense because these are the same institutions we are trying to protect. Moreover, the decision by Mr. Paulson has destroyed a long-held method for raising money—selling preferred shares as a substitute for equity—which is now something that has surely disappeared along with any major investment banks. No, no slack; there have been wrongheaded decisions made, and that is my viewpoint.

To provide some substance for my viewpoint, let me point to a letter to Congress sent yesterday by the American Bankers Association. They say that American banks have lost about $10 to $15 billion on the FNMA and Freddie Mac debacles and that 27 percent of American banks held the preferred shares in their portfolios. They point to the 85 percent that were community banks, and in a letter to the Treasury and other Agencies they stipulate that each dollar in capital represents $7.60 in lending and that the losses incurred from the nonpayment of the housing agencies' dividends will restrict lending by some $76 to $114 billion; they have asked the Treasury and Congress to pay some reasonable level of dividends. I give my absolute support to this proposal, and I wonder just how much and for how long the reputational damage caused by Secretary Paulson's ill-thought-out decision here will affect the finances of the United States.

I am but a single citizen with a small voice. As a private citizen, I wrote to Congress myself about these issues. I was raised to be a stand-up guy, and while I am totally in favor of Congress providing relief in this rather severe crisis that we find ourselves in at present, I am not in favor and will not cut any slack to support decisions that have been made and implemented that I feel have been a disservice to my country, and that, my friends is just that!

Let Us Look Now Further Down the Road

Yesterday, the Fed changed the rules for ownership in the banks that the Treasury penalized to allow for a larger share of outside ownership with less regulation. The Fed edict now allows for a 33 percent outside ownerships position. It had previously been 25 percent, without direct supervision by the Fed, including a 15 percent ownership in the common stock of any banks, and they have allowed, for the first time, seats on the board of directors for these outside owners. The truth is that the federal government participated in impairing the capital of many of these institutions and now seeks to allow outsiders to inject capital. I truly wonder where is the sense in any of this?

The Monetization of the New Debt

Here is an interesting side note to the bailout plan that deserves some thinking. If the cost to the taxpayers is $700 billion and the debt is monetized, which it surely will be, then we have added 7 percent to the M3 money supply, which, by my way of thinking, is going to cause a rout in inflation. No one has discussed this much, but the incredible leap in the price of oil, gold, and commodities yesterday suggests that there are some people thinking this through. Treasuries, up now on a flight to safety, may be the next big loser as the markets figure out the inflationary ramifications of this bailout. I continue to think that bonds linked to inflation represent one of the best values of any debt instrument at this time. and I point specifically to the new Citigroup 5-year offering with an 8 percent initial coupon and a 2.50 percent spread to the Consumer Price Index (CPI). The coupon at current CPI of 5.50 percent would be 8 percent, which is +504 bps to the 5-year Treasury and much more attractive, in my view, than Citigroup nominals.

Congress Understandably Balks

September 24, 2008

It has been remarked upon several times that Congress is not really dangerous unless it is in session. Not only are the boys hard at it now, but the press is actually paying attention to them. This has to do with the financial crisis, of course, and it gives them a chance to parade around, puff up their chests, and call everyone "right honorable," which in Congress talk means "you frigging thief" unless you are a member of the same party, and then it means "you frigging thief." It truly gets frightening when one congressman stands up and compares preferred stock to the telephone company's "friends and family" plan. God help us for electing these people, as I am afraid we are getting what we paid for, and it is obvious that we have been way too stingy.

Now, of course, the Treasury and the Fed are asking us to put our money up. The Fed chairman has told Congress—and I am not kidding here—that we need to pay more for some distressed assets than market value. Heck, every time I go to buy new boat shoes and the fellow says "$89," I offer him $103 just to be a good sport like all of the rest of you do, I am sure. I say this to Chairman Bernanke: "I already give enough to charities and I don't need you to do it for me, but thanks." The one piece of good news here is that you can now all fire your pricing services and save some money. The Fed is now going to tell you how to value what you own, and I have not seen one indication that they are going to make you pay for it. This may be the only favorable part of the whole $700 billion bailout.

It is truly amazing how times have changed. Under some former administrations, anyone proposing nationalizing private companies and bankrupting governmental agencies would have ended up at Farmer

Mac's Funny Farm, and now he is the secretary of the Treasury. What next—hire Hugo Chavez to advise Bush on how to take over companies and still remain president? Reuter's commented this morning, "In a mark of the urgency the administration attaches to the bailout, Vice President Dick Cheney traveled to Capitol Hill to urge Republican lawmakers to back the plan." This begs the question of where the heck was Cheney that he needed to travel to Congress; if he was where he was supposed to be, he could have just walked. Of course, politicians don't allow the vice president to walk much, as they fear "exercise in futility." I am not sure why Bush sent Cheney in any event; he is so disliked there that the only thing that comes to mind is some kind of weird political reverse psychology. Perhaps no one else wanted to go, and who could blame them? Secretary Paulson has also asked Congress not to let the courts interfere with his actions. There is a rumor that someone reminded him that the United States had a Constitution, and he seemed rather surprised and indicated that there was nothing about it in the training program at Goldman Sachs.

I have watched with interest as the chairman of the House Financial Services Committee, Barney Frank, has said that any institutions taking federal loans should limit executive compensation. He said any executive who took one was "selfish and unpatriotic." In the spirit of fairness, which seems to have fled the political scene these days, I think it is only right, since Congress provided oversight for the two bankrupt housing agencies, that Congress should also take a pay cut. Strangely enough, I have not seen any mention of this offered by our elected officials. Probably just an oversight in the press.

One piece of the current process is truly amazing to me. Bernanke and Paulson have stated and restated that we need to pass the $700 billion bailout package within seven days. I have been schooled in the notion that it took God that long to create the Earth, and then he had to rest; now appointed officials of the government are asking for the same time frame and expect results from this Congress? I would ask any of you who know what these boys have been drinking to tell me so I can avoid the stuff. Then there is the notion that the $700 billion should be coughed up before we know what we are buying; that kind of money represents about $2,000 for every man, woman, and child in the United States. Bernanke and Paulson have stated that they have no specifics as of yet and that they will design a process in the coming weeks to buy up the mortgage assets after consulting with outside experts. This seems equivalent to walking into Wal-Mart and telling the manager that you want to buy some clothes and handing them a large check and then waiting to see what kind of clothes they bring you. The store manager may tell you that he will consult with experts on attire before the clothes are delivered, but purchasing clothes in this manner does not seem the best approach to me, and no one I know at any clothing store has ever suggested it, so I find myself wondering about the idea of buying something before you know what it is that you are actually purchasing. Something is not quite kosher here! I would also like to know who these outside experts are going to be—what if Elmer Fudd is on vacation or Speedy Gonzales cannot be reached?

In a barely mentioned part of the $600 billion U.S. spending bill that was passed by the Senate overwhelmingly and will probably come to a vote in Congress on Wednesday is a provision to give $25 billion in low-cost loans to the automotive industry. This includes General Motors, Ford, and Chrysler. I have searched and searched through the legislation, but I cannot find any mention of limiting executive compensation for the automakers as part of the package. Must be a typo, I am sure. I do enjoy getting up early to read the newest financial articles, as they all say were are entering a new chapter in the American economy; I am no dummy and know this chapter well; it is Chapter 11, which I have tried to avoid all of my life, so I find it somewhat demoralizing that our political leaders are trying to hand it to us and do it in seven days. I have been hearing some rumors about the financial experts that Paulson and Bernanke might use, by the way, and the super secret plan entails getting all of the bank CEOs to converge in Hollywood with Howie Mandel and play "Deal or No Deal." To be honest, this is superior to any plan I have heard proposed by the administration.

Finally, in all fairness to Congress, I do not blame them one iota for balking at Paulson's and Bernanke's cry for help. To be honest, the presentation has been amateurish at best. To come and ask for $700 billion on the basis of economic emergency without a well-thought-out plan risks exactly what they are getting: hesitancy. They have detailed no specifics, said they will use outside experts that they have not named, said they will buy mortgage assets above market price using some formula to be conceptualized in the future with no rational construct yet presented, and yet at the same time demanding immediate passage is just a burlesque folly that any prudent man would suspect. To present a well-thought-out plan and to ask for advice, consent, and approval is one thing, but to present an apparition and ask for approval and expect that Congress would not ask if this was, in fact, a ghost should not surprise any person with any amount of common sense.

We Have Now Pledged $4.7 Trillion

November 24, 2008

The big news overnight was the U.S. government's rescue of Citigroup. I sent out the news and then the terms of the deal at about 2:00 A.M. EST, and you should all have them under separate headings. To me, the important news was that the new preferred is on the same footing with the outstanding Citigroup preferred shares, and then that the dividend will be cut to $0.01 per quarter for a minimum of three years unless approved by the government.

Here is one more case where the play is to own senior debt and not the equity. It may be advantageous, as some have suggested, to be the partner of the government and also take stakes in the outstanding preferred shares, but I am quite happy being the senior partner to the government, thank you very much; I think the better play is to own the senior debt. Now, the world being what it is, we may well see senior debt get coughed up this morning and at attractive levels, and I would give some thought to taking advantage of this situation. A corollary consideration now is AIG senior holding company debt. Here is another example of an opportunity to be the government's senior partner, as the Feds own the preferred shares. Depending on maturity, yields are available in the 12 to 14 percent range for AIG Holdco debt, and I think this opening has a lot of upside potential.

UBS

Reuters quotes the Swiss SonntagsZeitung newspaper overnight that the Swiss government may well have to inject more capital into UBS. The director of the Swiss Banking Commission said a takeover of UBS was unlikely and ruled out a merger with its rival, Credit Swiss. Now UBS's shares have lost more than 50 percent of their value in the past 30 days, and I have looked at their financials this morning and taken into account the rescue package that is already in place. I have reached the conclusion that their debt spreads just do not adequately reflect the risks associated with this institution, and I would caution you here, as I feel that the risk factor outweighs the reward unless there is a marked backup in spreads from current levels.

Corporate Bonds

Financial markets present many possibilities, of both a positive and negative nature, and we are being presented an outstanding positive one in this sector now, in my opinion. Long-term corporates have declined in value more than 18 percent through October, which is the worst decline on record going back to 1926, according to Morningstar. Never before have we seen spreads like this over Treasuries. I continue to think that present investments in this sector will be very rewarding in the times ahead, and I continue to think that it is the most compelling area in capital markets, as I think that equities are the worst place to be in a recessionary environment. I advise seeking strictly to senior corporate debt in the secondary market.

A Picture that Is Decidedly NOT Pretty

The U.S. government is ready to lend a total of $7.4 trillion of the taxpayer's money to various institutions. That number is just appalling and is my recent count of where we are now plus the new capital being injected in Citigroup. That number is 50 percent of everything produced in the country last year, and only $700 billion of this has been approved by Congress. The Federal Reserve is now lending an astonishing 1,900 times the weekly average for the three years before the crisis. These numbers are based on data supplied by Bloomberg and include $2.4 trillion to buy up commercial paper and $1.4 trillion from the Federal Deposit Insurance Corporation (FDIC) to guarantee bank-to-bank loans. The current financial crisis has now erased $23 billion or 38 percent of the value of all of the major companies in the world. The Fed has authorized $4.4 trillion of this number, and while most people concentrate on the $700 billion approved by Congress, this number is just dwarfed by the actuality of the Fed's actions. The FDIC has contributed to 20 percent of the total commitments, which amounts to $1.4 trillion in bank guarantees. The congressional TARP and other commitments by the Treasury amount to $892 billion or 12 percent of the total. Throw in a paltry $200 billion in help for the two housing agencies and $139 billion in assistance for the financial arm of General Electric and you can ascertain the total figure. The reality is that there is just nowhere to run and nowhere to hide anymore. If you throw in my viewpoint that we will have deflation now and inflation later, then you can even cross out the relative value of Treasuries beyond the guarantee of principal repayment. Senior debt of corporations where the Fed has put up capital at junior levels to senior debt is my best bet at present, but even there risk abounds; but my mattress is presently full.

Opportunity Knocks, Then Rings the Bell

January 29, 2009

When considering each and every plan that has been discussed to bail out the financial system and not knowing yet which one will be chosen or the specifics of how it will be enacted, it is worth noting that any and all plans under review do not negatively affect the debt owners. Now let us turn this around: All plans that are being considered, as far as I can tell, will have a positive influence on the banks and their balance sheets, and hence provide a boon to those of us who own debt. If we take this scenario and add in the historically high spreads between bank debt and Treasuries, then one may well conclude, as I have, that ownership of both subordinated and senior debt in the banks where the government would buy the common stock, under one proposal, would all mean that the debtholder would find himself in an enhanced position. If so-called toxic assets are removed from the balance sheets and the government continues to hold these junior positions, then there is some rendition of the children's game of "Do Over" in the works, while debt can now be purchased at spreads reflecting a troubled institution and not a new and improved version that may well be forthcoming for many companies in the financial sector.

To be honest, this is the stuff of dreams and prayers as the taxpayers take the risk at no cost to us while we get to own bonds with rather wondrous spreads to Treasuries, agencies, or the new FDIC debt. If you dropped to your knees and asked whatever Divine Being you believe in to help you—I am not sure it gets much better than this, and while the press is almost

> *He who refuses to embrace a unique opportunity loses the prize as surely as if he had failed.*
>
> —William James

totally focused in on the ramifications for the equity of these institutions, it is the debtholder that gets the boon! This obvious fact is not yet recognized in the consensus view or the present-day spreads and yields would not be in existence. Let the cheerleading crowd at CNBC remain asleep, I say; I am happy to have the money, thank you!

It is an amusing thing, in some respects, that an inverse ratio is now being built by our current economic crisis. The industrial credits are trading much tighter than financials to Treasuries, and yet the financials of the industrial sector are rapidly deteriorating due to the world's morass, and the probability of the government's helping most companies in this sector is about nil unless some credit such as General Motors has a huge number of employees and a financial arm that can mutate into a bank. So we have the industrials trading much tighter when they are in a state of decline, and the

> *In times of change, learners inherit the Earth, while the learned find themselves beautifully equipped to deal with a world that no longer exists.*
>
> —Eric Hoffer

banks have much wider spreads while the government pumps money into these institutions and/or buys their bad assets. It makes no sense to me, and I am obviously in the minority given the prevailing spreads, and while I listen respectfully to the countervailing arguments, I am not a buyer of the consensus wisdom. I see nothing ahead for the majority of the names in the industrial sector, except worsening financials, credit rating downgrades, and serious deterioration in their balance sheets. The bet is always made on the future, not the past, and the future of many industrials is in a precarious position.

The Soap Opera
As the World Turns
September 19, 2008

n a rather dramatic turn of events, the standard line, "Let them eat cake," has been replaced by "Let them eat Fannie Mae." It is quite something that in the American democracy, the saying of a French queen has been replaced with one supposedly attributable to an American secretary. The preferreds of Freddie are the new horror show and is now substituted for the Freddie of horror movie fame. I am just thrilled to see that we are paying all of the debts and obligations of AIG, and rumors of pending name changed to "American Insulated Group" abound, while we are not paying the obligations of the two now bankrupt but former government agencies.

When you are now asked to define the meaning of a GSE or a federally chartered institution, there is only one answer: How about them Cowboys? One can only hope that Congress, when reviewing Mr. Paulson's edicts, might make some changes in the decisions that have been mandated, but, to be honest, we might as well wish for the return of Peter Pan and the Lost Boys. Not that I don't, of course, even at my age, and I should like to meet them and Wendy, but I fear that I am to be denied those pleasures in this go-round of life. Of course, you never know, one day the Treasury could pop up and say the money we told you was there, that you relied on to purchase the preferreds authorized by the government, has now magically reappeared, and we will pay once again because the rationale of what we have done so far could lead you to any conclusion under the sun, including that it had been hidden by Peter Cottontail. This has all been so confusing that the noted biblical phrase has been turned and we now are robbing the son of Peter to pay Paulson.

This morning, I read that the government may now insure money market funds for a fee, so we can guarantee the short-term obligations of Lehman, I suppose, in an effort to fund all companies in Chapter 11 and help out our cousins at a British bank. This is another method to enhance the nuclear derivatives market, one guesses, and guarantee liquidity to whatever any money market fund placed in its portfolios to enhance yield and the return to the money market managers. It is not that I am against doing this or providing a comprehensive plan to shore up the financial markets, but the "America in Wonderland" playbook just seems more and more fantastical as each new chapter is written.

I am staring at the screen now and looking at the 2-year Treasury, down two full points. I don't believe I have ever seen that in one day. This is the mother of all whipsaws and Ma and Pa Whipsaw must be standing proud this morning, given the largesse of their offspring. The futures for the stock market are now standing very close to the man in the moon, and the world is bright and shining once again. I wonder if anyone will stand up and say, "It was just a joke. Sorry you didn't think it was funny, but we had good intentions." The one thing that can be honestly said is that everyone in the markets have now been treated equally; first the longs got slammed, and now the shorts have gotten slammed, and long live the spirit of equality!

Freddie Mac says that Lehman owes them $1.2 billion this morning. This is not a problem and does not require any genius to figure it out. Freddie—sell the assets to some money market fund, then take the money and buy the money market fund, which is now guaranteed by the government, and you will get all of your money back. What a wild ride; we are watching the invention of new, new economics, and who wouldda thunk? Another method would be to give the assets back to Barclays, have them put them in Tier III capital, now sure to be guaranteed by the government, and then to return the money to Freddie minus some small handling fee.

Next, I hear that the central government is considering letting the states participate. There are secret, secret talks that Vermont may buy Morgan Stanley and Utah will take over Washington Mutual, while Florida will be assuming ownership of each and every American real estate company in an effort to corner the market and increase property values.

Anything is now possible, and the financial world has become one very crazy place! Welcome to Disney World and Mr. Toad's Wild Ride.

Part IV

The Great Game

Chapter 14

Politics

Timeless wisdom, poignant thinking, and as a good a summation as any of what went on during America's financial crisis. Groucho may have missed a trick or two, but not too many, and he certainly never missed taking a shot at his brothers when he got the chance or engineered it. It may have been that our current flock of politicians came to learn at his well as they will stop at nothing to engineer everything. Sometimes the top spins so fast it makes me dizzy.

The great shame was that the same men that were responsible for not providing adequate regulations were mostly the same men that were entrusted to fix the chair that they broke. They couldn't put the thing together properly and they sure as hell did not know how to fix it regardless of how often that they insisted that they did. Graham should have stuck with his crackers and the rest should have been led away for their poor behavior but instead we got the three stooges in full regalia puffing out their chests and blowing in the wind as we all suffered

Politics is the art of looking for trouble, finding it, misdiagnosing it, and then misapplying the wrong remedies.
— Groucho Marx

In politics stupidity is not a handicap.
—Napoleon Bonaparte

from their dragon's breath. I know that we elected them—I am well aware of it—and so "we the people" bear some of the responsibility as well. I sometimes think that we forget that the people we elect will be the people that govern and if we held onto that thought during the elections we might end up with a better crowd.

The great tragedy of what has taken place is that it gave the Europeans a leg up to challenge to dominance of America as the world's reserve currency, as the safest place to invest your funds and as the lead player on the world's financial stage. To be quite honest, I am not sure if we will recover our former status. We acted just like the cowboys out in Dodge City that we had been accused of becoming. Rational thinking gave way to a Wild West mentality, and the more our politicians blundered and contended otherwise, the more ridiculous we looked. The worst of it was that the foolishness of the Bush administration gave way to the foolishness of the Obama administration so that both parties succumbed to the shriek of the political siren instead of putting politics to the side for the good of the country. It is amazing how often these people claim that they are acting in the best interest of the country and then how often it is not done.

> *Everything is changing. People are taking their comedians seriously and the politicians as a joke.*
>
> —Will Rogers

I think the only thing that might save the United States as the world's leading country is the worse behavior of the European politicians. The laws that they are taking about enacting and the taxes on the banks and the bankers and the limitations that are going to place on hedge funds and other pools of money may give us a second chance by fiat. If we regain our stature it will not be because we earned it but because the Europeans blew it. This does not strike me as a pleasant thought nor is it something of which I am proud but it may be the way it all works out. Fifty states may trump 27 countries after all, but the cards were not good and the playing of the hand even worse.

> *It is inexcusable for scientists to torture animals; let them make their experiments on journalists and politicians.*
>
> —Henrik Ibsen

Just dumb—you beat up and bash every bank and corporation in the country and call them liars and thieves and worse to stir up the lower economic classes of people, and then you wonder why these same companies are not hiring? Why should any right-minded CEO expand his business when he does not know what other tricks the politicians may have up their sleeves? Who knows what comes next; the FNMA Statue of Liberty play where you ask for more employment and then dismantle some company for doing just that on the basis of that they are not the right people? In my opinion, corporate America just has no faith—and I mean none—in what these people in Washington, D.C., are doing at present. If faith in politicians was like faith in God, the whole country would be atheists.

It has really been quite upsetting watching these people on television. It was as if they thought counterparty risk was defined as you giving a dinner party at 8:00 one evening and the danger was that your neighbor would do the same thing. The most curious thing was that they must have all drunk from the same water fountain as the most often-seen look on their face was the blank stare.

They often excused themselves claiming that they did not exactly know what a derivative was or what leverage meant as if this was an acceptable excuse. It frightens me when the people making the laws of the country do not understand what they are legislating. It made me wonder who was writing the laws anyway—some 23-year-old legislative aide fresh out of the University of Iowa who was stoked up on beer from the night before? If there was anything to blame in subprime, it was the mental capacity of our politicians that fits quite nicely into that description.

> *Mothers all want their sons to grow up to be President, but they don't want them to become politicians in the process.*
> —President John F. Kennedy

The Squeeze Is On

January 28, 2009

The Squeeze is on. There are many more precise and academic terms for the second stage of a recession, but I prefer my word as a wonderfully accurate depiction of what we are just now entering. If this whole mess started sometime in the fall and individuals and companies alike have four to six months of cash and credit; then we are just now beginning the Squeeze. This period has some endemic qualities that are just now coming to the fore. Let me offer up some examples: The crime rate will rise due to economic conditions; Ponzi/Madoff schemes will proliferate as the deterioration in the financial markets pushes people and institutions against the wall; you should expect and will get financial statements that are not accurate as everyone tries to smoke and mirror their house of cards; the people with money will not have it any longer or much less of it, as their investments have imploded, and this will also be true for institutions; business plans based on past performance will evaporate as well as the financials of many corporations because people/institutions stop buying and the value of assets, once the backdrop for economic expansion, have devalued and will devalue further, as no one can afford the old escalated prices for services and goods.

The picture is not pretty, but it is of no matter, as reality must be faced and faced squarely. None of this will stop until new money arrives, and that, in short, is just what many governments are trying to accomplish—bringing in new money. It is now accurate to say, I think, that the private sector is deleveraging as a consequence of their own excesses coupled with the federal government's abysmal job of providing adequate regulations and the major Western governments are leveraging up to prevent calamity as a consequence of these two forces. If you cut through the barrage of idiocy that I hear bandied about these days, it really gets down to how much and for how long the private sector delevers and then how much and for how long the public sector is willing to increase the public's risk to counterbalance the loss. That is the root of the real question in my opinion and then the consideration of the collateral damage that will accompany this process becomes the key topic to explore for those of us that invest money. This leads to one of the tougher subjects to muse about, which may be termed as *the Rules*. Here is where real thought becomes provoking, and it is a subject barely discussed as a macro concept.

The Rules

Governments make the rules; that is the crux of it, so when governments are printing money and using it to counterbalance the Squeeze, then you can bet 100 percent, in my view, on the notion that the Rules will get changed as the money is pumped out into the system. The consideration of just how the Rules will get changed may be the most difficult and important pieces of the puzzle. Examples of the change in the Rules to date abound; the bankruptcy of two federal agencies, the limits on executive compensation, the cessation of dividends as mandated by the government for receiving federal aid, and so on. The opportunities, to date, for the change in the Rules such as the ability to hold debt senior to the government or the opportunity to own

Daring ideas are like chessmen moved forward. They may be beaten, but they may start a winning game.
—Johann Wolfgang von Goethe

Federal Deposit Insurance Corporation (FDIC) debt that did not exist before as an alternative to Treasuries and agencies is another example. I have spoken before about my concerns for mortgage securitization owners, as I think it probable that the Rules get changed in that sector as the government helps homeowners to the detriment of those that own mortgages and one is forced to consider with great care what other Rule changes the government might mandate. All of this means that political risk must now be part of the equation along with investment risk.

My take now is that if you think the financial numbers are bad now, the Squeeze will make them worse and the changing of the Rules will bring unintended consequences. Great care must now be taken and an extreme amount of thought must be exercised to navigate our current path as managers of money. Financials must be scrutinized,

Greatness is not in where we stand, but in what direction we are moving. We must sail sometimes with the wind and sometimes against it—but sail we must and not drift, nor lie at anchor.

—Justice Oliver Wendell Holmes

and the triumphs of the past do not ensure future success in a world where economic conditions are deteriorating in an extreme fashion. We are now in the most radical of circumstances, which does not mean that you cannot win, but most assuredly means that winning is achieved by a whole new schematic. The comparison to some index holds little value when capital is lost and preservation of capital is the mantra of each and every day.

A Consideration of Political Risk

February 4, 2009

I find the events of recent days somewhat disquieting. The new administration keeps proposing people to run the country who haven't paid their taxes, and then they hue and cry about people who receive bonuses but who probably did pay their taxes, and one wonders which group should actually be in charge. Today, apparently, there is going to be a major speech by our president about limiting compensation, and this seems the focus of the government recently which, while it may be an important side note in the scheme of things, is hardly the basis to help cure our economic travails. It appears that we are focusing on the inane in the hope that the real problems we face will somehow just go away. All of this may be a ruse, of course, as we can concentrate on bonuses in the financial system, so we don't have to discuss the pitiful job that the government has done in providing regulations for the banking sector because the politicians do not want to attract attention to themselves. If one takes a rather grand view of things we find the administration lining up to give Wall Street money and then, at the same time, whipping them for it, so one muses if we have elected a group with a rather strange mentality. "Give them money and then whip them for it" so that only the mediocre are retained does not exactly seem to be the economic panacea we have been promised.

We have now had three appointees with major tax problems and perhaps someone should explain that to have someone "vetted" has nothing to do with the car made by General Motors. I did listen to our president as he addressed the Daschle withdrawal and was rather taken aback by his comment: "I screwed up." What will he say to the press now that the new performance czar has withdrawn for tax reasons: "I screwed up again?" I am in favor of change and a more open government like most of you, I would guess but I am not sure I am comforted by a continuing series of "screw-ups" about political appointments when we have not even addressed yet how the new administration will help rebuild our financial system. While I await the "Big Bang Speech" to come, I will tell all of you quite candidly that I find little solace in the direction we are heading.

At the forefront of my mind now is "political risk." While I do my best to stare at the continuing announcements of a multitude of company's declining revenues and profits, and one company after another slashing or cutting their dividends; I must tell you that my biggest concern, by far, is just what our elected officials are going to mandate. It is not just that I don't know what they are going to do; it is my increasing belief that they don't know what they are going to do and therein lies my greatest concern because I remain unconvinced that they get the joke. When I think about the real meaning of the "implicit" or "explicit" guarantee of our federal agencies or what it means for the other agencies that are not in conservatorship or what they might mandate for the mortgage-back securities market in an effort to save the homeowners or a whole host of other issues of the same ilk; I become fearful and there is just no way around this "gut feeling" that I have contracted like a bad cold one gets in their chest. The resonating truth is that I do now know what these people are going to do, and that makes prudent judgment as applied to investments a particularly difficult course to conjure up. I know that I want to be in corporate debt and not corporate equities, and I know that Treasuries are backing up as I have predicted, and I know that commodity prices have been slammed in a global economy heading south, but what I cannot rationally predict is what Congress and our president may do in these game-changing moments.

I have no answers to a number of the questions; I admit that right up front to all of you, but this doesn't mean that the tough questions should not be considered:

- If the government can bankrupt federal agencies and mandate that their preferred dividends do not get paid and also mandate that some of the companies that they have given money to cut their stock dividends to a minimum, then is it not possible that they could mandate that the preferred dividends or the hybrid securities of the companies that they help will also not get paid as a part of the package?

- If the government is going to defray, defer, extend, and so forth the mortgage payments for homeowners, is it not possible, when Wall Street is being treated as the Evil Empire, that agency mortgage securitization owners will have to absorb some of the losses?
- If taxpayers are the boon and investors are the bane, then in what other contexts will the investing class be held accountable or punished until the taxpayer gets his money back with interest?
- If there is little or no clarity to make investments does "Preservation of Capital" take on such a magnified importance that it erodes confidence to such an extent that the capital markets grind to a point near a halt?
- If the 1929 Depression serves as a history lesson are we much nearer the beginning of the decline and not the end?
- If inflation is the only way out of the morass, something I believe, then is making deflationary bets, past the shortest of terms, one more example of an emperor without clothes?
- If ratings are mostly based upon past performance, a view that I have, then has future performance in this economic downturn dislocated ratings from the reality of the future to come so that many companies will decline precipitously in earnings, profits and eventually in ratings that become lagging indicators?

What is clear is that the government is changing the Rules. What is not clear is the definition of the Rules!

Political Risk Knocks, Then Enters

February 17, 2009

Where is your "political risk" specialist? Where did you put him? You have opened the closet doors, peeked in that tiny office by human resources, even checked the cubicle by the water cooler and all to no avail. You don't need him that often after all. Usually, it is the analysts and those skilled in poring through financial data and the brain trust that can slice and dice mortgages like one of those Ginsu products on TV that are needed. Usually, you have no use at all for that pesky fellow who gets the joke about politics and the reality of great destruction that can be part of the game when one plays with "those who make the Rules," and one always hates playing with them anyway. The problem is that when the chips are down, the "Maker of Rules," also known as Congress, the President, Parliament, or whatever group you have controlling the purse strings, enters the fray by necessity and being the big bully that he is and not even understanding the game much anyway, you can rest assured that since he has the power to change the Rules, they will get changed.

I would like you to take a moment to consider this rather important fact this morning before darting off to your next meeting. When the 800-pound gorilla enters the game, the Rules are going to get changed, and to think otherwise is not only to be foolish but it may prove to be exceedingly costly. I would make the observation that the "Makers of Rules" are now fully engaged in the Great Game and that, if nothing else, one must prepare themselves and the portfolios you manage for significant structural changes that may well occur.

I have spoken about one such "political risk" already, which is the possible changes to outstanding mortgage-backed securitizations if the government decides that the investor class should bear some of the loss for helping homeowners remain in their houses. It is easy enough to blame the Wobbly Wogs of Wall Street for creating these financial products that no normal person can understand and then change the Rules so they bear some accountability for creating this mess. One can almost hear some senator or another proclaiming this in defense of the citizenry and then concocting a scheme, following the classic words of the Star Fleet Captain Lucian Picard, to "make it so." You should take heed and recall that for millennia the money changers and other evil-doers that deal with money are never considered to be citizens or tax-payers in the normal construction of things, but they are the outside panderers who get blamed for all of the catastrophes of the financial system when things go awry.

Politics being politics, one needs someone to blame and one wants to get reelected and the mob of Rome is not so far removed from the herd of the United States. I would like to remind those of you in the "but-terflies are free" crowd that the Federal National Mortgage Association (FNMA) and Freddie Mac are in conservatorship and that no one alive knows the exact meaning of the supposed "implicit" or "explicit" guar-antee or whether it applies to the mortgage securitizations or just the senior/subordinated debt, and I can almost hear the words echoing off the walls of Congress as someone starts calling for Wall Street to pay for some of the loss that has been created as homeowners must be kept in their abodes and who better than investors to get tagged with some of the loss. To think that this is not a real possibility is incredibly naïve and reminiscent of your long-held belief in the tooth fairy. What to do about the possibility of it all is another and more serious question but not to think that it could happen is foolish!

Now I personally do not think that the government is going to try to change the entire capital structure of the marketplace by decree-ing that their preferred stock is superior to senior/subordinated debt but it would not surprise me in the least to have the "Makers of the Rules" declare that their preferred stock was in a higher posi-tion than other preferred stock and that the people should be repaid first and the investors can just go hang if they don't like it. We have already seen the government restrict compensation, virtu-ally eliminate dividends, and place innumerable other demands on corporations that take the government's money, and it is only those reclining in heaven that may know where this process will stop. Rules

*In really hard times the rules of the game
are altered.*

—Walter Lippmann,
American journalist

will get changed in the name of the people and for the common good, and each of you should spend some time thinking this through because if you do not, you will get left in the desert sun to be dried out and find that your childish fantasies were just that: fantasies.

Just One Moment, Please

March 5, 2009

J ust one moment, please—just one second! I am a stand-up guy who got to where I am on my own two feet and did it honestly and within the boundaries that were laid out by the government. I am certainly aware that I am but one small voice in a sea brimming with noise, but there does come a moment in time when I will stand up and object, and I am doing so now. It may be all the rage and a popular methodology for politicians to gain support from the citizenry to attack Wall Street; the evil money changers of the modern era. This political tact has been validated as effective since biblical times, but if you are going to stand on the temple steps and come after me, then you must be prepared for me to respond.

I Respond to Our Elected Officials

You made the rules and you are responsible for their construction. You were supposed to regulate the rules that you made and you failed miserably in their implementation, and then again in the oversight that was necessary to police them. It was not that hedge funds were illegal or that leverage caps were ignored by the banks or that structured investment vehicles were disallowed or that banks were joined once again with investment banks so they could participate more broadly in the financial system and that they violated the law in some fashion by doing what you specifically allowed. I say to Congress: You bear the responsibility for all of this economic malaise more than any other person or entity in our country and I remind our president, who was in the Senate during this time, of just who was at fault.

I am not a recipient of Troubled Asset Relief Program (TARP) money or any other handout forthcoming from the government, and I owe forbearance to no one outside of common curtsey and respect that adheres to the stations of government. If my brethren on the Street wish to walk hat in hand up Pennsylvania Avenue and then stand idly by while we are vilified in the press and charged with crimes that we have not committed, I will not. It is not a truth of the Great Game, but it is certainly a truth of life that we all get up in the morning and must live within our own skin; I will shoulder the consequences of the wrongs I have committed, but I will not be silenced when accused of wrongs brought about by others and then blamed on me. One thing that I certainly have learned in this life is that if we collectively lie down and allow ourselves to be kicked that the kicking will not stop, and I chastise some of you who are far more well known than I and have a far louder voice that is listened to by the public to stand up and remind the pointers of fingers that Wall Street operated within the laws and regulations that were given to us. I do not rant and I am not angry, but I am resolute in my belief that Congress bears most of the blame for this financial crisis, and if many of you will not stand up and be counted, then I will stand up even if singularly and alone in the Coliseum while the mob reacts to the rabble-rousing declarations of our politicians. Thank you for your ear this morning, and I hope that my statements remind some of you of the importance of adhering to your values and then of standing up for yourselves when accused of crimes that you have not committed.

You cannot help the poor by destroying the rich. You cannot strengthen the weak by weakening the strong. You cannot bring about prosperity by discouraging thrift. You cannot lift the wage earner up by pulling the wage payer down. You cannot further the brotherhood of man by inciting class hatred. You cannot build character and courage by taking away people's initiative and independence. You cannot help people permanently by doing for them, what they could and should do for themselves.

—Abraham Lincoln

I should like to make one further comment: It is those of us that have worked hard and accumulated some money that are being asked to shoulder the burden, and this startling fact seems to have gotten lost in the politics of the moment.

Pact with the Devil

April 1, 2009

I received any number of comments yesterday from all around the globe regarding my thinking about "engaging" with the government and the consideration of "political risk" as part of the current investment process. My observations were meant, as always, to be illuminating about our current economic environment. There is kind of an epiphany here, as when it dawned on me that the noted opera composer of Italian origin, Giuseppe Verdi, shared the same translated name with the noted American football star, as they were both named Joe Green. In much the same way in which I was startled with this dawning of realization, I am quickly bridging the gap in my mind when political considerations become a part of our playing field.

First and foremost among the mental changes required is to understand that the people in politics do not share the same goals or aspirations as those of us that deal in financial matters. We are interested in making money, preserving capital, and competing with our peers to attract additional funds to manage, and are driven by the capitalistic mantra to produce revenues and profits and to receive salaries and bonuses commensurate with what we produce. Virtually all of these notions are so far afield from what drives those in politics that we may as well be negotiating with aliens when two of the three branches of government are engaged in making business decisions and not just regulating the process, which is where we are now because the government is providing funds to private enterprise in an effort of avoid financial collapse. In fact, you must reorganize your mind and step back and carefully consider what may be reasonably expected from those in power because, if not, you will make assumptions and decisions that are so far afield from reality that you will be left in the purgatory of poor thinking.

Since ancient Greece, Rome, and the empires of Spain, France, and England, the basic scenario has not changed anymore than the nature of human beings has changed. The money changers are interested in profit, while those in control are interested in power and therein lays the distinction on its basest level. The subsets of power in a democracy rely on reelection, public opinion, and the daily continuing struggle to both lead and follow the electorate

> *Nothing is more unpredictable than the mob, nothing more obscure than public opinion, nothing more deceptive than the whole political system.*
>
> —Cicero

in a delicate balance. The mob in Rome and the horde in the Germanic tribes are no different, not a whit, from the American citizens and taxpayers and those in power play to them, try to fool them, suppress them, elate them all in mad rush to retain their power to govern and hence to retain the good life and be important.

In plain fact, now, you have to shift your mind about and do some studying of history, not of the Depression or other financial calamities, but of how people are governed and the roles of those in power to attain a better grasp of what occurs when this government, any democratic government, has entered the playing field of providing the public's money to support private enterprise because the rules of engagement change and change dramatically when the "lender of last resort" is forced to actually lend. The cost of money is no longer a function of capitalism but becomes a function of power, and its retention, and there is the pointed illumination of separation and America, and much of the rest of the world, has now reached this line of embarkation that defines the new operating principles, and make no mistake about it—there are now new operating principles.

When the Congress proposes a retroactive tax to penalize those at AIG for taking bonuses because the government is bailing them out, there should be no surprise; if you were surprised, then you have not yet fully grasped the rules that get imposed when the government is forced from its normal "regulating mode" and into the "operating mode," which is what is now transpiring. In much the same manner as the lack of experience and lack of historical precedent frighten those at central banks when confronting deflation; democracies, and certainly the American democracy, has little experience and a whole host of political turmoils and considerations when entering the sphere of providing public funds and being responsible for their use and making a reasonable effort to provide for the eventual return of capital to the citizens.

It is like this: The government that understands baseball, and private enterprise that understands football, are now both engaged on a playing field where neither side understand the other's rules and everyone is being forced to play some game that they do not understand, have rarely played, and have no real comprehension of what the rules are or should be, so that the notion of winning is barely comprehensible as no one is quite sure of even how to play the game.

All the perplexities, confusion and distress in America arise not from defects in their Constitution or Confederation, nor from want of honor or virtue, so much as downright ignorance of the nature of coin, credit and circulation.

—President John Adams

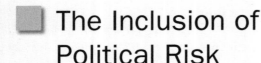

The Inclusion of Political Risk

April 6, 2009

This morning I undertake the sticky task of addressing American politics. The subject needs to be addressed in the most compelling manner now, as the politicians are no longer in the stands and playing to the crowd, but they have descended, without question, onto the playing field of the arena and they have joined the game. When the president of the United States calls the CEO of General Motors and fires him, then the unspoken rules of the last several decades have significantly changed. Make

A politician . . . one that would circumvent God.

—William Shakespeare, *Hamlet*

no mistake—I take no sides and I am not addressing the correctness or incorrectness of our new circumstances, but what I feel must be assessed is the "political risk" that now exists for institutional investors. It is not that economic considerations have given way to political considerations; it is that both issues must be carefully weighed now in order to make prudent financial decisions and that to make wise investments, without the inclusion of the political ramifications as part of your thinking process, is a mistake of the most serious kind.

Our current environment reminds me of the Kosher Dietary Laws. They started with a few biblical tenets such as "do not seethe the kid in his mother's milk," and by the time they had become firmly fixed, one could not keep them all without violating others. Having said that, Rule one is that the makers of the game, usually disposed to regulating what they have created, have now also become players of the game as they dispense the money of the citizenry. Rule two is that the politicians do not play the game under the same tenets and guidelines, or have the same ambitions, as those of us in private enterprise. This is a critical point and one that must be critically examined because the goals of the people in power are distinctly different from those of us trying to make money. Rule three is that you cannot beat city hall and that any attempt to do so will be met with frustration, aggravation, and vilification—or worse.

> *Politics is supposed to be the second-oldest profession. I have come to realize that it bears a very close resemblance to the first.*
>
> —President Ronald Reagan

As an example of all of this, when considering whether to join the new public-private initiative offered up by the government, we are faced with several political questions that may well trump the economic questions of whether to participate in this program. It may well be that the secretary of the Treasury is honorable and truthful in his naïvete when saying that the buyers of toxic assets using the taxpayer's money will be allowed to make a profit and not be held accountable by the government, but he does not speak and cannot speak for the myriad of participants in Congress when someone is held accountable for making too much money after having been given public funds. The drive to be reelected and to be seen as the protector of the common man to do so will motivate many politicians to hold up the "money changer profiteer" to the public light for the good and glory of Rome. Perhaps axiom one should be signified as "you will not go unnoticed" if you take the public funds and that the ultimate cost of your participation may

> *Politics: A strife of interests masquerading as a contest of principles. The conduct of public affairs for private advantage.*
>
> —Ambrose Bierce, *The Devil's Dictionary,* 1911

be far greater than any rewards that you may reap. If one prime motivator of a politician, which I believe is accurate, is not to lose the public's money, then motivator two would be not to allow private enterprise to make too much, however that is quantified, by the use of the taxpayer's dollar. The reality is that if you lose the taxpayer's money, you will be crucified, and that if you make too much, you will be crucified; I seriously wonder if the risks associated with this endeavor are worth the reward!

Yesterday, the secretary of the Treasury was on the Sunday morning talk show *Face the Nation*. He made two significant points, in my opinion.

1. "If in the future, banks need exceptional assistance in order to get through this, then we will make sure that assistance comes."
2. "Where that requires a change in management and the board, then we will do that."

I translate these comments this way: The largest banks will not be allowed to fail and they will not be nationalized though the government will take a proactive role in their management if necessary. These concepts seem to support my strategy to own the senior or subordinated debt in these same institutions when the government has taken preferred stock and warrants. To date, and that is all that can be said these days, it can be accurately stated that my concept is working as there has not been one failure to pay these senior obligations in these companies, nor do I believe that that the horizon holds any calamities for these indicated institutions and hence my opinion. While it is certainly not the consensus view, as signified by the yields available in these credits, it is my honest opinion that it is "safer" to be senior to the government than to assume the credit risks in many corporate names that are not subject to the same type of governmental authority or regulation where "credit risk" is the sole determinative in an economy going through serious deterioration. You may be more comfortable with assets where the credit risk is the only risk because that is what we know and understand, but that environment and the possibilities associated with it are now historical and not rooted in the present or the immediate future in my opinion. If all of your investments are now based on nothing but financial considerations, given the current returns associated with that decision, then I am willing to bet that you will not be competitive in the returns for your clients. In other words, the yields in your portfolios will not, in any fashion, match those of your peers who understand and assume both political and economic risks.

> *Take calculated risks. That is quite different from being rash.*
> — General George Patton

A Look Back—Heroes and Villains

September 1, 2009

O n the first day of the last quarter of 2009, I thought I would take a moment to look back. The play has been replete with winners and losers, noble acts and questionable conduct, smart moves and great stupidity—in short, all of the triumphs and losing propositions that compose both the comedy and the tragedy of the human condition. It is difficult to assess the events in stasis, but the drama must be squarely faced nonetheless if we are to learn anything.

I will begin with the players and in particular the person who was the worst of the performers, in my view: Hank Paulson. There are two possible conclusions when one regards what Paulson did: Either he made some incredibly dumb decisions or he played the Great Game with an edge that is understandable in private enterprise and unconscionable for a public servant. What was done to both Bear Stearns and Lehman Brothers could have been mitigated or, at least, handled better by the inclusion of public funds. The fate of Bear Stearns was somewhat understandable, while the Lehman conclusion was just a travesty, in my opinion. If one is nice and gentlemanly, one might say that his decisions were incredibly capricious and could have been better thought through; if one is less demure, one would be forced to say that what he did eliminated the competition for his friends and cronies at Goldman Sachs. There is no doubt in my mind, regardless of the reported actions of Dick Fuld and Jimmy Cain, that the financial world would be better served if those two long-standing institutions were still present, but Paulson closed the book on them and they are both gone. In my own view, the Lehman decision, given the size and complexity of the institution, pushed the financial world to the brink of collapse and was just unnecessary.

The next incredibly poor decision was to place FNMA and Freddie Mac in conservatorship. Due consideration leads me to the conclusion that this was a political move to get back at the independence of these two agencies. These were federally chartered corporations after all and conceived by Congress, and they could have been financially supported or brought back into the fold as "full faith and credit" agencies of the government without inflicting the unceremonious pain that was inflicted on the financial system of the country and the world by the very questionable act of putting them in conservatorship. The decision to stop paying the dividends on their preferred stock cast a pall over the American government's integrity that exists to this day. The country must be held to higher standards to protect our stated obligations and while legally the dividends could be stopped, I fear that in doing so we brought serious consequences on the nation that still exist. The message that has been sent to institutional and retail investors alike is a damning one that will not be easily forgotten. One may have hoped that the new administration would have corrected this serious mistake, but it has been swept under the rug like so much else as time has passed.

Recognizing the other side of the balance sheet, one must give both Geithner and Bernanke high marks. Not every decision was flawless in concept or perfectly executed, but the nod must be given to always acting in the best interests of the country and to solid financial creativity and finally to their own personal honor which well represented America in some very tough times. Our current president also is due some positive recognition for Bernanke's reappointment as the right thing to do for the nation. When the going is the most difficult, in times of war or severe financial stress, personal politics must be laid aside in favor of the higher interests of the country, and this was done.

When considering the reasons for our difficulties, I do not see the problem as a subprime issue or even the unregulated derivatives markets—both mistakes, no doubt, but not the prime mover. I believe that the real villain was overleverage all across the board. It is a particular shame that Congress is focusing in on executive pay as they play to the American horde. I wish our elected officials would concentrate on levels of leverage tied to sound financial criteria instead of stirring the masses with shrieks of horror at how much someone is being paid. We do seem to be moving toward some method of regulating derivatives—an absolute must, in my view—and for that we can thank those currently in power, but this should have been fixed long ago.

Brighter minds than mine will surely weigh in on this topic with the passing of years. Academics will muse and economists will pore over the data, but as a singular person enmeshed in the day-to-day acting of the Great Game as it played out, these are my personal observations.

There are new words now that excuse everybody. Give me the good old days of heroes and villains. The people you can bravo or hiss. There was a truth to them that all the slick credulity of today cannot touch.

—Bette Davis

Pay No Attention to What They Say

September 11, 2009

Mayor of Munchkin City: Then this is a day of independence for all the Munchkins and their descendants!

Munchkin: If any!

Mayor of Munchkin City: Yes—let the joyous news be spread! The Wicked Old Witch at last is dead!

Now these rather famous lines are close enough in meaning to approximate what the secretary of the Treasury said yesterday. In fact, in my opinion, the meaning here is a closer rendition to reality than what got said. The secretary announced that the witch was dead and then announced the beginning—and just the beginning, mind you—of programs that will start to be shut down now that the wicked old witch (the financial crisis) has met her demise.

Now I want to remind you, once again, to pay absolutely no attention to what gets said by anyone in the Treasury or the Federal Reserve Bank as we go through the process of returning to normality. Pay very close attention to what they are doing, program closings or the winding down of guarantees; but pay absolutely and positively no mind to how they are spinning the wicket.

Wizard of Oz: Pay no attention to that man behind the curtain.

Now you will be tempted, and some of you in the larger organizations may find yourself in your investment committee meetings nitpicking through what Bernanke or Geithner says, and you will get sucked into a giant black hole. These people are about to begin a process that will totally mislead you as they attempt to get the country back on its feet, and they will do it knowing full well what they are doing but with the certain conviction that they are on a higher moral ground. They are trying to propel America back to a solid financial footing, after all, and will use whatever means are necessary to accomplish that end. All fine, all good; just pay no attention to the hooks as they are baited.

You will read in the press all manner of pundits, economists, and Fed watchers who will strive to interpret the spoken and written words of the men in power. Ignore it, ignore all of it, or you, too, will find yourself at the unfortunate location of just exactly where on the planet you should not be when Dorothy's house lands on the Earth. In short, if you believe all of the stuff that is about to be uttered, proclaimed, and spread before the masses, you will get crushed.

I have spent 35 years of my life watching the Great Game unfold. I have been here before, have the T-shirt and get the joke—trust me here. I have warned that all of this was coming for some months now, and I know just exactly how this part of the game gets played out:

Watch what they do; pay no attention to what they say!

What Are They Doing?

1. The government is going to stop guaranteeing the money market mutual fund industry.
2. The FDIC is going to stop or severely restrict guarantees for banks.
3. The Fed's commercial paper funding facility is now down 87 percent from its high mark, and their cash auction program is now down 57 percent from its peak.

It is all of this that should be noted, examined, and extrapolated in meaning, while the reasoning provided for it or the comments on it must be ignored.

Now I know and you know that I am sitting in the wheelhouse of a boat on a canal at some small village in France. Fortunately, however, I have brought my mind with me on this journey, and it continues to work in a reasonable fashion regardless of any speculation to the contrary. Al and his hammer have not yet landed a killing blow. Dementia has not yet set in. To quote the great detective Hercule

Poirot: "The little gray cells still function." If there is just one lesson that you may glean from today's commentary, it is to just pay attention to the facts!

Some Extrapolation from the Facts

First, the Fed will begin to reduce its balance sheet. Watch this carefully because this will be step one before they begin to raise interest rates. As the balance sheet shrinks, begin to prepare your portfolios from an increase in rates. It is coming just as sure as the sun is rising on the horizon here in France. This certainty may be absolutely counted on; it is just the timing that is in question. Keep your eye on the London Interbank Offered Rate (LIBOR) rates; changes are likely to come here before any announcement is forthcoming from anyone. Cast a critical eye on the upcoming auctions of Treasuries and be especially mindful of the amount of subscriptions as a telling sign of money moving out of Treasuries and into other securities as liquidity and safety get replaced by a reach for yield. It is my best surmise that compression continues in bonds, especially in the laggards now such as Citigroup, Bank of America, AIG, Hartford, SLMA, Pru, and the like. Watch for niche plays such as I outlined yesterday, pick up some covered bonds, consider step-ups as an offset to rising rates, have some Treasury Inflation Protected Securities (TIPS) and Corporate Inflation Protected Securities (CIPS) in your hip pocket and consider taking some profits in very short bonds trading above par. As a general observation, I would say that the stock market is in for a great ride and that the end-of-the-year prices will be much higher than now.

Enjoy the ride as we leave the wicked witch dead in the dust!

Scarecrow: The sum of the square roots of any two sides of an isosceles triangle is equal to the square root of the remaining side. Oh joy! Rapture! I got a brain! How can I ever thank you enough?

Wizard of Oz: You can't.

The Wisdom of Jefferson

January 28, 2010

I make the observation after running capital markets at four investment banks that one should under promise and over deliver. This maxim has proved true over my long career on Wall Street and applies to not only business but to life. The result may be exactly the same but if you promise more than you can execute or more than you can put on the table at the end of the day then you will find that disappointment, if not anger, accompanies your unfulfilled word. Sometimes it is not the result but the shattering of faith that brings a man to his knees, and apparently our president has not had the proper instruction in this basic principle.

Let me be clear—I am not a disgruntled member of the opposition, nor am I making a political point about the rightness or wrongness of any particular scheme, so point no accusatory finger in my direction about some hidden agenda; it does not exist. What I am saying, however, is that no matter the greatness of oration or the eloquence of speech—in the end, delivery must be made or the promisor will be held accountable for what he has declared he will deliver.

> *The democracy will cease to exist when you take away from those who are willing to work and give to those who would not.*
>
> — Thomas Jefferson

My comments are not made in a vacuum and are not made just to express my feelings about last night's State of the Union speech as my main concern is the application to Grant's first 11 rules:

- Rules 1–10: Preserve Capital
- Rule 11: Make Money

Consequently when I consider the content of last night's address, devoid of oration, I truly wonder where we are being led or where we might end up. After our fearful financial gyrations reacting to the administration's proposed health care bill, which now looks like it will not pass—or if it does, the form will be nowhere close to what was initially proposed—and then to listen to all of the populist proclamations about our financial system, I cannot help but muse that this kind of rabble-rousing rhetoric may well backfire on those who make irresponsible proclamations from the steps of Solomon's Temple. There is no question that the government must regulate, but when it steps past that threshold, it has gone too far. In my view, if the government has a majority ownership, such as with AIG, or if a company is operating utilizing funds of the citizenry, such as in TARP, the government gets a say in the process, but when that money is repaid, then they have no more right to tell a corporation owned by shareholders how to run their business, and it is an affront to me that the government persists in that capacity.

> *I predict future happiness for Americans if they can prevent the government from wasting the labors of the people under the pretense of taking care of them.*
> —Thomas Jefferson

If the public is not happy with politicians, then we have established policies for elections that may not come often enough for some, but the people will get their say in due course. For banks, it is far simpler, and somehow that notion seems to have been lost. If on any day, any week, any month, an individual citizen is not happy with the policies of a banking institution, then he can change banks or a shareholder can sell his stock or a bondholder can sell his bonds and so cast his vote. Salaries and bonuses are the province of private enterprise and what will we find next: the disallowance of corned beef sandwiches at board meetings as proscribed by the government for dietary reasons?

> *My reading of history convinces me that most bad government results from too much government.*
> —Thomas Jefferson

Sovereign Debt

The crisis worsens; that is my take here and the conclusion is nowhere in sight. The spread between the German 10-year and the Greek 10-year gapped to record levels as Greek debt backed up by 70 bps at one point yesterday over their German counterpart and their 10-year bonds now yield 6.70 percent. The credit-default swap for Greece also hit a record on Wednesday up +53 bps to a record +378 bps. In Monday's commentary, I warned about Portugal's financials that were due to be reported to the EU, and my prediction was not out of line. The Portuguese government reported a 9.3 percent budget deficit, which was far worse than the EU projection of 8 percent. More than the numbers, and a sentiment expressed by a number of my clients, is the growing feeling that the Greek data, the Portuguese data, and possibly those of Spain are not accurate. I would expect ratings declines soon in all of these countries, and if the EU finds that any of their member nations are falsifying the numbers, then you may expect there will be hell to pay.

I was quoted on Bloomberg Radio yesterday about my view that the euro would fall to 125 against the dollar, and as I listened to their program, I also heard Nouriel Roubini's comments about the European Union. "If Greece goes under, that's a problem for the Eurozone," he said. "If Spain goes under, it's a disaster." I cannot help but to echo his view here and to warn that Spain, with its 19 percent unemployment rate and a serious decline in their financials, may be the next country to consider departing. The countryside may be beautiful, but the operative phrase for their debt at current spreads is "buenas noches."

Chapter 15

The Great Game

The Great Game—there is nothing like it on the planet. There is no iPhone application, no Xbox fantasy, no major league sport that compares to Wall Street. For 36 years now I have been privileged to get to play, and for all of this time I have regaled in the experience. From every corner on the planet the players make their way out onto the field, and there is plenty of space for all comers. Doctorate degrees, no degrees, the sons and daughters of kings, plumbers, and Sunday preachers—everyone is welcomed equally and given the opportunity to compete. The prize is money, lots of money, hoards of money and the power that comes along with it. Having the right name or going to the right school may get you through the door, but right there, at the second step, it stops and no one cares. You either know how to play and play well or you are excused. There is no academic course, nothing in business school, and no book that will adequately explain to you how to play. You barge in, you look around, you pay close attention, you mimic and innovate, and maybe, just maybe, you will learn how to play well enough to win.

I have known people who were great successes who came from the London School of Economics and other winners of the challenge that were hired out of a delicatessen in Brooklyn. There are those who thrive

at large institutions who play well from the chair that they are given
and guys running hedge funds that would die in the same chair. A good
backfield man is not necessarily a good frontfield man; everyone needs
to find his appropriate position, and there are no play books that give
you any directions. All that is available are a few *rabbis,* the term on Wall
Street for a mentor, that may provide you some guidance as everyone
else around you yells and screams at you that you can't make it and that
it can't be done, and yet, somewhere in your cerebral cortex, you know
you can and you go on.

There is no crying in the Great Game and there are no excuses. Good
intentions have gone straight to Dante's hell, and there is absolutely nothing besides either you got it done or you did not, you made money or
you did not—you succeeded or you failed. Screaming that "you tried"
is an automatic red card, and no matter the hours worked, the dedication
to your task, or the effort that you made, it is all for naught, as either
the pile of cash was increased or you wasted everyone's time. These are
incredibly difficult lessons for most people, and the vast majority of
applicants fall by the wayside because of them, but it is the essence of the
Great Game and either you get the joke or the joke is on you.

The vitals are easy to explain: a large dose of testicular vicissitude,
tenacity, brilliance, and, finally, experience. The last vital sign is the
most important of all and is not gained by the size of your intelligence;
experience is just impossible to replace or gain in any other way except
by the living of it.

As the seasons progress, there are the failures, the comeback kids,
the great successes, the lesser achievers, and all manner of players in
between. The CEO may be the quarterback, and the chief financial
officer (CFO) the goalkeeper, but there are attackers and defenders and
the gatherers of money and the investors of money and managers of
special squads and niches intertwined within niches, but in the end it
is all some contribution to the making of money that moves you from
Boardwalk to Park Place.

I can't help that I'm bigger than you.
You're such a genius, you figure out how
to handle me.

— Orson Scott Card, *Ender's Game*

When I look back at it all, I smile.
I grin at the whole adventure, and each
and every day I want to keep playing.
Some of the best and brightest minds on
the planet are engaged and the intrigue
that I felt in the early days of my career
has not faded. I never thought I would

get this far, but then I always felt that I could get a good ways down the road if I worked at it. It is not just the people from different countries, but the different mind-sets, the quantitative thinkers, the math geniuses, the motivators of men, the bureaucratic control freaks, the whole range of different people who flowed into the mix and who helped to shape my future. It is also a future that keeps unfolding—my book that is coming out, appearances on TV and radio, new friends that get my commentary who show up and engage and to be part of it all is both a pleasure and a blessing.

The Great Game, that is what I call it; the very best show on Earth!

The Wizard's Wishes for You

December 31, 2008

- I wish for you grand adventures filled with joy while the child in us all remembers the excitement of exploring what is just around the bend.
- Keep those lost on the way forever in your hearts and guard their memory with the fervent hope that you will see them once again.
- May your family and friends be gladdened by your presence as their lives are enriched by the pleasures of sharing this journey with you.
- Allow the chapters that life closes to be accepted with grace while you embrace the wind rushing through the opening door of the future.
- Always remember that the game is yours to win or lose and that the great thrill of achieving is more satisfying than the receipt of any prize.
- Do not allow the temptations of possessions to bring dishonor upon your soul or to garner shame upon those that you have chosen to love.
- Never forget that the roads chosen will chart your course and that the wisdom to be accumulated with age is the light to blaze your path.
- With life comes calm seas and raging storms and may your practiced eye and prudent judgment steer a safe course through all tossed your way.
- Do not fight with scarecrows or windmills, but always remember to smile gently and not lose patience with the unfortunate fellows that do.
- Take pleasure with the sighting of each rainbow and store them in your mind so that in times of distress you can recall them in your heart.

- Never accept obstacles blocking your way forward as you can go over them, under them, around them, through them or dance until they move.
- Always remember what is important and never lose sight of the frivolities of life that may seem important for the moment but are not.
- Keep faith with yourself and your family and friends and be slow to anger, quick to praise and respectful of every sojourner you pass.
- Learn from the mistakes of the trek, but do not be too harsh on yourself for errors made, as that is the chief manner in which we grow.
- Never-Never Land is past the second star to the right and straight on till morning and we will all get there soon enough; no need to hurry.
- Awake each day with excitement; there are pirates to fight, a yellow brick road to find, and new parts of Winnie the Pooh's forest to explore.

All of this is the wish of the Wizard for you: a thousand hellos, a very few goodbyes, and your spirit shining brighter than any star in the sky!

Please allow me to take the next moment on this New Year's Eve to say "Thank You" to the Wizard's Apprentice, Angela O'ffill. Angela, you have been loyal and honorable and have worked hard with me for many years now, and if you represent the next generation of Americans, then I have no fear for the future of Wall Street or our country. So, Angela, I doff my Wizarding hat this morning in public to you and say, "Well done!"

Just yesterday, Constar and Chesapeake filed for bankruptcy, while LyondellBasell, the chemical company, announced it is considering bankruptcy. I fear these are the signs of things to come in 2009. I wish I could present a pleasanter picture, and I am not without optimism, but reality is stark and stares us all in the face, and there is just no way around what is in front of us, I am afraid. It is going to be a year where many companies disappear, dividends are slashed, and preservation of capital is at the forefront of concerns. Do not be fooled by the momentary hiatus that generally

> *The general who wins the battle makes many calculations in his temple before the battle is fought. The general who loses makes but few calculations beforehand.*
> —Sun Tzu

accompanies the end of a year. Don't allow yourselves to be soothed by the temporary lull in volatility. The spectral ghost of things to come is emblazed with a black robe and hood, and his scythe is honed and razor sharp and blood will be spilled. As we face forward and square away for 2009, my best advice is to get out the armor, polish up the sword of carnages past, and prepare for battle.

To play the Great Game requires a vision, an attitude and the internal fortitude to execute your plan. There is always risk, and it is the ability to couple less risk with greater reward than separates the men from the fools. Times past may have allowed you to ride with the thundering herd and think that you have achieved greatness, but that day has closed, my friend, and these are the times of real trials and tribulations. I stand fixed in my own vision, which is not to be in equities, not to be connected to real estate or securitizations tied to real estate, to own the Federal Deposit Insurance Corporation (FDIC) debt if you must and not Treasuries or agencies, and that the corporate market has been radically changed in both risk characterizations and potential return by the government's taking positions in many financial names, while industrial and utility companies and their debt are left to their own devices. I am resolute in my opinion that it is now safer—not risk free and not without some peril, but generally safer—to own financial credits where you can achieve a superior position to the government by both the grace of God and the peculiarities of the current administration. As investors, besides the use of public funds, it has cost us nothing—not a penny, euro, or pound—to have the American government inject new capital in these credits and yet we can own debt senior to the American taxpayer, while history has demonstrated time and time again that our politicians will move both heaven and hell to make sure that the taxpayer's money is returned. It is akin to walking down a path through the jungle with the 800-pound gorilla in front of you and no other animal in existence with even the remotest chance of challenging this gargantuan beast. While the marketplace, as reflected by the yields in industrial credits and utility credits obviously hold a different view, I will take the protected position thank you as opposed to laying out my bet in unprotected territory when the times are as tough as currently prevail.

Difficulties mastered are opportunities won.

—Winston Churchill

The Hour of the Shire-Folk

April 28, 2009

I thought I would take some time this morning to discuss my thinking about my commentary. I have been writing it for almost eight years now, and perhaps the occasional return to the reasoning of my methodology is in order. This is prompted by a protracted discussion with a client yesterday where he inquired as to my thought process about a given subject and we politely exchanged views concerning a certain political risk.

During my lengthy tenure on Wall Street, it is clear to me that one can lose money in the blink of an eye, while making it is a longer process. Consequently, I try to focus more on the downside and what could happen, what might happen, than where one might add a few shekels to the portfolios. From the largest of you to the smallest and spread around the globe, I feel that if I can add some value to your thought process just a few times a year then I have made a positive contribution that justifies our doing business. My ego is not so big nor my self-respect so aggrandizing that I think I might offer novel thinking past that point. What I do think is that I can bring to the table sometimes is a viewpoint not considered or identify a risk that may have been missed or point out the magnitude of an issue overlooked that may prove helpful in your thought process. It is not that I try to predict the future; just warn about it. *Out of the Box* has a very specific audience—professional money managers all around the world—and is not sent out to the public. It is the thinking of Mark Grant standing alone and not the thinking of my firm, nor is it encumbered by investment banking or traders or any distractions beyond perhaps my three dogs.

I approach the world with a sense of humor that is evident in my writing. I wake up each day with a spirit of wonder and, all of these years later, I am still excited by the markets. I have made enough money; that

Ray, people will come, Ray. They'll come to Iowa for reasons they can't even fathom. They'll turn up your driveway not knowing for sure why they're doing it. They'll arrive at your door as innocent as children, longing for the past. Of course, we won't mind if you look around, you'll say. It's only $20 per person. They'll pass over the money without even thinking about it: for it is money they have and peace they lack. And they'll walk out to the bleachers; sit in shirtsleeves on a perfect afternoon. They'll find they have reserved seats somewhere along one of the baselines, where they sat when they were children and cheered their heroes. And they'll watch the game and it'll be as if they dipped themselves in magic waters. The memories will be so thick they'll have to brush them away from their faces.

—Terrance Mann in *Field of Dreams*

is no longer the reason I still play the Great Game, but I still love to play it, and each day brings a new adventure out on the field. To think, and then write, and then have the pleasure of interacting with some of the best and brightest minds on the planet—there is not much better than that, in my opinion, and I thank each of you for getting the opportunity to still be on the ball field.

When the topic is serious; when large amounts of money hang on a decision is when the tenuous space between the rock and the hard place gets the most difficult. I do not make the decisions; you make the decisions, and all I can reasonably try to do is bring all of the considerations into focus because, as good as any of you are, you may have missed something. Large institutions tend to get very insular in their reasonable paranoia about the Street or their competition knowing what they are doing. I take great care in guarding everyone's position after an exchange of ideas. My friend, the Wizard, reflects my own sense of humor about myself, and he is a great mentor to keep me on the straight and narrow path when the gravity of a situation is hard upon our backs.

It seems to me that we are currently in a time that is different from most of my years on Wall Street. We are all experts, in one form or another, in economic risks. Each of us may specialize in something or another but we have all been trained in this field of endeavor. What we have not been trained in and what is now as important, if not more important, frankly, is political risk. The referee has entered the game, the goal line is wherever he says it is at any particular moment, and the rules are a work in progress. The critical factor, in my view, to begin to understand this new dimension of risk is to understand that the referee and you have totally different motivations. You and every other player on the field are trying to win the game, but not the referee. The referee is playing to the crowd that is watching the game, and he wins only if the throng is enjoying themselves. You must keep this salient fact in the forefront of your mind or you will not understand his motivations and you will get blindsided by the "Master of the Rules."

My discussion with my friend yesterday focused on the law of contracts. The referee, our elected officials, wrote the law of contracts, enforce the law of contracts, can abridge the law of contracts on a whim that only the judiciary can set aside and then only if it were to violate the master playbook which is the Constitution. The rather startling truth is that if the present laws do not play well with the crowd, then they will get changed because that is what really matters to the referee; the consensus of those in the stands.

If we are to continue to be "Masters of the Universe," then we must recognize that the financial universe and the political universe have now melded for some period of time as the economic realities, like a kind of gravity, have forced the intercession. We, on the field, may visualize it as the seven seals in the tower of Mordor being broken and the Beast being unleashed upon the world once again, but the onlookers in the stands see it as the seven archangels of light arriving from above carrying the Book of Judgment to right the world in the final hours. The referee may well listen to your pleas, but, make no mistake, he will make his decisions based on what he perceives as the desires of those in the bleachers. To not get this joke is to lose the game, and you must not forget how to laugh.

This is my most special place in all the world, Ray. Once a place touches you like this, the wind nevers blows so cold again. You feel for it, like it was your child.

—Dr. Archibald "Moonlight" Graham, *Field of Dreams*

"I will take the Ring," he said, "though I do not know the way."

Elrond raised his eyes and looked at him. . . .

"This is the hour of the Shire-folk, when they arise from their quiet fields, to shake the towers and counsels of the Great. Who of all the Wise could have foreseen it?"

—J.R.R. Tolkien, *Lord of the Rings*

The Change of Rules

June 5, 2009

There may have been a time when there was a semblance of order that ruled the denizens of the Doubloons, but that has long faded as there are just too many sheriffs in town, each trying to impose their own order. There may have been a time when the boys took significant positions and liquidity was available, but that has faded into customer orders and games now played utilizing the "greater fool theory." Buyers are rushing into places where, just months before, they had feared to tread, and I shake my head as, one more time, the merry band of men follow Robin Hood into the woods.

This is a tough time to play the Great Game. The old rules are not the new rules, and the game book gets changed almost daily by the referees, who do not only act in concert but who might don their cap of owner, player, or coach, or head into the stands to join the throng at the drop of their hat. There may have been a time once, when understanding the complexities of the financial markets was enough. That time is long gone as we must now assess the winds of political change and the motivations of the people who can and do change the fundamentals of the free enterprise system. We play to appease the gods of capitalism, while those boys play to appease the horde, and while we hope we might do well enough to afford the box seats, they want to be on stage and listen to the applause of the crowd. In some significant manner, and this is not a joke, the people in power now control not only General Motors and AIG and a host of other companies where the public is the de facto owner, but each and every major bank in the United States until they are released from the talons of the Troubled Asset Relief Program (TARP), and that freedom is something they seem loath to grant. Power and control, once attained, is an addictive substance.

I write about this subject this morning because it is clear to me that many of you are not paying close enough attention to reality. You are trapped in the past and playing the game as if we were still there, when clearly we are not. Please close your eyes and then reopen them, as the scene has changed.

The promise given was a necessity of the past: the word broken is a necessity of the present.

—Niccolo Machiavelli

If you wish to argue about the nuances of nationalization or socialization, then please be my guest, but that is a task better suited to armchair observations when sitting in the overstuffed armchairs on a Saturday afternoon in your board rooms or at your club. The truth may be painful, but it is there nonetheless; the American government presently controls the game and in ways not seen in our lifetimes, and no amount of wishful thinking is going to change that choke as you think about reality. The CEO of General Motors is fired by the president of the United States, and then the company is taken into bankruptcy and then filled with money from the public's coffers—and you think things are still the same?

Corporate executives are being fired or allowed to resign, and boards of directors are being changed, and if you do not see the footprints of the people in power, then your sight has faded with naïvete or age. The financial system is the centerpiece of any state, and the princes of the populace have assumed control.

History has taught us the peril of our present situation and one may only pray that the marketplace will be returned to those who compete for gain as a better alternative to those who compete for control, but until the strictures of the authorities are loosened, I am afraid that we are subject to the wiles of the realm.

The arts of power and its minions are the same in all countries and in all ages. It marks its victim; denounces it; and excites the public odium and the public hatred, to conceal its own abuses and encroachments.

—Henry Clay, 1834

Captain Hook at the Aegean Sea

March 2, 2010

For those of you who are just beginning the adventure, you may not understand some of what I am about to discuss this morning. There comes a point in your career where you have enough money, however each person defines that and when you play for different reasons. Money is the poker chips of life, no doubt, but there is also the excitement of playing. I have just returned home after being gone for one month on my boat. It is a curious thing to embark on a voyage of exploration, to stand on the beach where Columbus first landed and pick up a stone and put it in your pocket to mark the experience. This is the part of life that none of us should ever relinquish, and it is the young boy or girl that lies deep within us who finds joy from the simple experience of just playing.

If you close your eyes, you may see a pool of lovely pale colors. If you squeeze them tighter, the pool will take on different shapes, and the colors will become brighter—so bright, that in a moment they'll go on fire. And in that moment, just before they do, you will see Never Land.

—J.M. Barrrie, *Peter Pan*

For 36 years on Wall Street I have gotten up in the morning full of excitement to see what is going on. For the past almost nine years, I have had an additional kick, which has been to share my take on the markets with all of you. The plain fact of it is that I love winning and cannot stand to lose, and I also have the personality trait that derives pleasure from helping my friends and clients to win. I refer to this as the "aha" factor, which is when I can see the path through the woods better than others who are competing against me. No one can take away from me or from any of you those few moments when the light dawns, the landscape is laid out in absolute clarity, and money gets put down on the table as a result of your sharpened vision. The vast majority of what I send out each day is the serious stuff of investing, but I always remember to take a few moments and to send you something in an effort to put a smile on your face.

There is a reason for this; to lose the joy of playing is an awfully serious mistake that will cost you dearly, first, in your ability to play the Great Game and, second, in your ability to enjoy life no matter your financial successes. Besides, who wants to venture out on the playing field without the support of Wizards and Sages and other fantastical creatures of the realm!

Second star to the right and straight on 'til morning.

—J. M. Barrie,
The Adventures of Peter Pan

This morning as Captain Hook stands upon the shores of the Aegean Sea and directs the confrontation between those notorious Greek pirates and the counting houses in Berlin and Paris, we get to watch a play on brinkmanship. Not only is everyone is bellying up to the bar, but they are telling those over-the-top stories that so often get told when merchants and pirates are in the same room and have imbibed so much rum that they actually believe the stories that they knew they first made up those many years ago. I suspect it will all get worked out in some fashion, as merchants and pirates need one another to survive, but the cost will be severe not only to their currency but to the state of their union. As we approach the end of the drama the stories are getting more farfetched, the bragging is getting louder and the face-offs will be reminiscent of the recent American/Canadian hockey game in Vancouver. It will be point, counterpoint, and no point at all, as our European cousins line up to protect the spoils of the continent so they can compete effectively with the unwashed in America and the calculating minds in China. "Stand aside," I say, and bet on nothing good coming from all of this; while one cannot accurately predict the nuances of the outcome, one can certainly predict that the end of all of this will do them all no good. I tell you now, the euro is going down further, the financials of a number of banks in Europe will take a beating as derivative contracts get forced out into the light, and the complacency concerning sovereign debt will be an attitude that

"So, Pan," said Hook at last, "this is all your doing."

"Ay, James Hook," came the stern answer, "it is all my doing."

—J. M. Barrie,
The Adventures of Peter Pan

is shoved 10 steps out on the plank and will carry much wider spreads
in the future. Corporate financials may be regulated by governments,
but sovereign financials are regulated only by the politicians who are in
power, and this is a new thought that is just beginning to dawn on the
majority of us who invest money. The old notion that sovereign debt is
safer than corporate debt may be little more than too much swill that we
have imbibed for too long.

Ship on the Rocks: European sovereign debt, European bank debt,
the euro, European equities, American debt tighter than +100 bps
to Treasuries

Ship in Calm Seas: AIG, Student Loan Marketing Association
(SLMA); select regional American banks (RF, M&I, Fifth Third,
etc.); American bank debt, both senior and sub; fixed-to-float
securities; American equities; Build America Bonds (BABs)

And on Every Note in Between

August 11, 2010

My clients come first, last, and on every note in between. This may sound somewhat odd to you, but that is the way I feel about it. I was recently trying to explain this to some folks of rather rarified air that were present on my boat from one of the lead banks. I chastised them, in fact, and I told them that their prop desk and everything else they did was secondary to taking care of their clients. I have always felt this way; these are my standards. I am often reminded of *Mr. Holland's Opus,* which I shall paraphrase, "You are my symphony. You are the melodies and the notes of my opus. You are the music of my life."

I sometimes see Wall Street in this way. Music is quite similar to the financial markets if you think about it—crescendo, small riffs, diminution, and thundering sounds that magnify every particle in your soul as they float past your ears. It is true that I do not make the final decisions, but I would like to think that from time to time I might make a difference in someone's viewpoint and that I helped them to win the Great Game in some fashion. Someone recently asked me if I had ever thought of retiring. What a dreadful question to be asked. Certainly, I have the money, but why on earth would you want to leave the playing field when you can still play? Not me, my friends; when I go, it will be ranting and screaming, and Angela will send you a nice note that the Wizard has returned to Oz.

Out of the Box has recently passed its 10-year mark, which is why I am thinking about all of this, I suppose. Five days

> *You are talking to a man who has laughed in the face of death, sneered at doom and chuckled at catastrophe.*
>
> —My Cousin, the Wizard of Oz

a week and sometimes more often if the world is upside down you get the best I am able to give. I am surprised I have had that much to say to myself, much less to any of you. I have learned some things along the way that I wanted to share with you this morning. First is that just because something is obvious to me does not mean that it is obvious to you. Recently, I had one of the biggest managers of money in the world on my boat for dinner, and he told me that I written something so profound that I had totally changed his viewpoint. Now I think I have my moments, but I have never thought of anything that I have written as "profound." What it was is that debtholders are more important than shareholders in determining a company's fate. It seemed to me that this truism was right in front of my nose all the time, and so I have learned that people have different-shaped noses. I have also learned that everyone's niche shapes their view of reality. My commentary has a diverse audience—from plain vanilla bond people to high yield, to distressed debt, to mortgage-backed people, to equity folks, to senior managers that supervise everything, to central bankers and people from Mongolia to Sweden and Missouri and China and back again. Everyone comes at the Great Game from their own unique perspective. Playing for such a long time has also taught me that there is no replacement for experience, just nothing, because it gives you the opportunity to acquire some wisdom as you roll through the seasons. I can certainly tell you that when times get tough, people from anywhere and everywhere ask to get added to my distribution list, the calls come pouring in for help, portfolios show up for guidance, and the number of conference calls in which I participate spikes up with the severity of the crisis. If there is any certainty about deflation, it is the egos that suffer from it when things go the wrong way. So, more often than not, I share my opinion, provide a little guidance, pat my friends on their butt, and send them back out on the playing field.

Only the man who crosses the river at night knows the value of the light of day.
— Chinese Proverb

We play the game in eighths and quarters, but it was never about that. A reliable warning, a decent idea—now that is where value lies.

Now there are some game-changing events in front of us that you should get prepared for in your portfolios; the single biggest one is the American elections in November. The current administration came into power based on an appeal to the lower economic classes and to the inexperienced, which we will define as young people and students.

Promises were made that have not been kept, could not be kept, and the vast majority of Americans, of all classes, are just plain angry; that is my assessment. If you underpromise and overdeliver, you look like a great guy, but if you overpromise and then underdeliver, you appear to be a schmuck. It is not that the vast majority of people in the United States now care about Democratic or Republican policies; we are past that, in my opinion. It is that people of all ilks are just plain aggravated with how our country's business is being conducted.

Stimulus, you know, is just a fancy word for *spending,* and we have overspent. I suspect the next group sitting in D.C. are going to put an end to it, as most Americans get the joke that you cannot keep spending more than you have earned for any extended period of time. The American Credit Crisis is only through the first phase, and the next one will be a cutback in spending programs that will necessarily impact the economy. I do not think a severe downturn is on the horizon, but I do think it is going to be a long slog through the marshes until we get out of the mess that we have created. The correct bet, I think, is a long period of very low interest rates.

The next creature rumbling toward us will be a string of continuing issues in Europe. Have no fear—this is not even close to being played out yet, as the tribal warfare will continue with nationalism and federalism locked in a protracted battle. There are more risks here than thought by many and I continue to warn and warn again about the risks here as John Bull, the Berliner Bearm and the girls at the Crazy Horse line up in a bizarre rendition of De Sade's domination on the continent.

When I look out on the next few years, I am neither optimistic nor pessimistic—just resigned. I have spent some time on the stern on my boat in the Boston harbor thinking about this. I think the correct term, at least the best I can come up with is *pay the Piper.* And make no mistake—the Piper must be paid. No one and no country can lead a life of "money for nothing and chicks for free" without getting around to being held accountable for their silliness. America and the world has lived past its means, and the Piper is awaiting payment.

Common Sense Dictates the Game Has Changed

August 26, 2010

Today, we will discuss the most basic tool that you need to win the Great Game. This is the baseline armament that you need to do battle, and it is no more or less complicated than what your father tried to drum into your head for all those many years: common sense. This is sometimes called *gut* or *instinct* or even referred to erroneously as *luck*. Yet it is none of these things, and these words will throw you off course. It is just good old rational thinking where you calmly appraise what is happening around you, where you appreciate what changes are occurring in the world and the financial world and where you make judgments based on this most basic of principles.

Common sense is not so common.
—Voltaire

This is not the stuff of epiphanies or having some information that someone else does not have or the use of quarks and quantum mechanics as applied to the financial markets. This is much more banal and much more important, and it gives you the ability to examine the world around you and make prudent decisions about how to proceed. You see, it is not just time that moves in one direction; it is also you, as you are forever in the "now" and always headed into the "future." There is no other way about it in this life and, consequently, whether you ever stop to think about it or not, that is just the way of your present existence. Consider, then, that all other people and all other events in this world are also moving in the same direction and that the ability

Common sense is often called instinct. Enough of it is called genius.
—George Bernard Shaw

to assess the "now" as to define the "future" is 100 percent the use of common sense that is rooted in one simple dynamic: *change*.

Let us then consider what has changed in the past several years. Let's take a really hard look at what conditions have varied enough so that some or many of our old assumptions are no longer valid. If we oper-ate on incorrect assumptions, then the world becomes convoluted and things do not make rational sense and we start inventing postulates to explain the markets when, in fact, I believe that is generally that our assumptions are

> *Common sense is genius dressed in its working clothes.*
> —Ralph Waldo Emerson

being based on old and incorrect data. It is the ability to first under-stand that something has changed and then to accept this change that leads you squarely down the path of a rational comprehension of the world around you. I do not pose this argument for the sake of some philosophical discussion, I assure you; I submit my notion here, so you can improve your handicap in the Great Game and win out against your fellow contenders.

The Game Changers

First and foremost is our recent economic collapse. The Great Depres-sion and the present circumstance from which we are endeavoring to emerge were the two most serious brushes with financial ruin in the last 100 years. That is my observation. While the Great Depression is and has been part of our collective consciousness, it was an event that began 81 years ago, and, humans being what we are, we have been aware of its consequences, but it was too far in the past for any of us to consider it in any other way than an exercise in academia; we were not alive to feel the pain. Our recent brush with financial disaster is something else again; we felt and are feeling the pain, and it should be no surprise to anyone that quite real change is the effect of being that frightened. As one example here is the consideration of bonds versus equities as investments and why each and every asset class in debt is so historically tight to Treasuries and will remain so for quite some time. People do not like to lose money, and they especially do not like to lose so much money that their life gets radically altered for the worse by its loss. Many people and institutions lost so much money, in fact, that they have decided not to be in the position again regardless of potential gain; the pain was just too severe.

The world has changed, and it has also changed because the concept that stocks, over time, would outperform debt was found to be an untruth and even if over time the stock market returns to the old highs there was just too much fear created by our experience so that the public is no longer willing to be at that much risk. The risk profile of our generation is now and will not be what it was prior to the financial crisis of 2009. Your ability to comprehend this will explain in very rational terms, then,

The philosophy of one century is the common sense of the next.
—Henry Ward Beecher

why there is no bond bubble, why the stock market is behaving poorly and why the yields available in debt instruments are no longer the same valuations that they were three years ago as compared to equity dividends. The capital structure, so long ignored, was profoundly and stringently brought into play, and it will not be forgotten again anytime soon.

Then there is real estate. There was an assumption, a very flawed assumption, that residential real estate would appreciate over some period of time. For the purpose of my example, I will leave commercial real estate to the side for a moment; it is really the same thing with the addition of rents, but somewhat more complex in its explanation, though you will see the truth of both in short order. Real estate is, in my view, one of the worst investments on the planet in any time except when there is inflation, which was the total and sole basis of owning it. Real estate has no inherent value and is nothing but a relative comparison at best, while what is built upon it is a depreciating asset—houses decay over time. Further, there is no maturity to real estate, a true perpetual investment, so that there is no appreciation as defined by a maturity. Consider a zero coupon bond; there is no current return and just appreciation as maturity is neared, but in the case of real estate, not even this is present. There is no payoff at the end because there is no end. Consequently, if inflation is no longer present, as in our current situation, whatever real estate you own is going to decrease in value as the house decays, there is less money available to buy the stuff, you can no longer borrow as much money or as cheaply except if the government provides the guarantee and here is another game that has changed and most likely changed for many years to come.

The tide comes in and the tide goes out, and common sense will now tell you that the tide is out.

There are a number of rational viewpoints about this, but in many ways the Great Depression was really ended by World War II. Since that point, in the 1940s, we have had inflation that has pushed up the prices of each and every thing. Then we fell of the cliff as we lived beyond our means and finally got caught, with the last great crescendo being immortalized by the wonderful song intoning, "Money for nothing and chicks for free." We did have that last breaking wave where life appeared to be that way with money available to anyone and everyone for anything at all, and then we hit the wall and we are now sliding down the financial embankment until we find a floor.

Europe has changed. It is no longer a series of countries that existed within their own national boundaries. A great experiment is under way, and it is one that no one understands very well because the experiment is in process. Common sense will tell you that the powers on the continent are pushing this way and that way on each other for political dominance shrouded by their own economic desires. It is a nonwar of power that is nowhere close to being decided, and as with any experiment, there are a multitude of risks as the process unfolds. It is not really that important to predict how the experiment turns out, but what is critically important is to understand that there are quite real risks that are present and could undermine the world's financial system if the experiment goes poorly.

Then there is China, the other great experiment that is under way. These people no longer represent a Maoist communist dictatorship of social revolution. This country is no longer a land of tea drinkers and rice eaters that live in isolation halfway around the world from America. Common sense should indicate to you that they are now major players in the game and that, while it is a one-party state, it is not a communist state but a group of people, as is normal, trying to remain in power while, with the greatest population on Earth, they push their social and economic agendas ever outward and for their own purposes.

The game has changed and how to win the Great Game has changed because of it, and common sense is now dictating that a totally new set of rules is in play. It is all quite understandable if you just turn your mind around. Change your mind and you change your world.

Chapter 16

You Know You Work on Wall Street When . . .

Wall Street is defined by itself and the definition is continually changing. There are the rituals, the terms of honor, your reputation, and the arcane words that are part of our language. Unlike any other business, it is all based on your word, you may do a $100 million trade, and there is nothing that is signed, no written contract, and it is just you and the other guy that say, "Done." No one trusts anyone until both time and many interactions have transpired, and then you guard the trust like some cherished family relic. It is a big world, and also a small world where anyone can be checked upon with a few phone calls. The playing field is divided into three main sections, America, Europe, and Asia. My commentary has bridged those boundaries, though, and I receive calls and emails from Norway to Mongolia. Not only do I wake up each day and plow into the recent

A person without a sense of humor is like a wagon without springs. It's jolted by every pebble on the road.

—Henry Ward Beecher

news that has changed the landscape, but I awake to communications that will chart the course of my day.

As one of the more senior players at this point in my career in the Great Game, and as a person that refuses to give up his sense of humor regardless of the seriousness of the subject, I sometimes make fun of myself and my colleagues.

For a time, prior to the American financial crisis, the game was a lot of fun, and life was less troubled and freer of aggravation. It is different now, of course, as we are all locked into a much more serious struggle, but this will not always be the case and was not the case when I poked some fun at Wall Street.

Humor is just another defense against the universe.
                                    —Mel Brooks

People hide behind compliance, and they get crotchety and overbearing so that I have to do a little butt kicking to remind them that high and mighty does not mean old and stodgy.

Many people might not understand all of the words that I have used. *Out of the Box* was solely the purview of very large institutions for 10 years, and this is the first time that my commentary has been made available to the public. When you read this book, bear in mind that the audience has been professional money managers, central bankers, the most senior people at insurance companies and the like, so that if things are sometimes not clear, I was not writing for the investor-at-large. The sphere of my commentary already knows the words and phrases or if too complex, he could turn to his buddy and ask. The idea has always been how to win while not losing.

I suppose that if I had penned "You Know You Work on Wall Street

Imagination was given to man to compensate him for what he is not; a sense of humor to console him for what he is.
                                    —Francis Bacon

I wonder if illiterate people get the full effect of alphabet soup.
                                    —Jerry Seinfeld

When . . ." during the past few months, it would have been earmarked by bashing from the administration, by being bad guys and by behaving irresponsibly, but then those who trumpet that message can kiss my patootie. Perhaps now, more than in a long time, I should provide some more humor to my brethren, but then serious issues always take precedence over being too cute.

Still, in difficult times, it is especially important to retain the sparkle in your eyes, as otherwise the lens that we glare though becomes a muddy brown. The people who live in the Street are, I suppose, not like other people. We live and breathe the stuff, or as one of the world's great money managers said to me, "It is my obsession." It is not just the money you understand; it is the Great Game itself and the continuing battle to win. Winning is everything, all things, and the only thing! The fascination is that yesterday's win is old news and, as we say, "You are only as good as your last trade." The great trader or salesman or money manager of last year may be the flop of the next year, and it is a continuous and ongoing process of reinvention that keeps you a success.

This and a sprinkle of fairy dust as a little help from any other realm is always appreciated.

> *Sometimes I lie awake at night, and ask, "Where have I gone wrong?" Then a voice says to me, "This is going to take more than one night."*
>
> —Charles Schulz,
> Charlie Brown in *Peanuts*

You Know You Work on Wall Street When . . .

January 13, 2006

J ust a few more because it is Friday and because I can do it. . . .
You know you work on Wall Street when:

- "Hiding a trade" does not mean the Steelers keeping their first-round pick a secret from the Dolphins.
- You own a necklace made from those Lucite deal logos.
- You apologize to your Bloomberg frequently so it won't shut down on you.
- You found your present girlfriend on Trader's Monthly.
- You have a clapper device installed on your Bloomberg.
- Your girlfriend's idea of safe sex is to lock the trading room's door.
- You take your compliance officer to lunch as often as you take a client.
- You keep a can of orange juice on top of your Bloomberg because it says "concentrate."
- Your trading room and your apartment are in the same building.
- Someone asks you the time and you say, "96 to 97, 1 by 1."
- You finance your money market fund purchases.
- You know that the head of your syndicate department is not connected to the mafia.

Grant's Rule 12 states: "When a Company Is under Federal Investigation for Fraud or Accounting Charges—Sell." This rule is not set in place because a company may necessarily be going bankrupt. This rule has served me well over the years because it prevents me from very unpleasant surprises on the downside. I have found it much cheaper to absorb the transactional costs than to have my head handed to me by points. Everything may work out just fine over some time period, but I am always free to reenter the credit when I feel comfortable. A perfect example of this is what is now happening with IBM. They are now under federal investigation for accounting issues, and the bar has been raised to a "formal" investigation. Who knows what the Securities and Exchange Commission (SEC) might find?

If the spread has not widened much because it is IBM, then great, I am out at a good price, and I can watch the situation develop from the safety of the sidelines. You do not know, and I do not know what the SEC has found to make the investigation a formal one, but I can certainly assure you that it is something they do not like. I invite you to consider the use of my rule this morning!

You Know You Work on Wall Street When . . .

January 28, 2006

You know you work on Wall Street when:

- You are on the trading floor and hear the word bifocal and immediately call compliance.
- You know that an "authorized share" is not getting your spouse's permission to go to a swinger's club.
- You are aware that "authorized float" is not that dollop of extra rum on a pina colada.
- You trade mortgage bonds and your view of "average life" is not a statistic on the life insurance company's actuarial tables.
- You can discuss a "back end load fund" in mixed company.
- You make a "balloon payment" and it isn't buying some rubber floating thingie on the beach.
- You are sure that a "bank line" is not the guy in customer service trying to pick you up.
- You do not think that a "bank wire" is the cord from the computer to the wall.
- You think there is more to a "barbell strategy" than a suggestion by your personal trainer.
- It doesn't occur to you that a "basis point" is the critical argument in a formal debate.
- You believe that a "basket trade" is not something that occurs at the straw market in Nassau.
- "Bear," for you, doesn't end in Bryant, begin with Smokey, or refer to your being naked.

- You know that a "bear market" is not the selling of grizzlies in Mongolia.
- You know that a "bear raid" is not an attack on your campsite in Alaska.
- You know that "opening bell" is not the son of Alexander Graham Bell.
- "Less than par" doesn't mean you have a serious head cold.
- You don't think that a "benchmark issue" is something to be decided by the Supreme Court.
- You are aware that "bid-to-cover" is not a father trying to get his daughter to change blouses.
- You are positive that a "bifurcation diagram" is not something for birth control.
- You have no doubt that the "big board" is not a reference to some kind of kinky sex paddle.
- You are aware that "Black-Scholes" is not some funny little cushiony thing you put in your shoes.
- You know that a "blanket recommendation" is not based on the quality of the wool.
- You have never thought that a "blind pool" is a swimming hole for people that can't see.
- You never think that a "block trader" deals in children's toys.
- You have been taught that the "blue list" is not a categorization of various types of depression.
- You have had enough experience to know that blue chips and cow chips are not the same thing.
- You know that "boning" is charging a lot more for an asset that it is worth and not something else.
- You know that "book profit" is not how much you made when you sold the signed Charles Dickens first edition.
- You know that "book to bill" is not a literary creation sent to Mr. Gross or Mr. Gates.

And finally . . .

- You know that "bottom-line growth" is not a term designed by Jenny Craig.

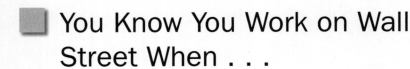

You Know You Work on Wall Street When . . .

March 10, 2006

You know you work on Wall Street when:

- Your partner wants to get intimate and you ask, "What's the bid?"
- You know what "early withdrawal" means, and we'll just leave that one there this morning.
- Your favorite channel is MTV and you spend all day humming "money for nothing and chicks for free."
- You never think that an eighth refers to King Henry.
- You don't think that the Elliott wave theory is used for predicting major tsunamis.
- You are sure that "whole foods" is not an emerging market.
- You know that an "endowment fund" is not some group of guys on *Sex and the City.*
- You do not believe that "enterprise value" is the cost of the ship on *Star Trek.*
- You know that an "equity carve-out" is not some fancy way to cut the turkey.
- You are aware that an "equity collar" has nothing to do with BDSM.
- You know that "escalator clause" is not related to Santa.
- You don't believe that an "exercise price" is the amount you must pay to the gym.
- You know that an "exotic option" is not some strip joint you could go to after dinner.
- You have no doubt than an "expiration date" has to do with options and not when someone is going to get hit on *The Sopranos.*

- You are cognizant that an "extension swap" has to do with maturity and not trading in your old boyfriend for a new one.
- You know that extraordinary call and booty call are not the same things.
- You know that "face value" has another meaning besides some girl in the Victoria Secret's catalog.
- You know that "fair value" is not the cost of the Barnum & Bailey circus.
- You know that a "fallout risk" has nothing to do with a low-cut dress.
- You know that Fannie Mae and Sallie Mae have no reference to next Friday night's date.
- You know that Freddie Mac was not a character in *Brokeback Mountain*.
- You know that the federal open market committee does not set the opening and closing times for grocery store chains.
- You know that Fedwire has no relation to barbed wire or even her brother high.
- You know that a "fill or kill order" is not some language used in the Marine Corps.
- Your financial position has nothing to do with the missionary position.

And finally . . .

- You know that "first call date" does not refer to Susie, Linda, or Janice.

You Know You Work on Wall Street When . . .

March 21, 2006

I peeked out from under the darkness of the morning at the bond world, and it was boring, boring. Nothing of great import last night and Bernanke told us nothing. Some days are just that way, not too much to comment on at all. So now I will really roll up my sleeves and attempt to amuse you. You must call and buy some bonds for every time you laugh, so if you aren't in the bond-buying mood, you have to stop reading this now. You can't, I know, and you won't, so get out pen and paper and make a check mark every time you chuckle, and Angela will expect to hear from all of you this morning. She will have a great day, some 6,000 phone calls, so she will be busy. It is good to keep her busy; she is only 27 and her mind might wander into untoward places. Okay, here we go . . .

You know you work on Wall Street when:

- You turned down having sex this morning so you could jump out of bed to see what Chairman Bernanke had to say.
- You rushed back to bed after you saw that Bernanke said nothing and got the old "If the Fed Chairman is more important to you than I am" speech.
- This morning you are thinking, "nothing of note in the speech, no sex, my partner is aggravated with me, and why do I work on Wall Street?"
- You realize that something has happened to you because between the ages of 18 and 24, you would not have turned down sex if Armageddon had arrived.

- You notice that your erectile dysfunction disorder rises and falls with the value of the portfolios you manage.
- You have given thought to naming your new puppy Bloomberg.
- You know that FASB does not mean Fat Albert Stood Bareheaded.
- You know that GAAP is not that chain of stores.
- You know that GDP, or gross domestic product, is not some moldy old food left in the refrigerator.
- You are aware that "gift inter vivos" can be spoken about in mixed company.
- You have learned that golden handcuffs have to do with contractual obligations even though your neighbor insists they are for something else.
- You know that a grant date is the date on which an option or other award is given and not the guy who writes *Out of the Box* going out for dinner.
- You are pretty sure that greenmail has another meaning besides the letters you got on St. Patrick's Day.
- It would never occur to you that a growth manager was some guy helping a thirteen year old get taller.
- You have no doubt that the Hang Seng Index and the Won Hung Lo Index do not refer to the same things.
- You know that head and shoulders refers to technical analysis and is not a new dandruff shampoo.
- You know that a hedgehog is not some greedy old guy running a fund.
- You know that horizon analysis is not sitting on Grant's boat and watching the sun come up.
- You know that horizontal analysis is not giving your bed partner a 1–10 rating for their performance.
- You know that hyperinflation is not Uncle Fred blowing up the beach ball.
- You know that a T–bill is not some transvestite you met in South Beach.
- You know that trading in stocks and bonds does not mean you publish a BDSM catalog in Poughkeepsie.

And finally . . .

- Every time Moody's cuts the rating on one of your holdings, you are reminded of that rock-and-roll band, The Moody Blues, and you feel sick just like when you smoked that funny stuff at one of their concerts.

You Know You Work on Wall Street When . . .

March 13, 2009

I t has probably been five years since I did my rather infamous take entitled "You Know You Work on Wall Street When . . ." With so many things having changed and a little humor needed these days, I thought I would revisit the subject. Here you go!

You know you work on Wall Street when:

- The giant trading room that your firm built is now staffed by you, Vinny the kid, Andrapov with the heavy accent, and the cousin of the head of mergers and acquisitions.
- You used to have four screens, but now you share a Bloomberg with some guy that has never returned from sick leave.
- In midafternoon, when speaking on the phone in the trading room, you are amazed by the echo.
- You have clients that now take your calls because it is just your firm and E-Trade that covers money managers with less than $100 billion in assets.
- Last week you met with your sales manager, and for the first time ever he said, "Call whom you like; it doesn't matter."
- You wake up one morning and realize that "customer order" has replaced "firm position" and that no trader in the firm has uttered "we'll make a bid" since prior to the New Year.
- Your firm took the TARP money and now the head of sales, the head of trading, and the head of risk all report to the government's compliance officer, who occupies the corner suite that used to belong to the CEO.

- You recently ran into the old head of your derivatives desk and she looked odd in her Burger King uniform.
- Your new employee handbook forbids using the words *subprime mortgage* during business meetings with clients.
- The employee cafeteria is now the vending machine hallway.
- Your Brioni suit is now worth more than your Manhattan apartment.
- The doors at St. Patrick's Cathedral and the bid/ask spreads in many credits now are now of approximately the same dimensions.

Currency Intervention

The last time a major central bank intervened in the currency markets was in 2004. Switzerland has ended the streak and one wonders if this is just the first shot across the bow. It no longer seems unlikely that there may be devaluation trades made now by a number of key players in an attempt to remain more competitive on the global stage. There is some speculation that Japan may be the next participant in the game. Something to keep your eye on now!

The Banks

Many of the American lead banks are reporting they are making profits through the first two months of 2009. If the first quarter gets reported out this way, then we can translate this into their not needing any more federal assistance. If we add this to the probability that the current mark-to-market accounting rules will be eased for "hard-to-sell" assets, then the extrapolation is that bank credits may improve and hence tighten against the benchmarks. None of this is etched in stone at this point, but the situation seems to be showing some improvement. Since it is unlikely that you can take advantage of this after the fact, it may be a good moment in time to begin increasing your exposure to some of the bonds in this sector. In particular, I would consider JPM, Bank of America, and Wells Fargo in the banking space, and then American Express and GE in the larger financial space. A quick look at the equities of these names will show some of the biggest percentage gains ever during the last several weeks. Financial shares in the S&P 500, as a group, have increased in value 33 percent in just one week, and this is worth noting. It is my view that there are a number of credits in the bank/finance space that widened recently in a disproportionate fashion to the real risk. If you cross out the noise about nationalization and insolvency, provocative comments that I never bought into in the first place, then current spreads represent a real opportunity, in my opinion.

You Know You Work on Wall Street When . . .

September 12, 2009

thought I would ponder Wall Street this morning. So here is what I am going to do. . . .

You know you work on Wall Street when:

- Yield is not the amount of corn you produced.
- The stock market has no fence around it.
- Preferred stock is not prime meat.
- A convertible may or may not have a top.
- A new issue isn't your friend's firstborn child.
- The NASD isn't some new band from Portland.
- An index future is not the possibility that you will give someone the finger.
- Crude oil isn't that stuff you buy at the adult bookstore.
- A repo isn't when you lose your car.
- A T-bill isn't a relative of the spoonbill.
- Your daughter has "LBO" on her Christmas list.
- Your son wants Disney stock and has no interest in visiting the park.
- The home shopping network operator recognizes your wife's voice.
- Your husband thinks a "subdivision" is part of a financial ratio.
- You live in New York and "taking out the trash" means getting rid of your daughter's boyfriend.
- You know that a hot tub is not a stolen bathroom fixture.
- You understand that "credit" has more meanings than just a reference to a card.
- You know that "get out of jail free" cards have been banned by the SEC.

- You know that the French Riviera is not a foreign car.
- You know that "Canary Wharf" is not that cute little place with all the birds in Key West.
- You have a hefty bag tied outside your office window in case you ever decide to jump.
- Your brother-in-law is also the CEO of your firm.
- Your son is named after J. P. Morgan.
- You honestly believe that women are turned on by your screaming in the trading room.
- You have no idea what the term *over yonder* means.
- You know that Dom Perignon was not a mafia boss.
- You know that a Volvo is not part of the female anatomy.
- You own special suspenders for formal occasions.
- You have considered writing "To make money, call . . ." in the prominent bathrooms in your city.
- Most of your casual attire has a logo.
- You think the national anthem should be changed to "money for nothing and chicks for free."
- After making love, you ask your partner to move the Blackberry.
- You have the first deal you did emblazoned in a Jell-O mold.
- You have a suspicion that "the Bloomberg" and "Mayor Bloomberg" may have some connection.
- You have pictures of Bill Gates and Warren Buffett over your fireplace.
- You keep Chinese railroad bonds framed on your office wall in case they ever come back.
- Foreplay consists of turning CNBC off.
- You can't marry your girlfriend because your firm would fire you both.
- You know that "interest rates" have some other meaning than how well your date went last night.
- You spend more time in front of a Bloomberg than with your wife and children.
- In tough trading situations you secretly think, "What would Curly do?"
- Your child's first words are "That trade is done."
- Your last words before sex are "The market is closed now, baby."
- Your girlfriend is a trader and makes your market 5½–6.
- The name of the hedge fund you work for is tattooed on your ankle.

- You know that an "out–of–the–money call" is not placed collect to your parents.
- Your wife says, "I just couldn't find a thing at Cartier's today."
- You can quote the market for apartments in Manhattan.
- You don't think that an asset–backed is a member of the opposite sex with a big behind.
- You know that Wall, Street, & Broad are not attorneys.

■ *About the Author* ■

Mark J. Grant was raised in Kansas City, Missouri, which is the heartland of America. He carries his traditional roots into his commentary, which seeks the "preservation of capital" above all other considerations. He has been sharing his thoughts with large institutional investors for more than 10 years now, as well as running Structured Finance and Corporate Syndicate for a number of years at a publicly traded investment bank. Mr. Grant has run capital markets at four investment banks and has been on the board of directors of four investment banks, which is a diversity of background shared by very few people on Wall Street. He has also been the president of a public company in telecommunications and on that company's board of directors.

Mr. Grant currently lives in Fort Lauderdale, Florida, with his two Aussie rescue dogs, who are also known as the two Sages. He also sometimes resides on his boat "Wishes Granted," which is often found in the islands of the Bahamas or points South. Mr. Grant carries the title of "The Wizard," which is a nickname bestowed on him by several money managers and in that context recently celebrated his 600th birthday. He has participated in the financial markets for more than 36 years and has a wealth of experience that he shares each day with central banks, managers of money, trust departments, insurance companies, mutual funds, hedge funds, sovereign wealth funds, and other large institutional investors. Mr. Grant's commentary is also published daily by MTN-I, one of the preeminent enterprises in London, which focuses on international structured finance.

■ Index ■